TOURISM AND ECOTRAVEL

TOURISM AND ECOTRAVEL

Geetanjali

CENTRUM PRESS
NEW DELHI-110002 (INDIA)

CENTRUM PRESS
H.O.: 4360/4, Ansari Road, Daryaganj,
New Delhi-110002 (India)
Tel: 23278000, 23261597, 23255577, 23286875
B.O.: No. 1015, Ist Main Road, BSK IIIrd Stage,
IIIrd Phase, IIIrd Block, Bangalore-560085 (INDIA)
Tel: 080-41723429
Email: centrumpress@gmail.com
Visit us at: www.centrumpress.com

Tourism and Ecotravel

First Edition, 2010

ISBN 978-93-80540-16-0

PRINTED IN INDIA

Printed at Mehra Offset Press, Delhi

Preface

Recognition of tourism as an agent of change - its growing importance in the world economy and the effects that it can have for the environment - was given at the United Nations General Assembly Special Session (Earth Summit II) in New York in 1997. The basis of this recognition was that tourism must be developed in a sustainable fashion, to ensure the conservation of resources for future generations to make their livelihoods from tourism, just as their parents do now.

Tourism is one of the world's largest industries and so the author has done in-depth research into its impact on the host community and the environment. It is not all bad news, however. The book provides an overview of tourism and the "promises of tourism." It also lay out the adverse effects of tourism (on both "guests" and "hosts") in colorfoul detail.

The book makes a strong case for "rethinking" ecotravel (which, although different-and laudable- in intent, is equally damaging to the environment); arguing that the entire industry needs to be rethought, from top to bottom. This book provides a wealth of resources for use by those who wish to join in the campaign to rethink tourism.

Author

Contents

Chapter 1

Traveller, Tourist and the Debate

Criticisms of tourism are not new - they have been around as long as people have travelled for leisure. This chapter examines what is distinctive about today's critique of tourism. It argues that 'traveller-tourist', the axis around which snobbery (and the inverted snobbery of those who rail against travellers as 'elitist') has often been expressed, does not fit so well with today's moral distinctions.

FROM GRAND TOURS TO COOK'S TOURS

Historically, the extension of tourism has always been subject to criticisms - usually from those who wanted to preserve its benefits for themselves. It is easy to see this as a common brand of elitism, with the more privileged trying to differentiate themselves from the uncultured masses. Pronouncements in this vein were commonplace in Victorian Britain, and still today Martin Graham, Chairman of the Federation of Tour Operators, can echo the language of the past, asserting, and [sustainability] hasn't really made any difference to the great unwashed.

A lot of people muck up their own back yard, and do just the same on holiday.' One hundred and forty years ago Thomas Cook responded to his critics and defended tourism in a fashion that is also pertinent for today. His customers, he claimed, could be identified by their 'courteous and joyous fraternisation', in contrast to the '"independent" tourists who paid up to three times the cost for the privilege of thus sitting solitary in a crowd of free and elastic spirits'.

On the face of it, it can seem that there is little new in the critique of tourism. Tourists in search of a fortnight of fun and frolics, or just rest and relaxation, remain subject to the critical eye of the concerned. Yet much has changed in the way tourists are derided - there are important aspects of the moralisation of tourism that are distinctly new.

The origin of the word 'tourist' comes from the Grand Tourists. The Grand Tour played the role of a right of passage for the British aristocracy especially in the latter half of the eighteenth century, although Grand Tourists preceded and succeeded this heyday.

The Grand Tours were linked to the acquisition of a classical education but represented more than this for the young heirs to estates and fortunes - these travellers were in search of worldliness and a culture that would mark out their right to rule. They presided over the birth of the modern idea of fashion and cuisine as they sampled and brought back ideas from their travels from Paris, Florence, Naples and Venice.

The Grand Tours were no fleeting visits. In fact, the travelling itself made this impossible - often travel, even for the elites, was arduous. Accounts of the Grand Tourists often make reference to the physical fatigue and illness associated with travel at this time.

Daniel Boorstin in his seminal essay 'The Lost Art of Travel' quotes an eighteenth-century account thus: 'Under the best conditions six horses were required to drag across country the lumbering coaches of the gentry, and not infrequently the assistance of oxen was required.' The origin of the word travel is 'travail', meaning work, and travelling at this time required great endeavour.

However, alongside the acquisition of culture and the difficult journeys across land and sea, the Grand Tourist exhibited a good deal of the hedonism, licentiousness and recklessness often associated with more mass forms of travel. Young English aristocrats could 'give loose to their propensities to pleasure' according to one observer, and indeed, Casanova's *Memoirs* were an account of his travels through Europe's capitals between 1826 and 1838. By the end of the Napoleonic wars in 1815 the Grand Tour, previously the preserve of the aristocracy, was increasingly encroached upon by the ascendant industrial elites. The latter provided the means for the extension of travel - the iron from which the railways were constructed, the steam technology that powered the trains - and also comprised a growing class with the means to travel.

The tension between town and country, between industry and landed wealth, was to be played out in the cafés of Rome and Naples, where those of landed wealth looked down upon the sons of those whose wealth was gained through industry.

As tourism developed, tourist perceptions changed. Areas of wilderness such as the Lake District and mountainous regions such as the Alps, previously regarded as obstacles to travel, increasingly became the object of travel for travellers influenced by Romanticism.

The Romantic spirit of the time is most closely associated with, and best articulated by, the Romantic poets. Prominent amongst these was Wordsworth, who campaigned against the railways coming to his beloved Windermere. Romanticism in essence represented a reaction to modernity - to the growth of cities, urbanisation and industry. It upheld individual emotion against collective experience, and nature against human endeavour.

Whilst Romantic travel predates the Industrial Revolution - Rousseau's taste for naturalness over the corruption of development led him to champion the Alps when to many travellers they were seen as an impediment to travel - there is no doubt that industrialisation and the modern ideas of liberty, fraternity and equality, championed by the French Revolution, generated a Romantic reaction that has profoundly coloured tourism in the modern era.

Romanticism not only coloured the tourist's viewpoint, but also shaped the criticisms of the growth of leisure travel. The growing number of tourists exemplified man encroaching on nature, and was therefore undesirable from a Romantic standpoint.

Such criticisms were expressed by those who considered leisure their birthright. The extension of travel beyond the aristocracy to the capitalist class was part of the latter's ascendancy.

It is hardly surprising, then, that the Grand Tourists should resent this upstart class intruding on their precious Naples and Venice - it signified the end of their dominion. This tension between modern society and the reaction to it has informed the 'traveller-tourist' debate historically.

The Romantic reaction to modernity took in the means of travel as well as the new bourgeois tourists. As early as the 1870s, Ruskin saw the train as devaluing travel, as it 'transmutes a man from a traveller to a living parcel' - sentiments held by many who criticise the package charter holiday industry of today.

He also likened it to concentrating one's dinner into a pill. Ruskin's criticism was against bourgeois tourism, but more broadly against the train as a symbol of modern, industrial society. Ruskin rejected the advantages of speed itself: 'All travelling becomes dull in exact proportion to its rapidity.'

Ruskin's reactionary Romanticism was taken to task by Thomas Cook, who celebrated the possibilities opened up by rail travel as: 'Travelling with the millions'.

It was the new industrialist tourist who provided much of the market for Thomas Cook's Tours from the 1840s. Cook made travel that bit easier for his clientele by making arrangements for smooth passage, good accommodation and finance (he invented the traveller's cheque) for the growing number of travellers.

Cook also pioneered package travel for the working class from the 1850s. Soon large numbers of workers and their families were taking advantage of trips to the seaside - Cook's tours are often regarded as the first mass package holidays.

The growth of leisure travel was bound up with the economic progress wrought by the industrial revolution. The development of industry created both new needs and new possibilities for meeting them. However, in an important sense, tourism was also a spur to industrialisation itself. Tourism brought wealth to coastal areas, which benefited the populations of these areas greatly. Indeed, in certain periods in the nineteenth century, resorts were the fastest growing class of towns. In this sense, tourism was itself part of the industrial revolution, rather than just a product of it.

As well as the development of technology and industry, the new-found mobility for leisure was premised on developments such as holidays with pay for some workers (although this did not become the norm until the 1938 Holidays with Pay Act), the establishment of Wakes Weeks and Bank Holidays as regular holiday times, and growing incomes enabling increasing numbers of workers to engage in tourism. By 1911, 55 per cent of the population of England and Wales were taking day trips to the seaside.

But for the critics of Cook, the new possibilities and new wealth evident in the tourism industry were overshadowed by the notion that this was travel as consumption rather than travel for culture. Novelists, commentators and scholars satirised and scolded the growing number of tourists.

The distaste expressed by some at mass, working-class tourism was infused by a broader fear and loathing of the masses that emerged as a reaction to industrialisation, urbanisation, the growth of the organised working class and events such as the Paris Commune that resonated around Europe and struck fear into ruling elites.

The antipathy towards the growth of tourism was directed against the perceived crudeness of these new tourists. They were, as the working class, regarded by many as a race apart from those born into wealth, the latter considered to possess the wherewithal to benefit from travel.

On the subject of these early mass tourists the Reverend Francis Kilvert famously commented in his diaries in 1870 that, 'Of all the noxious animals, the most noxious is a tourist; and of all tourists the most vulgar, ill-bred, offensive and loathsome is the British tourist.' Kilvert's comments were unguarded, direct and posited the culture of the masses as inferior to those of his station. In this vein Cook's Tours were criticised for extending travel to the lower orders.

For one commentator of the time, cities were deluged with droves of these creatures, for they never separate, and you see them forty in number pouring along a street with their director, now in front, now at the rear, circling them like a sheepdog - and really the process is as like herding as may be.

Cook himself had a fatherly approach to his tourists, typical of the outlook of Victorian philanthropists. His first tours for working-class people were temperance trips, where tourists could enjoy a good dose of preaching and bracing walks. An early trip was to the unlikely destination of Leicester, the purpose being a temperance meeting.

Bad behaviour was clearly an affront to the missionary in Cook, and on one occasion he was driven to comment that, 'to the shame of some rude folk from Lincolnshire, there have been just causes of complaint at Belvoir Castle: some large parties have behaved indecorously ... conduct of this sort is abominable, and cannot be too strongly reprobated.'

However, Cook was notable for defending the extension of travel from its detractors. The opportunity to travel for leisure was, for him, part of a more civilised society and the means of travel were a symbol of industrial progress, a progress that was for everyone. In this spirit Cook referred to his tours as 'agencies for the advancement of human progress' as, after all, 'railways and steamboats are the result of the common light of science, and are for the people'.

Cook criticised the sheer snobbery of the critics of tourism of his day. For him it was foolish to 'think that places of rare interest should be excluded from the gaze of common people, and be kept only for the interest of the select of society', and he added that, 'it is too late in this day of progress to talk such exclusive nonsense'.

Cook's defence and celebration of progress resonated with the outlook of many people, too. One of Cook's most celebrated ventures, to take ordinary people to London for the Great Exhibition of 1851, attracted vast numbers of customers from all social classes.

The Great Exhibition, and other international expositions of the time, were widely fêted as celebrations of scientific endeavour and industry. Cook even wrote a pamphlet on why people should visit the Great Exhibition in which he described it as 'a great School of Science, of Art, of Industry, of Peace and Universal Brotherhood'.

Cook's tours to the countryside also revealed something of the class divisions that were evident in popular tourism. These outings have been described as 'tense occasions' as 'country landowners, however obliging, could not look with complete calm on invading groups of working-class people whisked in by train from nearby towns, for they embodied changes that were only partly understood and were already partly feared'. Hospitality towards one's newly mobile potential adversaries did not come easy.

Having extended the range of his tours from Britain to Europe, and from Europe to Asia and on to Africa, and having established tours within the remit of all social classes, Cook set up a register for people who wanted to be the first tourists to the moon. This was no publicity stunt (people put their names down), rather it reflected a sense that society had, and would continue to, overcome geographical limits to travel.

The first fifty years of the twentieth century were dominated by two world wars. However, tourism developed in this period too. For the working class, improvements in living standards, holidays and transport led to the growth of seaside holidays.

The advent of the motor car challenged the pre-eminence of rail travel as the main mode of leisure travel. Car ownership grew to 2 million by 1939, and the car was celebrated as a harbinger of a new freedom for leisure travel.

It is, however, since the Second World War that the modern package holiday abroad has become established. In 1949 Vladimir Raitz audaciously approached the Aviation Ministry to get permission to run chartered flights from Gatwick to Calvi in Corsica, where customers would sleep in tents by the beach (the height of fashion) and drink at a bar brought in specially from Paris.

The aircraft used were decommissioned Second World War military aircraft - the war had bequeathed aircraft, airfields and technology that facilitated the rapid growth of international tourism. The modern package holiday was born and grew rapidly as ever-increasing numbers of people were able to travel as tourists.

Overseas package holidays developed rapidly throughout the 1960s and 1970s, managing 10 per cent growth per year between 1960 and 1974. Despite a distinct blip in 1974 due to the oil crisis (which put up the price of airline fuel), and the subsequent recession, tourism has continued on an upward trajectory since.

But whilst Raitz regards his industry as ringing progressive changes - 'democratising' foreign leisure travel to increasing numbers of people and boosting the economies of destination areas - it is the boom years of the package holiday industry that are associated with destruction, crudity and ugliness by tourism's contemporary critics.

The results of this boom included Torremolinos on the Costa del Sol, a byword for unethical holidaying or affordable fun, depending on one's view of package travel. For tourism's critics, Torremolinos represents everything that is wrong with the package holiday boom - large scale, cheap, transformative of the environment and of culture.

It is roundly criticised even in some of the tourist guides to Spain. For the Lonely Planet guide to *Andalucia* it is 'arguably Europe's finest example of how overdevelopment can ruin spectacular landscapes'. In Cadogan's *Spain,* it is a 'ghastly, hyperactive, unsightly holiday inferno'. The Costas are clearly associated with the excesses - in terms of the physical developments and also the behaviour of some of the visitors - of mass package tourism.

In amongst the carping criticisms one guide points out that on the back of tourism revenue, a considerable amount of money has been spent on the promenade, green spaces and the trawling of thousands of tonnes of sand to build up the beach at Torremolinos, ideal for bathing, families and beach sports.

However, such initiatives fail to impress many advocates of New Moral Tourism, relying as they do on development rather than nature. In fact, whilst the development of the Mass Tourism industry has generated a good deal of development, often in poorer regions in Mediterranean countries, the creative aspects of this development are overshadowed by an exaggerated sense of destruction and loss.

Criticisms of the package tourism industry such as these are the starting point of the New Moral Tourism, leading to an impulse to change the industry and the behaviour of its clients. But what is different about the critique of modern Mass Tourism? To what extent is the New Moral Tourism actually new in a qualitative sense? There are two important points to be made here.

First, whilst Cook was part of a tradition that was prepared to defend the extension of travel as an emblem of society's progress, few are prepared to do this today. Cook regarded the extension of tourism to the working class in the following way: 'These are the days of the million ... [who can] o'erleap the bounds of their own narrow circle, rub off rust and prejudice by contact with others, and expand their sails and invigorate their bodies by an exploration of some of nature's finest scenes.'

Very few are prepared to put this case today. Advocates of New Moral Tourism typically argue the opposite, that in fact Mass Tourism is characteristic of mass society, a society in which growth has spiralled out of control, with severe consequences for the cultures and environments of the world. It is in this spirit that 'ethical tourism' dominates discussions, with dissenting voices often adopting a cynical 'we're all doomed anyway so what's the point' posture.

In this sense, the discussion of tourism is best understood within the broader assault on the idea of human progress, an idea championed by many 150 years ago, but today often dismissed as at best utopian and at worst fascistic.

Whilst in Cook's era possibilities appeared to be boundless, today there is an acute sense of limits to man's capacity to go further, faster and in greater numbers. The recent grounding of Concorde, an aircraft that had in the 1970s epitomised the spirit of progress in travel, seems to sum up this mood. In fact the means of travel are generally regarded as more problematic than liberating. Notably the car, erstwhile symbol of freedom, has become a symbol of environmental degradation. It is not uncommon for people, including car owners, to see themselves as 'anti-car'.

Space tourism may have been a prospect relished by Cook, but today it is regarded with incredulity by many, for whom it seems to epitomise an arrogant humanity, intent on colonising other planets. Only ailing ex-Soviet facilities prospectively offer space tourism, to a clientele of super-rich Americans - a telling symbol of the post Cold War era.

Even seaside piers, which in the past 'involved an attempt to conquer nature, to construct a "man-made" object which at all times and forever would be there dominating either the sea or the sky', are now in disrepair and falling into the sea. Nature, it seems, triumphs over human endeavour. Surviving piers today are championed in the spirit of nostalgia for simpler times past.

Secondly, the debates on tourism in the nineteenth century were to a large extent, demarcated along class lines. The aristocracy were unhappy about the loss of the exclusivity of travel as a new business and middle class emerged. Working-class tourists, the 'great unwashed', were to be avoided both by travelling first class and by travelling to different places.

From the 1880s distinctly working class coastal holiday destinations came into their own, and divisions between resorts frequented by the working class, and the gentry and nobility became entrenched, reflecting the class divisions of the time.

Some argue that something similar is true today; that the complaints at the growth of Mass Tourism reflect a desire on the part of the 'new middle classes' to maintain the exclusivity of their holiday pursuits. However, today the critique of tourism is more broadly accepted and often appears not to carry the same snobbishness or elitism that Cook railed against.

Package tourists are not so much directly criticised for having inferior moral standards to New Moral Tourists, but are instead criticised for damaging other cultures; the culture of the host populations and hence also cultural diversity. This is different from the past, when tourists were considered to lack the cultural sophistication of the elite. The consequence of this is that today's critics of tourism identify themselves as radicals, champions of 'culture' and 'the environment', unlike in the past when antipathy towards tourism formed part of an unashamed conservative outlook. New Moral Tourism is thus presented as a selfless critique; for others, not just for oneself.

Eminent Victorian gentleman Sir Lesley Stephen spoke of 'Cockney-ridden' resorts, but pointed out that at least the resorts confined the 'swarm of intrusive insects' to one place. The last hundred years have seen the aristocratic sense of superiority decline.

Today advocates of sustainable tourism see some value in popular resorts in so far as they keep a lot of people in one place, minimising potential environmental damage. The language of the Victorian critic is unacceptable today, but the sentiment that 'the mass' of people, mobile, constitute a problem is all the stronger for being re-presented in terms of environmental and cultural threats.

Whilst Thomas Cook's tours of 130 years ago were criticised for carrying those without the etiquette and cultural understanding of the elite, JMC, the brand used by Thomas Cook package holidays today, is more likely to be criticised for damaging environments and cultures.

FROM 'TRAVELLER-TOURIST' TO NEW MORAL TOURISM

The debates over travel in the nineteenth century bequeathed us 'traveller versus tourist', an axis around which the critique of tourism has often been discussed. This is still very much in evidence today, witnessed in tour operator advertising, travel literature and in the broader discussion of the nature of modern tourism.

However, as we shall see, travel today is far from immune to the criticisms of its deviant offspring, tourism. Today's critique of tourism, premised as it is on a view of people in opposition to nature and cultures, has extended itself further to encompass the erstwhile critics themselves.

The propensity to turn in on itself and to become *self-critical* is an important, new, characteristic of the New Moral Tourism. Today's debate is less 'traveller versus tourist' (although the tourists are the ones generally in the frame), and more a critique that starts out focussing on the package tourist and, following its own logic, ends up criticising the attempts at ethical tourism themselves.

The cultural associations of post-war travel include the Hippy Trail in the 1960s and 1970s. Well-heeled university students, rock stars and assorted hippies established the Trail, stretching from London, picking up in Europe, and on through Asia to Kathmandu.

They were self-consciously seeking a spiritual enlightenment, and reacted against what they perceived to be a materialistic, modern society tainted by the Vietnam War. They embodied a rejection, be it a temporary one, of western culture, and placed themselves at the centre of the counter-culture.

For the radical thinker Marcuse, Man had become 'one dimensional', and through travel young radicals sought a more human dimension. Travel for them offered a spiritual alternative that had little connection to the growing holiday industry.

The counter-cultural character of the 1960s traveller was epitomised by Jack Kerouac. Kerouac, born into white Middle America, rejected the American dream ticket in favour of a ticket to nowhere in particular - his travel was hedonistic and directionless. Kerouac immersed himself in the culture of oppressed black America - jazz culture.

Whilst Kerouac's *On The Road* remains iconic for some travellers, his legacy is unclear. On the one hand, Kerouac's rejection of the American way of life may resonate with New Moral Tourist's moral elevation of the host's culture above their own. On the other, whilst Kerouac is associated with an amoral, directionless detachment from his society, the moralisation of tourism embodies a search for direction and is associated with moral regulation of oneself and others.

Another icon of post-war travel is the Lonely Planet

guidebook series. The first Lonely Planet guide was written by Tony and Maureen Wheeler, two enterprising travellers left broke by their travels in the hippy heydays of the early 1970s.

It contained useful advice on the merits of Kashmiri and Afghan marijuana - it was not a mainstream publication. Lonely Planet bought into the idea of travel as an alternative to tourism - something more individual, authentic and experimental. Lonely Planet guides today often deride the resorts favoured by package holidaymakers.

Alongside these icons, the symbols of the post-war package tourism industry include Butlin's holiday camps, Horizon Holidays (the first package holiday company to charter aircraft and fly tourists to Majorca and elsewhere) and Blackpool's Golden Mile. Unlike the symbolism of travel, tourism is, for its critics, naff.

So the traveller has generally been presented as a very different animal to the tourist. Travel has long been associated with experience and individualism - travellers are not part of the 'faceless' Mass Tourists, as they are so often portrayed by the ethical lobby. To be a traveller was to take an interest in the local culture - for Tony Wheeler, founder of Lonely Planet guidebooks, to experience it 'at ground level', rather than travel within the 'tourist bubble' of the package holiday industry. American writer Daniel Boorstin set the tone in the 1960s.

For Boorstin, 'The traveller was active; he went strenuously in search of people, of adventure, of experience. The tourist is passive; he expects interesting things to happen to him ... he expects everything to be done to him and for him.'

The self-perception of the traveller is the 'thinking tourist' - someone prepared to strike out, experiment with different ways of life, and not be part of a packaged product put together by global companies.

He is someone who takes an interest in the culture and the environment of his host. One could surmise from this that the New Moral Tourist was with us all along, in the guise of the traveller. However, the modern travellers - backpackers, trekkers, ecotourists, gappers - have in many ways increasingly merged into the Mass Tourist - they are increasingly subject to similar criticisms.

The critique of travel is most widely expressed against the burgeoning 'backpacking community'. A report on the behaviour of backpackers paints an unflattering picture - one akin to some of the condemnatory commentaries of package tourists. Dr Heba Aziz of the Roehampton Institute in London draws the conclusion from her research of backpackers in Egypt that they inhabit their own 'international backpacker culture' consisting of sex, drugs, pizzas and pancakes.

They hang out with each other in 'den-like coffee shops with thick cushions and hookah pipes' pouring over 'The Book'. 'The Book', as readers of modern backpacker literature such as Alex Garland's *The Beach* and William Sutcliffe's hilarious *Are You Experienced*? will be aware, is the Lonely Planet guide. The conclusion of the research is that travellers, just like tourists, are rather insensitive and crude.

And far from breaking away from the tourist bubble to discover other cultures, they are portrayed as happy to create their own culture ably assisted by the Lonely Planet empire.

The tone of this report is echoed in many unflattering commentaries on the backpacker. One recent opinion piece in *The Times* newspaper likened backpackers to 'great lumbering dungbeetles ... slumping like so many uncollected bin-bags around the Trafalgar Square fountain'.

To be young and to travel seems to invite cynicism, if not downright hostility, from some of tourism's critics. The perception of the traveller no longer conforms to that of Boorstin - active, in search of culture and experience - instead they are presented as destructive Mass Tourism in disguise.

Also travellers have often stood some distance from the charge of environmental and cultural degradation, an accusation commonly levelled against Mass Tourism. Today that distance is diminished. One theme that emerges in the new critique of the traveller is that they are at the cutting edge of extending the numbers of people travelling, in a world in which international travel is viewed as already bumping up against limits. Therefore if it is accepted that globally numbers of people travelling is a problem then the travellers inevitably get tarred with the same brush as tourists.

Due to growing incomes and lower-cost travel opportunities, independent travel has grown markedly in recent decades. STA Travel, specialists in independent travel, sent half a million British youth abroad in 1999, many on RTWs (Round The World Tickets) - a tenfold increase on a decade ago. It is estimated that backpacking has increased sixfold over the last ten years, reflecting these trends - upwards of 200,000 people go backpacking annually from the UK alone.

Other estimates put travellers at around 10 per cent of international visitors. In particular, lower oil prices and improved technology, coupled with increased competition resulting from airline deregulation, have brought down the cost of travelling by air. In recent years the rapid growth of the low-cost 'budget' airlines such as Easyjet and Ryanair has also improved the opportunities to travel independently in Europe.

Just as important perhaps is what could be regarded as the more flexible existence of young people. Breaks (either voluntary or as a result of short-term contracts or redundancy) in one's working life are more common. Also people are starting families later in life, hence extending the period in which footloose travel is a possibility.

Whilst travel has in the past been associated with youth, now the years of youthful freedom have extended into 'middle youth' as more people put off settling down into their thirties and later. Tony Wheeler has pointed out that these days backpackers include everyone from broke teenagers to the 'Hilton Hippies', who travel backpacker style but stay in expensive accommodation; or the 300 doctors at a convention who venture into the Australian outback and stay at a backpackers' lodge.

Of course, all this applies to some more than others - career breaks are a pipe dream for those without a career.

The view that this growing band of travellers simply adds to tourist numbers is developed by Brian Wheeller of Birmingham University. For this critic, travel companies promoting ecotourism - definitely in the camp of travel rather than tourism - are simply engaged in a marketing ploy providing a cosy, environmentally friendly feel-good factor for western tourists - meanwhile, global capitalist growth in tourism continues unchecked but in a more acceptable guise. Wheeller argues that, whatever the label, it is all pretty much the same when it comes down to it - it is all pretty negative.

However, the impact of independent travellers is not only seen as a question of numbers - if this were the case the criticisms would be barely distinguishable from those of Mass Tourism. It has been pointed out that backpackers act as *pioneers* of Mass Tourism.

In seeking out more remote, less popular locations, the backpacker leaves in their wake a nascent tourism industry. Businesses, local and foreign, spot possibilities to develop the industry, companies cite the location in their brochure and word of mouth increases awareness of the place as a destination. Over time one thing leads to another and a few adventurous trekkers becomes large numbers of youthful pleasure seekers.

One industry expert has noted this role of 'traveller as a destination pioneer' on what was once the Hippy Trail. In a research paper he quotes as evidence Murgha Mack of Top Deck Travel: destinations which were first explored by intrepid backpackers often evolve into mainstream areas for tourism ... For example, we have carried backpackers overland to Kathmandu for many years, but it is only in the last few years that it has come to be visited by the less adventurous traveller.

And then after the less-adventurous traveller comes ... the tourist! The travellers spread the tourism net further and further afield as they keep 'a step ahead of the growing army of other travellers and institutionalised mass tourism markets in the continuing search for ever-increasing exotic destinations'.

The Hippy Trail, one of our icons of travel mentioned earlier, is now superseded by a trail of 'mass backpackers', who are regarded with the glumness previously reserved for the package tourist.

Travel is also implicated in damaging cultures in a similar fashion to the claims made against Mass Tourism. In Goa and on the eastern coast and islands of Thailand the allegation against independent travel is that it has become commercialised and as such is indistinguishable from mass package travel. This commercialisation, it is argued, has implications for both the host and the tourist.

For the hosts it means they are subject to far-reaching cultural change. The economy becomes geared up to sell to tourists at a profit. An important element of this process is the 'commoditisation' of culture. Here long-standing aspects of indigenous culture become staged as rituals for the travellers/ tourists.

These rituals may lose their true meaning and value for the community practising them. Their role in cohering the societies is less in evidence as they become bought and sold. Hence travellers - those who look for the traditional, the authentic - may in fact, it is argued, be doing the most harm to the object of their fascination.

For the traveller it is held that the experience of travel is diminished by its commercialisation - a commercialisation that proceeds apace. This is ironic, as travel can be seen as an attempt to escape the commodification of human relationships - the influence of the cash nexus on how we relate to one another. This aspiration, to escape the modern, commercial world, may be confounded, as the attempts themselves are subject to the same commercialisation.

This is not a new theme. In the 1960s German writer Hans Magnus Enzenberger argued that, 'Liberation from the Industrial World has become an industry in its own right, the journey from the commodity world has become a commodity.' Rudy Koshar in his book *German Travel Cultures* usefully describes the process of commodification as one of a 'simultaneous multiplication and narrowing of possibilities that late modern and commercial society brings'.

More opportunities are available formally, but it becomes increasingly difficult to break out of the particular *way* we consume, relating to each other through the cash nexus. The search for something different - alternative - is seemingly confounded by the commercialisation of travel. Travel becomes commercialised and merges into tourism.

In this vein travel has been problematised by both conservative and radical thinkers. Conservative American critic Daniel Boorstin bemoaned the end of travel in his classic *The Image: a Guide to Pseudo Events in America.* He saw it as denigrated by the decadence of mass production, mass transport and mass communications. People were disinterested, duped, or both.

For Boorstin, we are offered, and have become satisfied with, 'pseudo events' rather than the real thing, exemplified by the popularity of 'tourist attractions' over interest in people and places.

Dean MacCannell, writing from a radical perspective, raised a similar theme in his ground-breaking *The Tourist: a New Theory of the Leisure Class* in the early 1970s, written at a time of rapid increase in international Mass Tourism, and also the heyday of the hippy trail.

For MacCannell, many people sought out authenticity through their travels. This authenticity was denied to them at home, stifled by the dominance of a society defined by consumerism and the cash nexus. Yet for MacCannell, this search for authenticity is all too often stifled by the commercialised nature of travel and tourism - the search for a more human and humane existence is often in vain. MacCannell hence saw tourism as a metaphor for the contradictions of modern society, a perspective that strongly informs the debate today.

Boorstin and MacCannell are often contrasted to one another - Boorstin dubbed 'elitist' as he seems to view the majority as having been dumbed down to accept 'pseudo' experiences, and MacCannell the radical who portrays tourists as aware of the lack of authenticity in their everyday lives, aspiring to something else; something better.

However, the shared theme between these authors is a sense that commercialisation spreads itself ever further and wider, to the detriment of the people concerned, in this case host and tourist. Travel as an attempt to distance oneself from this is either difficult or impossible. Travel is increasingly a part of mass consumer society, something that both authors bemoan. Hence travel is perhaps Mass Tourism - travellers are just fooling themselves.

Our second icon of travel, the Lonely Planet Guide, provides an example of this sense that travel has merged into Mass Tourism. Lonely Planet, once associated with independence, freedom and adventure, is in the frame for spawning generations of 'mass backpackers'.

For their critics, these backpackers are really Mass Tourists by another name. In this vein, the Lonely Planet guides have been described as 'a blueprint for the modern package holiday', as 'the book dictates where to stay, where to eat, which day trips to take, what to buy'. In Alex Garland's book *The Beach,* and in the subsequent film adaptation, the Lonely Planet guide is described as 'The Book', a metaphor often used for backpackers' guides.

The Book conjurs up the image of the backpacker following religiously the instructions from this 'higher authority' - travelling where The Book recommends, staying where The Book decrees and generally acting as a disciple of the new religion of travel. For critic of travellers Heba Aziz, the guides are deemed to have 'institutionalised' travel, making it similar to, and as damaging as, package tourism.

Today Lonely Planet is a major international operation with millions of sales annually and over 250 publications. And if you haven't got The Book you can access The Web Page from the internet cafés found in every backpacker ghetto. Hence Lonely Planet seems to epitomise the commercialisation of travel.

By the critics, its customers are increasingly portrayed less as free-spirited, free-thinking travellers, and more as naive disciples, following The Book religiously, and turning traveller heaven into tourist hell.

The implicit assumption of the assault on travel guidebooks is the same as that underlying criticisms of mass package tourists - that the consumer is an uncritical recipient of falsitudes from a rapacious industry. Travellers, the 'thinking tourists', become part of the faceless, homogenous mass.

Leaving aside the gross cynicism of some of the criticisms of the guides, the charges are surely unjustified. The humble guidebook is just that, a guidebook, with advice that one may choose to follow or ignore. Travellers can take it or leave it. Tony Wheeler, Lonely Planet founder, himself admits to meeting travellers who used his guides to identify places to avoid.

'WE'RE ALL TOURISTS NOW'

A backpacking acquaintance of mine sees himself as a traveller rather than a tourist. The only exception, he says, is when he meets other backpackers - then he is only too keen to distance himself from the pretensions of his fellow travellers!

It is common to argue that travelling and tourism are more or less the same thing. However, there are perhaps differences, even if they are more to do with how people like to conceive of themselves than anything else. In general, for travellers the *getting there* is likely to be at least as important as *being there*. Even for the less-experienced, more conservative traveller, travel is associated with an experiential dimension lacking from tourism.

Paul Fussell in his book, *Abroad*, referring to those who see themselves as travellers and look down upon tourists, asserts: 'The anti tourist deludes only himself. We are all tourists now.'

This argument that 'we are all tourists now' tends to translate as 'we are all *as bad as* tourists now' cited in the context of a downbeat discussion of the perceived cultural and environmental problems created by tourists and travellers alike. Arch-critic of ecotourism, Brian Wheeller, makes a similar point, arguing that 'new wave tourism' is a sheen on a destructive industry: of those considering the issues, popular opinion is that mass tourism with all its stereotyped negative connotations is bad, guilty of causing tourism's impact problems and should be 'dealt with' accordingly.

New Wave Tourism, on the other hand, is seen as the complete antithesis to this, sensitive, sophisticated and sustainable, the perfect antidote to be encouraged and enjoyed. While advocating a more caring industry, it fosters the image of a return (if there ever was one) to the golden age of enriching and educative travel.

It echoes Senecas (*sic*) 'we should choose a place which is healthy not only for our bodies but also for our morals.' That this appraisal is perhaps less than objective, coloured (green?) by the fact that many of those voicing an opinion do not regard themselves as mass tourists, or as being part of mass tourism, is completely ignored. For eco tourism, read ego tourism.

'Just once, I went for a run on a Harley motorbike. I thought "Where's the farthest I can go? I'll go to Alaska", It's like 700 miles. A friend of mine, Larry, came along, and if he hadn't, I don't think I would have done it. It rained every day and, God, it was a misery. I realised I had a 26-year-old brain and a 52-year-old butt. But every time I'd look in the mirror, Larry was back there and the two of us pushed each other along.

It took us about a month and it poured every day apart from two days when it snowed. We got there and Larry said: "What do you think?" I said: "Hell, I don't know, let's go home ..." And we turned right around and came back again. I sold the Harley and I don't care if I never see another one.'

Wheeller rightly conveys the sense in which New Moral Tourism is an etiquette that contributes to the moral authority of those adopting it. However, his riposte to 'New Wave Tourism' does not proceed to defend package holidays, but to suggest that ecotourism is just as fraught as its mass counterpart. It is this pessimistic standpoint, rather than the notion itself that we are all tourists, that I would take issue with. Tourism, or travel - whatever your preference - should be celebrated. Tourists and travellers should be defined less by the risks they pose, and more by the opportunities (including purely pleasurable opportunities) they create.

And if there is such a thing as a traveller, as distinct from a tourist, is there anything worth celebrating in this classification, often considered elitist, snobbish and pretentious? In many ways the association of travel with life experience may be just so much hot air.

For some, travelling abroad is a break from what they perceive as the routine and stress of modern western existence. If so, the year out could easily be interpreted as simply running away from real life to immerse oneself in a temporary fantasy world for as long as finances permit.

And why cannot 'experience' be gained in other ways? Is the teacher who takes a year out to go trekking and work in Peru more experienced than the one who focuses on her subject for the year and enjoys a fortnight all-inclusive in Spain? Is the student who reads in his bedroom any less wise than the one who volunteers to work in conservation in the Seychelles? And more to the point for many travellers, is working in a bar in Australia so different from working in a bar in London?

I have no reason to defend travellers, never having been part of this fraternity. And it is tempting to go along with the critics who attempt to knock oh so worldly backpackers off their pedestal by rubbishing their experience and pointing out their supposed role in environmental degradation.

But the premise of the attack is that people and cultures are fragile, and that we should restrict any desires we have to see the world from a recognition that we are complicit in trashing the planet. This clearly is an attack on all of us, travellers, tourists and everyone else.

New Moral Tourism, then, has tended to broaden the scope of what is to be criticised. The package holiday, Mass Tourism, is the obvious culprit if one starts from the premise that cultural encounters are fraught, that development has spun out of control and that there are simply too many tourists. Backpacking, having expanded rapidly, logically must, and has, entered the frame too.

But what of ecotourism, advocated as a solution to the problems of Mass Tourism? Here is a form of tourism explicitly linked to conservation rather than destruction. Ecotourism, according to the World Tourism Organisation and The International Ecotourism Society in America, is the fastest-growing tourism market (be it from a very low base). So surely, following the logic of the moralisation of tourism, is it not also a risky activity?

In fact, this is precisely the criticism some have made. Ecotourism - for its advocates lying at the opposite end of the moral spectrum to Mass Tourism - is increasingly subject to similar criticisms. One writer, Anita Pleumaron of the Tourism Investigation and Monitoring Team in Thailand, expresses in stark terms the dilemma for the conservation-minded ecotourist.

In a paper titled 'Ecotourism or Ecoterrorism' she argues that ecotourism is usually just as destructive as package tourism. Ecotourism, unlike tourism to already-developed regions, threatens 'the expropriation of "virgin" territories'. Moreover, 'travellers have already opened up many new destinations', bringing the Mass Tourism that New Moral Tourism seeks to avoid.

In similar vein, Erlet Cater, advocate of ecotourism, sees dangers in its development: 'There is a real danger that eco tourism may merely replicate the economic, social and physical problems already associated with conventional tourism. The only difference ... is that previously undeveloped areas are being brought into the locus of international tourism.'

Martha Honey, Director of the Ecotourism Programme at the Institute for Policy Studies in Washington DC, makes a similar point, asserting that

By definition, ecotourism often involves seeking out the most pristine, uncharted and unpenetrated areas on Earth. Often, these are home to isolated and fragile civilisations. In some areas, ecotourism is at the front line of foreign encroachment and can accelerate the pace of social and environmental degradation and lead to a new form of western penetration and domination of the last remaining 'untouched' parts of the world.

Here, not only is ecotourism complicit in destructive practices, but it is actually 'at the front line of foreign encroachment'. This conjures an image of cultural purity degraded by outsiders. For these authors mass tourists have a single redeeming factor - that they are less interested in 'encroaching' upon wilderness.

The contradictions of ecotourism are also well expressed by a writer in the American Audubon Society magazine: 'Tour boats dump garbage in the waters off Antarctica, shutterbugs harass wildlife in National Parks, hordes of us trample fragile areas. This frenzied activity threatens the viability of natural systems.

At times we seem to be loving nature to death.' Such comments are typical of the dilemmas within the advocacy of New Moral Tourism. There is a real irony in all this. Advocates of New Moral Tourism have long criticised package tours as destructive of the environment. Ecotourism was their ethical alternative to the rapacious mainstream industry. Now it stands accused of having the same destructive capacity.

There can be no fixed dividing line between Mass Tourism and New Moral Tourism today, as the latter's criticisms of the former have increasingly turned in on themselves. New Moral Tourism is not just critical of others, but is self-critical too. The premise of the New Moral Tourism -

HOLIDAY SNAPS - 'INDONESIAN TOUR GUIDE'

'With the tourists everything is organised, so they don't destroy as much. The traveller wants to see something new and wants it to be cheap and then tells others about it. I prefer tourists ... the travelers are uncontrolled - they don't want to go to the places already prepared for them, they want to go to other places and then they spoil them - and they don't spend any money.' that cultural encounters are fraught, that environments are under threat from leisure travel - has meant that increasingly all tourism has come under scrutiny. As one critic puts it, despite ethical intent, 'even small groups of people, or for that matter the lone traveller, no matter how sensitive, may have a disruptive effect on local culture'.

Moreover, for some the discussion has gone full circle. Cynical critics of New Moral Tourism brands argue that as they involve going to remote places and linking with communities, they may in fact be more destructive than Mass

Tourism. Such cynics take delight in arguing that perhaps Benidorm and Blackpool are the best examples of environmentally and culturally benign tourism, as the impacts are kept in one place and can be more easily managed. Such arguments portray a dim view of the tourist. These critics clearly regard holidaymakers as willing prisoners in beachside jails. Their critique is a false one - it shares the premises of New Moral Tourism, although at least it is prepared to take it to its logical conclusion.

New Moral Tourism is a fluid, moralistic perspective rather than a defined set of products or activities - although clearly some activities are deemed 'bad' and others broadly 'good'. It is an inclination to see others, and oneself, as potential problems to environments and cultures. It embodies an impulse to lay down a moral code to police the boundaries between tourists and their hosts. Never mind Mass Tourism, travel, for leisure or education, for relaxation or fantasy, is worth defending from this.

Chapter 2

Fragile Places, Fragile People

Two overarching assumptions of New Moral Tourism are that environments and cultures are fragile in the face of growing numbers of tourists. This chapter questions these ideas and suggests that in assuming this, advocates of New Moral Tourism do few favours to the host societies they purport to be sensitive towards.

NATURAL LIMITS

The negative views of the tourist referred to in the previous exist alongside and are mediated through a critique of the environmental and cultural problems placed at the door of tourists and the tourism industry.

These problems are considered severe, sometimes bordering on apocalyptic. One influential book opens with the assertion: 'A spectre is haunting our planet: the spectre of tourism.' The emphasis on the destructive capacity of tourism is striking. For one critic:

Over the last 30 years or so, mass tourism has had the effect of ruining landscapes, destroying communities, diverting scarce resources, polluting the air and water, trivialising cultures, creating uniformity, and generally contributing to the increased degradation of life on our planet.

Tourists are commonly charged with being responsible for damaging the environment and destroying cultures. For the critics, the Costa del Sol is no more than a 'concrete jungle' and Goa is rapidly going the same way.

It is clearly a serious charge - one that has prompted non-governmental organisations (NGOs), campaigns and aid agencies to devote their energies to reforming the industry, and reforming the tourists themselves. In the former case, new forms of tourism are proposed to replace package holidays, and in the latter case, codes of conduct seek to change the behaviour of the tourist.

Over the last fifty years tourism has increased greatly - there are now around 700 million international tourists annually, compared to 50 million in the mid-1950s. The rapid growth of leisure travel is often presented as being of frightening proportions.

There is also an overriding sense that the travel 'carrying capacity' of the planet has been reached or exceeded. Even at the level of the United Nations, some believe society is 'bumping up against limits'. In fact, one could also argue that such a remarkable growth is a drop in the ocean when we consider that it represents approximately one in ten of the world's population.

Whilst there is much concern at the global picture, the issue of tourist numbers is most often discussed in terms of the carrying capacity of a resort, region or village, defined as 'the maximum use of any site without causing negative effects on the resources, reducing visitor satisfaction, or exerting adverse impact upon the society, economy and cultures'.

Carrying capacity seems relatively straightforward - the number of people a particular geographical area can cope with, that in turn sets limits to the extent of tourism development.

Yet whilst carrying capacity provides a useful marker for planners, the usage of the term tends to assume a static state of affairs. Carrying capacity is often implicitly assumed as fixed in the New Moral Tourism worldview, determined by the pre-existing relationship between people and the natural environment in a particular place.

In fact, development itself, including tourism development, can *transform* the carrying capacity. Better transport, drainage, facilities - for residents as well as tourists - would surely be part of well-planned developments, and would enable greater numbers of people to visit if this was deemed appropriate.

It is ironic that carrying capacity is more likely to be seen as an issue where population density, and density of tourists, is actually low, and conversely is less likely to be problematised in major cities and established resort areas.

Concern over capacity is often fraught in rural parts of the developing world, where just a few tourists, it is held, can damage fragile environments and cultures. The problem with this is that it becomes a Catch 22 situation in which development is deemed inappropriate due to carrying capacity constraints, and in which these constraints are never challenged due to the dearth of development.

For example, one study argues that trekkers in the Himalayas are pushing against the carrying capacity and hence the sustainability of the regional environment. The wood demanded and the biodegradable litter created by the several hundreds in the 1950s was sustainable within the system's productivity, but the demands and refuse of the many thousands in the 1900s are not.

Here the carrying capacity is determined by the pre-existing relationship between people and the environment in this area. There is no suggestion that greater numbers of tourists could generate revenue that may have the effect of altering this relationship.

Some would argue, though, that the carrying capacity, if exceeded, will put off ecotourists, trekkers and green tourists and damage the economy - that in a sense attempts to expand may be self-defeating. This is, however, a wholly different argument, which amounts to saying that the market won't stand for environmental change. It may be entirely rational to place a carrying capacity on an area of land to this end. However, it has little to do with fragility.

The notion of carrying capacity is sometimes modified to allow for 'Limits of Acceptable Change', or 'adaptancy', referring to the limits to changing carrying capacity progressively over time. Such an approach is more sophisticated, and undoubtedly useful in planning.

However, it cannot answer the question as to what these limits are - for the advocates of New Moral Tourism, environmental and cultural imperatives rein in substantial change by branding it as destructive. LAC, and the notion of adaptancy, also present change as an exogenous variable to the societies in question. It can easily be interpreted in a mechanical fashion that denies the creativity of the host societies.

FRAGILE ENVIRONMENTS

Of course, some areas may be regarded as being more 'fragile' than others - there is an argument that different areas, defined by their culture as well as geography, have a differential ability to cope with development. Two authorities define fragile environments as 'environments that are less suitable for dense human colonisation' and point out that such areas may be attractive as potential tourism destinations due to their natural beauty.

But in what sense are these areas less suitable for human habitation? Industrial development, cities, developed infrastructure and other features of modern societies exist in many different climates and geographical conditions, from London to Rio de Janeiro, and from Seoul to Addis Ababa. The reasons for development in some parts of the planet and for a lack of development in others are primarily social rather than the result of natural suitability or fragility.

Indeed, if natural suitability were a criteria, California would never have been built, and rebuilt, on the San Andreas fault line, parts of Holland would be in the sea and Hackney Marshes would still be a marsh, rather than a residential area in London.

Two authorities, Harrison and Price, see fragile environments as including those that exhibit 'marked seasonality, which means that many human activities are limited to quite clearly defined parts of the year'. Such activities are listed as 'cultivating crops, collecting naturally growing foods, hunting, or fishing [which are] typically limited to relatively few months - or even weeks - of the year'. These months or weeks may also be the seasons for tourism, hence the propensity for tourism to damage such fragile environments.

Yet societies that rely on the land in this way are often less developed, exhibiting high infant mortality and low literacy levels. The dilemma here is that if the problematic consequences of incremental development are seen as a reason to question the appropriateness of any development, then the environment remains fragile.

It becomes a self-reinforcing process. The authors are correct to point out that 'Tourism should not be viewed in isolation from the environments and cultures on which it is imposed' but similarly, those environments and cultures do not exist outside of an existing level of development and can be understood only in their relationship to this, not as prior features of a society.

Posed in this way, it is possible to view environmental capacity problems less as too much development and more as the partial nature of development (lack of infrastructure alongside resort developments) *or even the overall lack of development*.

Harrison refers to 'fragile lands', which he argues is similar to the conception of fragile environments utilised at the United Nations Rio Earth Summit in 1992, and to that of another author, Deneven, writing about environmental fragility in Latin America.

The latter emphasises that such fragile lands should be managed according to traditional land-use systems. In essence he argues that these fragile environments impose specific limits to development on their respective communities. However, it is unlikely that traditional land-use systems will enable the inhabitants to develop economically in any systematic fashion.

It is highly unlikely that the 'sustainable agriculture' advocated will enable the inhabitants of such areas to join the still rather exclusive club of holidaymakers. Of course, there can be sound scientifically-based reasons why particular environments may be ill-suited for particular developments.

However, as Urry and MacNaughten have pointed out, popular appeals to the environment only occasionally take as their primary point of reference scientific enquiry. Rather, they are more often to do with 'specific contestation about instances of nature which [have come] to symbolise a wider unease with the modern world'. Such sentiments, they argue, reflect an 'aspiration for more meaningful collective engagement and moral renewal'.

The moralisation of tourism lies within this trend. The contestation of particular environments, and how they should, or should not be used for tourism, often takes an a priori circumspect view of development. This is presented as cultural sensitivity towards the host community, and hence also as a more moral type of behaviour.

It is also worth noting that there is a lack of coherence in the environmental claims even in their own terms. The moralised view of tourism often holds dear the *specific* environment of the host community, above a broader view of the global environment.

More often than not New Moral Tourism involves long-haul travel - this is as true in the green travel guides as it is with the commercial niche market tour operators. Yet other environmentalists, such as Friends of the Earth, highlight air travel itself as the most environmentally damaging aspect of modern tourism.

FRAGILE CULTURES

Moreover, Deneven also argues that, 'social fragility, in terms of organisation, markets, prices, incomes, social relationships and politics ... can be more critical than environmental fragility'. Development is problematic not simply in relation to the environment, but also in relation to the existing balance *between people and the environment*.

Similarly, writer on ecotourism Erlet Cater refers to the potential for even the most sensitive of tourism developments to bring problems to 'delicately balanced physical and cultural environments'.

This is a crucial point in the environmental critique of tourism development - that there is an existing balance that embodies something positive not just about the environment, but also about culture. Environmental preservation is justified not just for its own sake, but with regard to this relationship.

Hence the environmental critique of tourism is at one and the same time a critique of its cultural effects, with culture viewed as this existing relationship between people and nature.

This approach is underwritten by the United Nations, whose Agenda 21 documentation asserts that, [indigenous people] have developed over many generations a holistic traditional scientific knowledge of their lands, natural resources and environment ....

In view of the interrelationship between the natural environment and its sustainable development and the cultural, social and physical well-being of indigenous people, national and international efforts to implement environmentally sound and sustainable development should recognise, accommodate, promote and strengthen the role of indigenous people and their communities.

The quote makes explicit that it is the relationship between local (in this case indigenous) communities and the natural environment on which they rely that is central to development. Formulations such as these suggest that nature and history take precedence over technology and aspiration for equality in sustainable development.

The application of modern technology, and the levels of development required to make inroads into inequality and poverty, may not rest easily with this deference to indigenous knowledge and local culture, a deference strongly evident in the moralisation of tourism. Local culture - people and their relationship to their immediate environment - is regarded as fragile in the face of development.

'Fragile environments', then, embodies the notion of fragile communities - the people who live within these environments. The relationship between fragile environments and fragile communities is typically discussed as follows:

Just as traditional uses of soils, waters, plants and animals - often developed over centuries (or longer) of experimentation to minimise change in communities' biophysical life-support systems - may be rapidly degraded by external influences, the communities' societal structures are equally susceptible to change by external human forces, whose magnitude and potential impacts are not always predictable. In relation to tourism development, cases where tourism has caused social and economic dislocation are well documented. The problem, however, is that reference to fragile communities suggests that development *as a category* is destructive. Hence the preservation of existing social and economic patterns becomes something intrinsically desirable in the face of this fragility.

The discussion of fragility effectively creates a vicious circle of fragility, or perhaps more accurately, poverty. Poorer regions in the Third World, often based upon subsistence agriculture, are inevitably going to be affected greatly by development. Yet in order to overcome their fragility, development - thoroughgoing, transformative development - is precisely what is required.

The anti-developmental content of the language of fragile environments and cultures is evidenced in a discussion of the Annapurna Conservation Area Project in Nepal. Two authors comment that 'village youths are easy prey to the seductiveness of western consumer culture as tourists are laden with expensive trappings such as high-tech hiking gear, flashy clothes, cameras and a variety of electronic gadgetry'. They argue that the Nepalese culture is in grave danger of corruption by tourists.

Yet what is really so wrong in aspiring to own a camera and wear fashionable clothes? In fact the real problem here is that for so many Nepalese, like other Third World peoples, the prospect of owning a camera is a distant one because of the poverty that prevails there. The forms of 'sustainable tourism' advocated by the authors are designed to leave these societies as they are - culturally authentic, but grindingly poor.

Further, the authors of this research argue that in the past, 'basic needs have been accommodated by the resource base'. They go on to argue:

Numerous indigenous systems evolved to manage natural resources. Although not perfect, the systems have helped to maintain the quality of the Annapurna environment. Over the last two decades, the explosion in trekking tourism has upset this delicate ecological balance and has contributed significantly to a loss of cultural integrity in the Annapurna region.

Limits imposed upon the indigenous people are not a product of their environment or their culture, but of *the relationship between the two.* In this way, a carrying capacity that precludes transformative development is championed as arising from a holistic approach.

Of course, there will always be situations in which resentment occurs. The point is, though, that this has little to do with tourism development *per se*, but is more likely to be an expression of broader inequalities. Tensions can occur in Nepalese communities arising from, for example, the exposure of Holiday snaps - *The Beach*

Alex Garland's *The Beach* is a compelling read, and its theme strikes a chord. The beach in question is a place far from civilisation, inhabited by a self-selecting band of western youth. They live out a dream on their own Beach, hidden away from the rest of the world. But the dream turns in on itself.

Especially since the release of the $50 million movie version, starring Leonardo DiCaprio, *The Beach* has become something of a cultural reference point. The story behind the film's making is equally telling. The filmmakers have been accused of damaging the environment on Phi Phi Leh, the small Thai island used for filming.

The removal of some existing vegetation (giant milkweed, sea pandanus and spider lily, which then died in a plant nursery before it could be replaced) and the planting of palm trees in its place (removed after filming) has been a focus of the environmental protests that accompanied the filming.

Protesters have brought a legal case against the Thai Forestry Department, the Agriculture Ministry, the Thai film agent and Twentieth Century Fox. The protesters donned DiCaprio masks and chanted slogans to make their point.

Others have argued that Phi Phi Leh was already suffering some ill effects from tourism, and that the film crew cleared rubbish away prior to filming. Evidence of this is to be found in the Rough Guide, which warns that 'unfortunately the disregarded lunch boxes and water bottles of day trippers now threaten the health of the marine life' in the area. Prior to filming, an environmental audit was carried out.

After filming, Reef Check, a UN-endorsed coral conservation group, commented that there was no evidence of damage. Yet despite the efforts of the filmmakers, and the stated environmental commitment of the film's star, Leonardo DiCaprio, the film remains tainted by allegations of environmental insensitivity and a $2.6 million lawsuit.

The Beach has become a metaphor for the vain search for spiritualism away from western society. So the argument goes, when too many seek out the beauty of a remote place, it ceases to be remote and loses its beauty - for *The Beach* read Goa five years ago, or even Torremolinos ('a small fishing village ruined by mass tourism') twenty-five years ago.

Now environmentalists are worried that the film will popularise travel to Phi Phi Leh and other Thai beauty spots and threaten the natural environment.

Yet others have pointed out that although the palm trees are not authentic the island is cleaner than before. And inhabitants in the region have been far keener to benefit from the commercial spin-offs from the film than to protest.

Nepalese youth to trekkers exhibiting a level of wealth unavailable to them. But to cite tourism as the cause of such problems is to take a very restricted view. Broader inequalities are neglected in a discussion that is essentially about people's behaviour. The defence of cultural difference (from tourists) is prioritised and the aspiration for equality is the casualty.

PERCEPTUAL LIMITS

Carrying capacity can be seen as perceptual rather than based on an environmental imperative. It can be viewed as the numbers of tourists and amount of development possible before *perceptions* of the environment are tainted in the eyes of tourists or residents.

There is a commercial issue here - it may well be in the interests of the host to promote a particular type of tourism involving a high spend, which may involve restricting building and tourist numbers. However, there is no evidence that in general hosts prefer fewer tourists, even where tourist numbers are very high.

Malta, for example, a small island state and one of the most densely populated countries in the world, attracts large numbers of tourists on package holidays. Yet opinion polls on the island indicate that the Maltese would welcome more tourists - they are seen as a boon economically, and far from animosity, tourists are welcomed.

Perhaps this positive view is due to the fact that the island has enjoyed consistent development and increases in income alongside the growing influx of tourists. The Maltese experience suggests that perceptual limits, or at least those perceived by the host societies, cannot be understood outside the broader context of development and prospects for development.

However, the New Moral Tourism often cites perceptual limits as given features of communities under scrutiny. It is certainly true that one can find cases where communities have raised objections to plans for tourism development on the basis of its impact on their livelihoods or way of life. However, this is as likely to be an objection to the partial or limited nature of developments, as it is to too much development or too many people.

One model often cited in the academic discussion of tourism's impacts is Doxey's Irridex. The Irridex provides a linear scale on which to gauge the host's level of acceptance of tourists. It suggest that over time, and with greater numbers, a higher level of tension occurs - that there is a carrying capacity based on the willingness of the host community to accept large numbers of tourists. Initial 'euphoria' with the growth of tourism becomes 'apathy', followed by 'annoyance' and finally 'antagonism'.

In fact what is most striking about the model is not its limitations as a linear model for something as complex and multi-dimensional as a cultural encounter, but that a cultural encounter should be problematised in this way in the first place. The level of tension between different cultures is the starting point of the model.

The model suggests that 'a few people are OK, more people are increasingly a problem'. Yet anyone who has visited a popular holiday destination in a bad year when bookings are low will know that the opposite can be true. The Irridex typifies the a priori assumption of the host culture as fragile, and the consequent desire to establish perceptual limits.

THE OUTLOOK OF NEW MORAL TOURISM

The concept of carrying capacity is applied in a similar fashion in debates on population control, a fashion that could be described as Malthusian. Malthus, writing in the nineteenth century, believed that global population growth would outstrip the growth of the resources needed to provide for that population leading to famine.

Today there is often, particularly in the Third World, perceived to be too many people in relation to a limited resource base. Greater population, the Malthusian position has it, puts a strain on the natural environment that will be manifested in its degradation, with in turn severe implications for the survival of populations.

However, contrary to Malthus, societies have tended to uncover and harness far greater resources as populations have grown, and, it can be argued, precisely because they have grown, facilitating a greater division of labour within societies. So whilst Malthusian analysis tends to see 'people as problem', as a drain on resources whose growth cannot keep pace with increasing numbers of people, there is much evidence to support seeing 'people as solution'.

The application of carrying capacity to tourism development has a Malthusian character, be it more often applied at a local rather than global scale. Tourism growth is typically viewed as inherently problematic in relation to a fixed stock of resources.

Yet the ability to harness and develop resources has been vastly enhanced by increasing amounts of tourists and tourist revenue in many resort areas.

More people may pose environmental problems, but they also create possibilities for the resolution of these problems, at greater levels of development and with more opportunities for people as the result.

One small example of this principle is the beach at Benidorm. The much-derided resort of Benidorm caters for tens of thousands of tourists in a relatively small area. Yet it enjoys exceptionally clean beaches. The revenue from tourism enables the local authority to finance keeping the beaches clean, maintaining them as a resource.

One could make a similar case with regard to drainage systems and other facilities in many other successful Mass Tourism resort areas, which have often been upgraded to the benefit of hosts and tourists alike through wealth generated by the tourism industry. More people, it turns out, help finance a solution than simply pose an environmental problem.

Closer to home, the dredging of thousands of tons of sand to build up the beach at Bournemouth on England's south coast has attracted many tourists and sustained a growing industry. Increased tourism revenue has helped to finance improvements for tourists and residents alike. Increased numbers of visitors have been instrumental in improving facilities in the town.

However, horizons are typically lowered in the Third World, where limited developments, based on 'natural capital', are favoured as more environmentally sensitive in the New Moral Tourism outlook.

In a world in which tunnels under the Channel are possible and artificial islands can be built to accommodate air travel in Japan, one may have expected a more upbeat assessment of society's ability to develop the environment to provide a better life. However, the elevation of nature above development is intrinsic to the designation of rural parts of the developing world as 'fragile'. One author makes this point succinctly:

Our present admiration for untouched nature, increasingly tinged with guilt about our neglectful stewardship of its dwindling reserves, is a luxury belonging to a fairly advanced stage of social development. Before this had been achieved, nature struck people, if not as enemy, at least as a challenge. Civilisation started by clearing the wilderness. Yet it is the wilderness that, for some advocates of New Moral Tourism, is seen as fragile, subject to severe capacity limits and in need of *protection* from 'civilisation', which we can in this context read as development.

It is most often the Third World that is presented as under threat from modern development in the form of tourism. It is ironic that so much of the concern over numbers of tourists is directed at their perceived impacts on cultures and environments in the poorest countries, as the Third World is peripheral to international tourism flows.

It receives far fewer tourists (and generates fewer still) in relation to land mass and in relation to population size than the developed world. It is, though, the designation of rural environments in the Third World as fragile that provides a rationale for the emphasis on carrying capacity

'Fragility', though, is not given in an environment, but is premised on a limited and limiting view of the potential for development in the Third World, a view that can hold sway when prospects for development have been lowered to the level they are today. The problem is not too much development bumping against natural limits, but too little development to transform societies and push back these limits.

Rapacious development from tourism developers and hedonistic tourists with no regard for their hosts, is generally the last of the problems facing Third World countries seeking to better themselves. Rather, it is the partial and limited nature of development that can produce tensions.

From this perspective it is at least as true to argue that the problem is not too much development, but too little, and perhaps not too many tourists, but too few. In the developed world, too, tourism has been described as an industry that 'kills the goose that lays the Golden Egg' - we like to holiday to pretty places, but because so many of us do, these fragile places become spoiled. In the phrase of one report, we are 'loving to death' areas of natural beauty. There is an issue here.

Places of natural beauty should be maintained, but for the enjoyment of people rather than as bastions of nature. Mass

Tourism has done far more to increase access to diverse environments (natural and man made) than it has spoiled them for others. And elsewhere the Golden Goose is alive and well - last seen strutting Blackpool's Golden Mile.

'Tourism and travel, as global industries, have many different impacts on both the environment and the cultures of the world. Fragile natural resources like beaches and coral reefs can be destroyed by too many tourists or irresponsible development. Animal habitats can be devastated by visitors, and indigenous cultures can be altered forever by tourists and foreign corporations bringing money and goods.

'No matter where you go or how you travel, you will have an effect on the environment and the people you visit. But travelling responsibly can have minimal negative impact, and, in many cases, can actually help conserve the environment and preserve indigenous cultures.'

Chapter 3

Freedom Under Scrutiny

Tourism, especially in its 'traveller' form, has always been associated with freedom. Travel has changed profoundly, but today's backpackers still experience a rare freedom. For many young people, their travels lie between the ages of parental guidance and the strictures of work - perhaps a time for experimentation, radicalism and a little recklessness.

Package holidays are also about freedom. They traditionally carry the image of footloose, carefree relaxation. The holiday is the opposite of work - a chance to leave behind the discipline of working life, and perhaps also the moral strictures of home life.

Yet the innocent notion that you can 'leave your cares behind' seems less straightforward today. Alison Standcliffe from Tourism Concern reminds us that this involves 'closing your eyes to the things you normally care about'. Another author sees the 'increasingly hedonistic philosophy of many people' as militating against making tourism 'sustainable'. Hedonism, once a virtue of tourism, has become a threat. In place of spontaneity, caution and wariness are characteristic of the New Moral Tourism. This cautious approach is captured in a guideline from one of the growing number of codes of conduct for travellers and tourists:

Away from home and free; it is tempting to do things I would never do. I shall avoid this danger by observing myself critically whilst on holiday and behave with restraint. I want to enjoy myself without hurting and offending others.

Freedom is under scrutiny. For the critics of tourism, we have too much of it, both as individuals and as a society. But what is the extent of our freedom to travel? In the more wealthy countries in the world international leisure travel has become commonplace over just a couple of generations. Much of this has been achieved through the package holiday revolution spurred by growing disposable incomes and holiday entitlements. More recently low-cost airlines have also contributed to the ease of travel for footloose young people.

However, tourism's critics present the growth of tourism in apocalyptic terms. Jenny Jones, Chair of the Executive Committee of the Green Party, tells us that a 'staggering' 500 million travel abroad each year. If tourism were a country, we are told, 'it would be the third richest in the world'.

In the face of such dramatic pronouncements it is worth reminding ourselves that globally it is the barriers to travel, not its ease, that are most in evidence. It is all but impossible for the vast majority of the world's population to travel freely where they want to, even if they have the income to do so. Immigration controls operate as international pass laws - apartheid in South Africa has ended, but global apartheid has never been more in evidence, even for those wanting to travel simply for leisure.

There is a sick irony in the fact that Third World peoples are often fêted as rich in culture and spiritual depth within their own lands. Tourists can learn much, ecotourists tell us, from more sustainable lifestyles, closer to nature, in the Third World. Third World peoples can be visited and their cultures enjoyed and learnt from - but they can rarely reciprocate.

As soon as they want to travel here, they are no longer envied for their spiritual insight, living a simple life close to nature, but are transformed into 'economic migrants' or 'bogus asylum seekers' - a dire threat, we are told, to the western world.

Kenyans, when not dressed in traditional costume in the Masai Mara, or protecting wildlife for the enjoyment of well-heeled ecotourists, become part of the mass; a homogenous threat 'out there'. Wives are kept from husbands, children from their parents, by the fortress-like travel restrictions imposed in Europe, the USA and the rest of the developed world.

The expansion of travel has been described as the 'democratisation of travel'. This democratisation has proceeded apace, but still enfranchises only a small minority of the world's population, at least in terms of international leisure travel.

Yet for Jost Krippendorf, author of the seminal *The Holiday Makers: Understanding the Impacts of Leisure and Travel*, our freedom to travel 'threatens to engulf us'. If this is true then it paints a dark picture for those who are less free.

In 1991 a plane load of Jamaican tourists coming to the UK were stopped at the airport and turned back. They were over to visit family and friends for Christmas - a commonplace occurrence given Jamaica's expatriate links with the UK.

Normally, visas were recommended (although not officially necessary) to ensure a smooth passage through immigration, but on this occasion the British High Commission had told people to travel without, as the visa office was being rebuilt with security screens between prospective tourist and visa staff. The Jamaicans' Christmas was spoiled not by an administrative error, but by a system of checks that treats tourists of a certain colour as prospective criminals.

MODIFYING OUR HOLIDAYS

Tourism's critics are concerned with a kind of freedom. Much of the discussion of tourism today posits natural and cultural limits to its further expansion. Here, freedom is invoked by the critics - *freedom from* tourists is pitted against *freedom to* travel. Tourists are viewed through a dark lens by the critics - always as a threat to the environment or cultures, but rarely as an opportunity.

The critics argue that we should mould our desires, and indeed our lives, around what they consider to be environmental limits. For example, *The Green Travel Guide* argues that the traditional summer vacation is a behaviour pattern borne of habit, bad habit. Rather than spend a summer fortnight of fun and relaxation at a popular holiday destination, we should try to 'break this mould':

A day or two away from work may prove beneficial, and

a longer holiday taken off-season can be much more environmentally sustainable: air traffic is less congested, resorts and other tourist destinations less crowded. Short breaks allow the Green traveller to explore his or her own local environment, without adding to the strains of mass tourism, or to stay at home, whether it is to spend time with our families, catching up with other aspects of our local community lives, or in other forms of recreation.

The implication here seems to be that tourists do not know what is good for themselves, as well as the environment!

The guide goes on to add that increasingly people are 'downshifting' their lives - moving away from a routine nine to five, or even 'supershifting'; living in a way that enables one to choose when one works.

One guide to downshifting, written by two journalists who themselves downshifted, includes a section on how holidays fit in to this philosophy. Downshifters can, they argue, turn their diminished income into a virtue by holidaying closer to home or volunteering for environmental working holidays.

The package tour operators that one may have booked with when one had less time, pre-downshifting, are predictably criticised as destructive to the environment.

Concepts such as downshifting shed some light on the changed working arrangements for a minority of people, often those able to work more flexibly due to technology or wealthy enough to sacrifice earnings in favour of leisure.

But technology has not transformed the working day for most people; often people do the same job at the same desk, but with a computer on it, 'empowering' them to be 'multi-skilled' and 'flexible' enough to work harder, sometimes for longer. And many work hard to afford a few luxuries such as a holiday.

Ironically, taking a broader view of labour market changes over the last twenty years, the people who have the most flexibility with their time - the mass of young people channelled into burgeoning education programmes - are as likely to find themselves scraping together the cash for a once in a lifetime inter-rail around Europe or a fortnight in Turkey.

Jenny Jones of the Green Party also advocates holidays at home, which are, of course, more environmentally friendly. Drawing a link between environmental protection at home and abroad she begs the question:

How many residents of Newbury have been there? If more of them realised what they are about to lose local opposition to the bypass would be insurmountable. Will they instead allow the road to be built, and eventually use it to drive to Europe, to spend a holiday somewhere in the countryside not unlike what is being trashed on their doorstep?

It may be of interest to the residents of Newbury, a town in Berkshire in the UK, amongst others to note that this author speaks from the privileged position of having 'been there - done that'.

In the byline at the end of the article she mentions that she has worked and travelled in Jordan, Syria, Israel, Turkey, Crete, Ethiopia, Cyprus, Egypt and Abu Dhabi, as well as having lived in Seychelles and Lesotho. A case, perhaps, of 'do as I say, not as I do'?

Also this critic has missed the point about youth travel. Walk down the main thoroughfare of many cities around the world and you will often see young travellers - only they are all from overseas. And this is the point. Travelling is appealing to many young people not for the cultural experience or heroism, but simply because there is something about being young and *abroad*.

With the restrictions of family and school behind you, and the rigours of work ahead, the chance to travel often falls at a transitory period in people's lives. It is hard to feel liberated from these pressures travelling around Berkshire ... but the idea of being abroad has an entirely different appeal.

ETHICAL CODES: MORAL REGULATIONS FOR THE TOURIST

The advocates of a New Moral Tourism are not only concerned with the industry, but are profoundly interested in the tourist - your behaviour on holiday. The last five years have seen the emergence of a plethora of codes of conduct to advise and prescribe with regard to personal behaviour. The sentiment behind these is well expressed in the foreword to the recently compiled *Green Travel Guide* written by Robin Pellew of the World Wide Fund For Nature (WWF):

increased leisure and available money for travel, by train and air, opens up ... remote parts of the world to the adventurer and imaginative tourist. Faced with these realities, it is necessary that codes of conduct for ... visitors to foreign countries and different cultures are set in place to ensure the minimum impact on the environment and a maximum sensitivity to the local population and their ways of life.

New opportunities borne of increased travel possibilities have accompanied a growing consciousness of environmental and cultural risks, which these codes seek to address at the level of individual behaviour.

Below is outlined a selection from codes of conduct relating to the behaviour of travellers and tourists.

TOURISM CONCERN

Tourism Concern is probably the British campaigning NGO with the strongest profile. Alongside their numerous campaigns and educational resources, they also issue a general statement of 'Tourism Dos and Don'ts'.

Tourists are advised to: 'Save precious natural resources'; 'Support the local trade and craftspeople'; 'Always ask before taking photographs or video recordings of people'; 'Don't give money or sweets to children'; to 'Respect local etiquette - loose lightweight clothes are preferable to revealing shorts, skimpy tops and tight-fitting wear in many countries.

Similarly, kissing in public is often culturally inappropriate'; 'Learning something about the history and current affairs of the country helps you understand the attitudes and idiosyncrasies of its people and helps prevent misunderstandings and frustrations.' Overall, the leaflet states that it is 'Promoting awareness of the impact of tourism on people and their environments'. Tourists should 'Be patient, friendly and sensitive. Remember - you are a guest.'

Tourism Concern have recently established their 'Code

for Young Travellers'. What is interesting about this and other similar initiatives is the way that a small number of people can put forward a code of ethics that purports to apply to all young people. Even more intriguing is the way that numerous tourism companies want to identify themselves with such a project. The Rough Guide intends to publish the code in its guidebooks.

Now adventurous young carefree travellers will be confronted with a list of dos and don'ts in the front of their guides. If the guidebooks are, as they have been dubbed, backpackers' 'bibles', then the Tourism Concern Code is the equivalent of the Ten Commandments.

This American-based advocate of New Moral Tourism advises travellers as follows: 'Interact with residents in a culturally appropriate manner'; 'Reflect daily on your experiences and keep a journal'; 'Support the local economy by using locally owned restaurants and hotels, buying local products made by locals from renewable resources'; 'Get permission before photographing people, homes and other sites of local importance'.

The emphasis on the *local* is typical - benevolence towards the peoples visited is invariably seen as best accruing at a local level, rather than a national one. The codes also often invite us to consider the protocol of travel photography - how many of us have thought it necessary to ask before photographing sites of importance?

CERT was founded in 1994 by a couple on safari who were appalled at a tiger being burnt in a fire caused by a carelessly discarded cigarette. It exists to promote tourist and industry behaviour that helps to protect the environment. One of their three main aims is to 'promote environmental awareness among travellers and holidaymakers'.

Whilst the thrust of CERT's campaigning is aimed at the industry, there is also an emphasis on the consumer as an agent for environmental responsibility. Included in a list of advice for the traveller are the following: '"When in Rome ...". Respect local customs and sensitivities and follow high standards in courtesy';'"Stay on track". Off-road driving, off-track trekking and off-piste skiing can damage sensitive soil and vegetation irreparably. Keeping to marked paths and designated routes minimises the impact of tourism'; '"Don't trade in extinction".

Buying products made from endangered species threatens their existence. The sea turtles of Sri Lanka have been brought closer to extinction because of tourists buying turtle products'; '"When on the beach". Buying shells and hence encouraging the seashell trade, damages marine ecosystems and is nearly always unsustainable.

If you are near coral, remember this is made up of millions of tiny animals and takes centuries to grow. Treading on coral or anchoring your boat to it can cause long-term damage.' Tourists are also advised to learn about the local culture as this will 'help you become a more sensitive traveller'.

CERT's educational work is exemplified by a 1997 campaign, in conjunction with Her Majesty's Customs and Excise and British Airways Environmental Branch, asking children to design a poster encouraging tourists to shun souvenirs made from endangered species.

Given the abject state of the economy in some Third World tourism host areas, one wonders whether this campaign was more sensitive to wildlife than to people trying to make a living under difficult circumstances.

FRIENDS OF CONSERVATION

The Friends of Conservation, an Anglo-American organisation, with offices also in Kenya, issues a 'Conservation Code' for tourists. The preservationist emphasis is clear in the opening lines of the code: 'Tourism is the world's largest industry. It can play an important role in maintaining indigenous cultures and is an invaluable source of foreign currency for many African countries.

With a little consideration you can help to preserve this unique part of the world for future generations.' Above all, then, the tourist should be involved in preservation of uniqueness with regard to culture and environment. Whether this is to the benefit of future generations of the inhabitants or future generations of tourists is unclear. The code proceeds to list a number of dos and don'ts for tourists: 'On Safari'; 'At the Coast'; on 'People and Customs' and 'Shopping'. The advice includes the customary warnings regarding not dropping litter and not wearing clothing that may offend.

It also emphasises the illegality of buying souvenirs made from coral, rhino horns, elephant tusks and shells. Friends of Conservation are involved in education not only of the traveller, but also of the host population, and their listed projects include're-creation of habitat' and 'Anti-poaching support'.

SURVIVAL INTERNATIONAL

Survival International is an organisation devoted to supporting the rights of 'tribal peoples' around the world. Their leaflet advising travellers is titled 'Danger: Tourists' and outlines a number of dos and don'ts. Survival argues with much justification that, 'All too often tour operators treat tribal peoples as exotic objects to be enjoyed as part of the scenery.'

Yet Survival's own view is that the integrity of the tribal people's way of life is paramount, and development is therefore regarded as destructive. In this vein they warn that, 'Tourism may distort and irreparably alter the local economy.

Tribal peoples who were once self-sufficient or depended on local trade may now become dependent on the tourist dollar.' The preservationist emphasis in Survival's literature not only protects the people from the outside world, but also from any prospect of material development.

TRAVEL AGENTS

The influential American Society of Travel Agents (ASTA) has produced 'Ten Commandments for Ecotourism'. The code contains the following advice: 'Respect the frailty of the Earth. Realise that unless all are willing to help in its preservation, unique and beautiful destinations may not be here for future generations to enjoy'; 'To make your travels more meaningful, educate yourself about the geography, customs, manners and cultures of the region you visit.

Take time to listen to the people. Encourage local conservation efforts'; 'Learn about and support conservation-oriented programmes and organisations working to preserve the environment'; 'Whenever possible, walk or utilise environmentally sound methods of transportation. Encourage drivers of public vehicles to stop engines when parked.'

The assumption in the ASTA code is that of New Moral Tourism - that the environment - cultural and natural - is delicate, and we should organise our leisure lives around it, preserving diversity.

Their Ten Commandments are exemplary of the desire to present conservation holidays as a moral standard rather than an individual choice.

It is notable that although codes of conduct are primarily directed at the tourists, some seek to encourage 'ethical' behaviour by their hosts too. The Annapurna Conservation Area Project (ACAP) *Minimum Impact Code* asks tourists 'to respect Nepali customs in your dress and behaviour' and also to 'encourage young Nepalese to be proud of their culture'. Such advice is commonplace - the tourists are encouraged to see themselves as supporters of the local way of life, even when the locals are deserting it.

Jost Krippendorf also argues the need for education for mutual understanding in his seminal *The Holiday Makers* on the grounds that each group, tourists and hosts, needs to become aware of the other's expectations and needs.

Krippendorf puts forward his idea for a more 'human' tourism including proposals to 'inform the host population about tourists and the problems involved in tourism', to 'encourage holidaymakers to try new experiences and behaviour, and to learn how to travel and to prepare', and to 'educate people for travel'. He even advocates that this education should be formalised from the classroom to the travel agent.

The idea that there needs to be a prior written advice for hosts and guests in this way suggests that each party not only speaks a different language, but that they inhabit different worlds.

The notion that human conduct requires rules of engagement in the fashion put forward by the codes is striking. Clearly the advocates of codes do not regard hosts and tourists as capable of negotiating their own way through cultural differences and moral dilemmas, which, after all, is surely part of the experience of travelling.

The logic of the angst-ridden critique and the growth of well-meant advice is that tourism should be *for* something ... something more, that is, than enjoyment and relaxation. In this vein, one advocate of ecotourism demands: 'tourism remains a passive luxury for thousands of travellers.

This must change.' In place of luxury, New Moral Tourism offers harsher experiences. Suggestions offered from the Green Party in the UK include learning coppicing, organic gardening, vegan cooking and blacksmithing. Tour

HOLIDAY SNAPS - EXCERPTS FROM THE CODES

It is no longer good enough to travel footloose and fancy free. Tourism is accompanied by constant warnings to limit one's behaviour and to be ethical. From the environmental group Arc's pamphlet 'Sun, Sea, Sand and Saving the World' to Friends of the Earth's advice to question whether you 'need' to travel at all, tourism is now the terrain of moral codes and not a little guilt-tripping.

The often impulsive and reckless desire to strike out across Europe or further afield is no longer a good enough reason. A love of music, dancing and drinking provide no defence against the charge of immoral tourism. Excess moral baggage has to be lugged around if tourism is to be acceptable to some. Prominent Green campaigner George Monbiot sees tourism as desirable only when it is carried out by the few who are socially responsible:

travelling ... shapes many of those who become the social reformers, the human rights activists without whom every nation on earth would have succumbed to barren dictatorship. These are among the few for whom travel does broaden the mind, for whom exposure to injustice abroad may lift the veil from injustice at home, for whom the conditions suffered by the oppressed of the world, once seen, cannot be tolerated. Whilst they number as tens among the millions, their enlightenment surely means that tourism, for all its monstrosities, cannot be condemned.

For Monbiot, then, tourism is about social reform rather than enjoyment. Those who travel in a carefree and footloose manner are to be condemned for their lack of enlightenment and the damage they cause to the environment and other cultures.

In similar vein Mark Mann, a trenchant critic of Mass Tourism, advocates in his *Community Tourism Guide* that tourists should 'go deeper into local culture, engaging at a deeper level with local people and their needs'. The language used here is that of the social worker rather than the holidaymaker. The need to 'engage with culture', 'respect diversity', 'support communities' and 'make a difference' has replaced fun, relaxation, hedonism and adventure in the vocabulary of the New Moral Tourist.

Codes of conduct can, of course, contain a fair degree of common sense. In this respect, it is less the advice and more the impulse behind formalising common sense that is notable. In advising tourists to respect local culture, there is clearly the assumption that tourists do not do this. In advising tourists to dress appropriately, there is the assumption that such advice is merited for many of us.

The formalisation of common sense through codes of conduct is exemplary of an important trend, that the negotiation of new countries and new cultures is increasingly presented as inherently problematic. The tourist must be on their guard at all times in case they should cause offence.

They should interact with local cultures, but at the same time maintain a respectful distance from these same cultures. Even whether or not to give money to beggars has come within the realm of the codes. This problematisation of basic human functions is at times striking - it is easy to forget that we are talking about something as prosaic as holidays.

It is worth noting that the taking up of the codes by eco tour companies, and even by purveyors of Mass Tourism, marks a significant departure. Rather than satisfying customer needs, sections of the industry are increasingly concerned with telling their customers what those needs should be.

The sovereignty of the individual has been challenged by the assumption of the ignorant individual, in need of moral enlightenment from a plethora of environmental NGOs and even from tourist guides and tour operators.

In a sense the code-makers treat tourists and travellers like children - unable to think and act as autonomous adults. The assumption of the traveller as childlike threatens to demean the positive function of travel. It shields the subject from confronting and dealing with problems for themselves. It eschews the taking of risks, and hence diminishes the possibilities for learning from our own mistakes.

It limits freethinking by contributing to a climate of restraint. Whilst travel takes us to other places and other cultures, our own risk-averse, wary culture accompanies us, lest we should forget about it, let go and start to have fun.

The codes of conduct can also treat the host as a victim - those affected by incoming tourism are presented as victims of a cultural encounter. There is rarely any attempt at a cost-benefit analysis, weighing up the overall pros and cons of development projects.

Rather, negatives are given priority above positives, losers over winners, victims over beneficiaries. In addition, counselling local people on how to conserve their own environments contributes to a conception of less-developed countries as in need of paternal care.

Of course the impulse towards codes of conduct is not specific to tourism. The advice industry has boomed in many areas of life such as personal health, parenting and diet. Everyday aspects of life - what we eat, how we bring up children - are increasingly imbued with a pervasive angst and uncertainty. It is no surprise that holidays should fall within this trend, too.

Taken together, this 'Culture of Fear' as sociologist Frank Furedi terms it, amounts to a challenge to our moral autonomy. The new emphasis on ethical tourism implies a need for moral regulation at the interface of the tourist and their host. When decisions that may affect others confront us on our travels, whether it is tipping, taking photographs, how to dress or who to purchase from, we have already been told what the answer should be.

Hence interpersonal conduct is presented as inherently problematic, and the codes reflect an impulse to police this terrain. Freedom, adventure and hedonism are being eroded by this culture of caution.

As well as the codes, Good Tourist guides have emerged as a counter to Mass Tourism, promoting new forms of tourism such as ecotourism, responsible tourism, nature tourism and green tourism.

Three of the most prominent of these are *The Good Tourist, The Green Travel Guide* and *The Community Tourism Guide*. They show little restraint in their moral condemnation of Mass Tourism.

In *The Good Tourist*, the authors suggest that before going on holiday one should 'Environmentally Audit Yourself'. Questions to be considered in this personal audit include asking yourself: 'Why go on holiday? If you really don't want to go away, don't! ... Don't follow the crowd.' It urges: 'Get to know the locals ... it is surprising how, despite the tourist hordes, the desire to be hospitable to guests survives.'

Mark Mann, author of *the community tourism guide*, is quick to differentiate the holidays in his guide from 'the bland facade of mainstream tourism' and the 'tired tourist treadmill'.

The guide urges us to 'forget tourism's escapist fantasy and accept that our holidays take place in the real world - and have a real effect on real people'. Escapism and hedonism are replaced by a self-conscious concern and wariness on holiday in the New Moral Tourist's view.

Stark condemnations of tourism, a pursuit that for most people is fun, exciting and carefree, are commonplace. Mass Tourists appear to be neither enlightened about their destructive impact, nor, given the continuing draw of package holidays, willing to engage in a programme of moral rehabilitation offered up by the purveyors of the New Moral

Tourism through codes of conduct and a surfeit of well-meant advice.

In fact the attempt to provide guidelines for individual conduct on holiday is misguided. The advice offered is often derived from a *particular* ethical outlook, one that stresses the pre-eminence of nature over development, but that is then presented as a universal set of rules for all.

Tourists to the Third World may seek to spend their holiday cash in a local community rather than in hotels. This may yield some limited benefits for the rural community, but cut into the service economy in the towns and cities.

Refuse to buy a coral necklace and you may contribute to coral preservation, but the vendor may be a little poorer as a result.

If we campaign against golf courses on the basis of their use of water supplies, we may conserve the latter but deny people the income from high-spending golf tourists and the consequent possibilities for improving infrastructure.

There can therefore be no rules or codes that apply generally. Individuals may decide differently in different circumstances for a variety of reasons - these are matters for consideration and debate.

To try to regulate these decisions by drawing up ethical guidelines is a foolish task. It suggests surrogate parenthood - something young travellers perhaps felt they were leaving at home. Even more foolish is to take conservation as the starting point, when in the Third World societies to which the codes most frequently are applied, *development*, not conservation, is such a pressing need.

No one today is arguing for more freedom for people to travel. There is a sense amongst the critics that we have already surpassed society's limits. The implications of this are that leisure pursuits that many take for granted in the developed world are not to be extended any further.

Freedom is viewed in its negative form - freedom *from* tourism is the motif of many of the critics. The result of this is that as individuals we are increasingly subject to a surfeit of well-meaning advice.

Some of it is banal and patronising, and elsewhere its claims to be ethical are highly dubious. The traveller seeking adventure is circumscribed. The sun-worshipper is frowned upon. The fun lover is reminded that they are complicit in a 'destructive industry'. Leisure travel has never been subject to such moral proscription.

Chapter 4

Sustainability and Tourism

Although improvements in economic methodology and approaches to include the environment as an integral part of the economic system, and the use of a variety of environmental planning and management techniques may aid environmental conservation, concern over the negative effects of development upon the environment has led to calls for a new conceptual approach to development.

This conceptual approach is termed 'sustainable development', and at the beginning of the twenty-first century, it has become the new paradigm for all forms of development, including tourism.

THE ORIGINS OF 'SUSTAINABLE DEVELOPMENT'

In contemporary terms the term 'sustainable development' is usually credited to the Brundtland Report, officially the report of the World Commission on Environment and Development. The origins of 'sustainability' as opposed to 'sustainable development' lie in concerns over conservation and can be traced back to the conservation movement of the mid-nineteenth century.

The concept of 'sustainable development' first originated in the World Conservation Strategy published by the World Conservation Unit (IUCN) in 1980.

However, the popularisation of term did not occur until its use in the Brundtland Report seven years later, perhaps because by 1987, environmental awareness and consciousness were at a much higher level than they had been seven years earlier. The report was based upon an inquiry into the state of the earth's environment, led by Gro Harlem Brundtland the Norwegian Prime Minister, at the request of the General Assembly of the United Nations. Concern over the effects of the pace of economic growth on the environment since the 1950s led the United Nations in 1984 to commission an independent group of twenty-two people from various member states representing both the developing and developed world, to identify long-term environmental strategies for the international community.

The key environmental concerns of the United Nations were the high levels of unsustainable resource usage associated with development, and the role of pollution in major environmental problems such as global warming and depletion of the ozone layer, which threatened human well-being.

Accompanying the heightened awareness of environmental problems was also a realisation that the environment and development are inexorably linked. Development cannot take place upon a deteriorating environmental resource base, neither can the environment be protected, when development excludes the costs of its destruction.

Although 'development' is a common term in today's language, it is only since the 1950s that development has been studied as an academic subject, the time at which colonial territories started to achieve independence. 'Development' and 'growth' are often used as synonymous terms but there is a critical difference between the two.

Growth means to get bigger or larger, whilst development refers to a change in state, for the better. The difference between development and growth is aptly summed up in the following comment from Scottish National Heritage (1993:9):

To grow means to increase in size by the assimilation or accretion of materials. To develop means to expand or realise the potentialities of: to bring a fuller, greater, or better state. When something grows, it gets quantitatively bigger; when it develops, it gets qualitatively better, or at least different.

The pace of economic growth since the 1950s has been

rapid; for example, although industrial production grew fiftyfold in the twentieth century, 80 per cent of this growth took place since 1950 (WCED, 1987).

Whilst this rapid pace of industrial growth has helped to increase the living standards and life expectancy for many, the number of people in the world who continue to live in absolute poverty (i.e. having below sufficient income to meet the basic needs of food, shelter and clothing) has increased to 1 billion people or approximately 20 per cent of the world's population, although according to the *New Internationalist* (1999) the figure of one billion represents the same number as in the 1930s when records began.

The way development has been pursued, characterised by a general lack of concern for the environment, has led to the use of natural resources in a way that is unsustainable, that is, many finite resources are being exhausted whilst the capacity of the natural environment to assimilate waste is being exceeded.

It was the predominance of the negative aspects of these changes that led to the calls for sustainable development. The term gained greater attention following the United Nations Conference on Environment and Development (UNCED), held in Rio de Janeiro in June 1992, popularly referred to as the 'Earth Summit'.

At the Earth Summit a programme for promoting sustainable development throughout the world, known as Agenda 21, was adopted by participating countries. Agenda 21 is an action plan laying out the basic principles required to progress towards sustainability.

It envisages national sustainable development strategies, involving local communities and people in a 'bottom-up' approach to development, rather than the 'top-down' approach which has typically characterised national development plans.

Although tourism as an economic sector was not debated in Rio, five years later at the 'Earth Summit II' in New York, it was debated as a recognised economic sector. In the recommendations and outcomes of the report it was stated:

The expected growth in the tourism sector and the increasing reliance of many developing countries, including small island developing States, on this sector as a major employer and contributor to local, national, subregional and regional economies highlights the need for special attention to the relationship between environmental conservation and protection and sustainable tourism.

In the last decade of the twentieth century, the term 'sustainable development' became widely used by governments, international lending agencies, non-governmental organisations, the private sector and academia. An encapsulated history of the concept of sustainable development is displayed.

THE MEANING OF SUSTAINABLE DEVELOPMENT

The fact that the term 'sustainable development' can be adopted by governments, international lending agencies, non-governmental organisations, the private sector and academia, some of whom could be viewed as having divergent and politically opposed objectives, is a reflection of the inherent ambiguity of the concept.

This ambiguity permits a variety of perspectives to be taken on sustainability. Much of this ambiguity can be traced to the most commonly quoted definition of sustainable development taken from the Brundtland Report:

Richardson describes this definition as a political fudge, aimed at compromising the opposing views of commissioners from different states, to keep everyone happy.

However, the remainder of the Brundtland Report makes it clear that within the scope of this definition other key issues relating to development have to be addressed, such as the alleviation of poverty, degradation of the environment, and issues of intra- and inter-generational equity.

It is important to realise that sustainable development is not concerned with the preservation of the physical environment but with its development based upon sustainable principles. The Brundtland Report stresses the need for the alleviation of global poverty, not only as an ethical objective, but also as a key method to ameliorate the pressures being placed upon the physical environment. Subsequently the report lays out the principles of how the environment should be developed:

Economic growth and development obviously involve changes in the physical ecosystem. Every ecosystem everywhere cannot be preserved intact.... In general, renewable resources like forests and fish stocks need not be depleted provided the rate of use is within the limits of regeneration and natural growth.

Emphasis is therefore placed upon the conservation of the resource base rather than the preservation of individual flora and fauna. In terms of the use of finite resources, such as minerals and fossil fuels, actions such as resource management, recycling and economy of use are highlighted to make sure that the resources do not run out before substitutes are found.

A central theme of the Brundtland Report, poverty alleviation through sustainable development, is critical for the long-term environmental well-being of the planet. Poverty is a major cause of environmental destruction, a relationship that is particularly exacerbated in regions of the world where the population is growing rapidly, and forced into more marginal environments.

The link between poverty and environmental destruction is emphasised by Elliot (1994:1) in the following passage:

In the developing world, conditions such as rising poverty and mounting debt form the context in which individuals struggle to meet their basic needs for survival and nations wrestle to provide for their population. The outcome is often the destruction of the very resources with which such needs will have to be met in the future.

Poverty has been worsened in many areas by population pressure and the growth in world population in the twentieth century was rapid. In 1900 the world's population was 1,600 million, by the beginning of the new millennium it has risen to 6,000 million, and according to the United Nations by the year 2025 it is estimated it will be over 8,500 million.

DIFFERENT PERSPECTIVES ON SUSTAINABLE DEVELOPMENT

That there should be differing perspectives on the meaning of sustainability is perhaps unsurprising, given the range of priorities, interests, beliefs and philosophies underpinning human interaction with the environment. Two broad ideological approaches to the environment are recognisable, 'technocentrism' and 'ecocentrism'.

Technocentrism is characterised by a belief that technical solutions can be found to environmental problems through the application of science, thereby placing its faith in quantifiable solutions to problems.

Its reliance upon quantification allows for a divorced objectivity in decision making, rendering subjective considerations over the environment, such as feelings or emotions, as being unworthy of consideration. Such a reliance upon objective measurement means that the environment's complexity as a system can be overlooked and differing viewpoints ignored.

As Reid (1995:131) remarks: 'Technocentrism's readiness to quantify problems and solutions and its forecasts of success make it attractive to decision-makers who may be ignorant of the complexities of issues filtered through viewpoints, interpretations and value judgements of which they may be unaware.'

Through a lack of appreciation of the complexity of the environment as a system, there is also a lack of realisation that most development decisions have consequences for the environment that extend beyond the physical boundaries of an individual project.

Within the philosophy of technocentrism the physical environment is viewed as a resource to be exploited by humans as they deem appropriate.

As for the degree of democracy in decision making, technocentrism is characterised by a preference for centralised control rather than local decision making, as Pepper (1993:34) writes: 'There is little desire for genuine public participation in decision making, especially to the right of this ideology, or for debates about values.' An alternative ideological approach to how we view the environment is ecocentrism.

Ecocentrism is closely associated with the philosophies of the romantic transcendentalists and characterised by a belief in the wonderment of nature. Ecocentrics have a lack of faith in both modern technology and technical and bureaucratic elites, and subsequently advocate alternative technologies as a way forward.

This is not only because alternative technologies are likely to be more environmentally benign, but also because they are more democratic in the sense that they can be owned, maintained and understood by individuals with little economic or political power.

Ecocentrics' position on technology may be termed 'Luddite', that is, they are not opposed to new technology, but are opposed to technology that places its ownership and control in the hands of a powerful elite.

Doyle and McEachern equate the term 'ecocentrism' with 'deep ecology', recognising that it has four main characteristics.

These are as follows: that all beings, whether human or non-human, possess an intrinsic value, the antithesis of the technocentric instrumental viewpoint of nature; that all beings are of equal value and there is therefore no hierarchy of species in nature; that all nature is interconnected, with no dividing lines between the living and the non-living, the animate and inanimate, or the human and non-human; and that the earth is finite in its carrying capacity.

These views are in contrast to the 'dominant world-view' on development, which incorporates a pioneering and frontier mentality, assuming an unlimited supply of natural resources and an unlimited waste absorption capability in nature. Differences in views of development between the 'dominant world-view' and 'deep ecology'

The equating of the dominant world view with the attitudes of technocentrism is not difficult and according to O'Riordan (1981:1) the balance of power in decision making in society lies with the technocentrics: 'Technocentrists tend to be politically influential for they usually move in the same circles as the politically and economically powerful, who are soothed by the confidence of technocentric ideology and impressed by its presumption of knowledge.'

Dominant World-view	Deep Ecology
Strong belief in technology for progress and solutions	Favours low-scale technology that is self-reliant
Natural world is valued as a resource rather than possessing intrinsic value	Sense of wonder, reverence and moral obligation to the natural world
Believes in ample resource reserves	Recognises the 'rights' of nature are independent of humans
Favours the objective and quantitative	Recognises the subjective such as feelings and ethics
Centralisation of power	Favours local communities and localised decision making
Encourages consumerism	Encourages the use of appropriate technology
	Recognises that the earth's resources are limited

Within these two broad ideological approaches a range of contrasting positions can be taken on sustainable development. Baker *et al.* conceptualise a ladder of sustainable development moving upwards from a technocentric approach at the bottom to an ecocentric position at the top.

At the bottom of the ladder is what they term the 'Treadmill' approach, focused on accruing material products and pursuing wealth creation.

This approach is strongly technocentric in character, with little concern being displayed for the environment, beyond believing that human ingenuity can solve any environmental problem created by development.

The second rung of the ladder is occupied by 'weak sustainable development', in which the aim 'is to integrate capitalist growth with environmental concerns'.

In this perspective emphasis is placed upon continued economic growth, but the environmental costs of development are to be reflected in economic calculations and accounting procedures.

Unlike the 'treadmill' approach, 'weak sustainable development' recognises the finite nature of many natural resources, and also recognises that the environment's capacity to assimilate waste is not limitless. Emphasis is therefore placed upon furthering the development of economics as a discipline to permit a better evaluation of environmental assets.

A criticism of this approach is that it limits the value of the environment to that which can be quantitatively measured, neglecting its cultural or spiritual worth.

The third rung of the ladder is occupied by an approach more synonymous with ecocentrism than technocentrism. 'Strong sustainable development' advocates that environmental protection be a precondition of economic development.

Subsequently, within this perspective the environment becomes the key consideration, rather than economic growth as in the latter two scenarios. This perspective requires that development policies aim to maintain the productive capacity of environmental assets, and preserve other environmental assets deemed worthy of protection as they are, for example tropical rainforests.

'Strong sustainable development' takes qualitative aspects of the environment into account and 'local communities' will be involved in decision making over development issues. All the available instruments of policy, including legal, fiscal and economic measures, should be used and adapted to support this approach.

Occupying the top rung of the ladder is what Baker refers to as the 'Ideal Model'. This approach is underpinned by a strong ethical dimension, the viewpoint being taken that nature and non-human life have an intrinsic value, which extends beyond their usefulness to humans.

The measurement of growth expressed in quantitative terms ceases to be relevant as the 'quality of life' becomes the objective of development rather than the 'standard of living'.The policy implications of this viewpoint are that environmental protection will place severe restraints on the use of the earth's resources and economic activities.

This approach represents a 'radical' approach to sustainable development, involving structural changes in global society and economy. Indeed, according to Baker, ecologists would argue that the 'Ideal Model' represents a new paradigm in its own right.

The advocation of radical changes in society to achieve sustainable development concentrates on power relationships in the wider political economy. This entails addressing the root causes of non-sustainability, including the distribution of power and wealth, the roles of transnational corporations, class-based politics, and gender inequalities.

The distribution of intra-generational equity, even though it was an issue raised in the Brundtland Report as having direct consequences for poverty, is notably absent from most government agendas. Radical approaches to sustainable development challenge the values and principles of capitalist society, as Doyle and McEachern (1998:37) comment: 'Radical environmental political theorists are involved in paradigm struggles, each seeking to create new sets of key values and principles that directly challenge existing, powerful paradigms.'

Radical political positions over the interpretation of sustainable development, that emphasise different degrees and elements of structural change include 'deep ecology', 'social-ecology', 'eco-socialism' and 'eco-feminism'. The values of *deep ecology* in contrast to the values of the dominant world view have already been illustrated.

To reiterate, the emphasis of deep ecology rests on the intrinsic value of all life, and acknowledging that all life is equal. This means that deep ecologists take the viewpoint that human beings are not the sole purpose of the evolutionary process but just another animal species.

In this philosophy there is no theoretical separation between humans and the rest of nature. These beliefs have led to campaigns for the preservation of wilderness in North

America, Scandinavia and Australia. Subsequently, deep ecologists are sometimes enthusiastic supporters of population control programmes in order to reduce destructive human pressures upon the earth, which has led to accusations of them holding fascist tendencies.

The politics of *social ecology* are rooted in anarchist traditions, with their associated hostility to the state, liberals and Marxists. Social ecologists subsequently advocate maximum individual autonomy and the decentralisation of society into local communities as opposed to the concept of the nation-state.

According to Roussopoulos (1993:122), social ecology: 'represents the greatest advance in twentieth century eco-philosophy'. Its development is closely associated with the American ecologist Murray Bookchin who adopts two key positions in his philosophical approach to social ecology.

The first is to recognise that the many types of hierarchical structures that exist in society are socially constructed and determined, and represent the source of all forms of domination within society, and also between humans and nature.

The second position, which distinguishes social ecology from deep ecology, is that although humans are part of nature they occupy a rather more exalted place in the evolutionary scheme.

Eco-socialists in contrast to social ecologists, attempt to integrate ecological principles with the political theories of socialism including Marxism, rather than anarchism. The concern of eco-socialism lies equally with the problems of social justice, such as the inequity of wealth distribution in society, and ecological concerns.

Just as there are many types of socialism there are many varieties of eco-socialism. Although eco-socialism can be allied to Marxism, the theories of Marx that assume a limitless abundance of nature are not accepted by eco-socialists. A distinguishing feature between social ecologists and eco-socialists is their belief in the nation-state. Eco-socialists do not accept that environmental problems can be tackled at a localised level, favouring central government and the strengthening of pan-national bodies, like the United Nations. Consequently, a necessary precursor for environmental protection is for eco-socialists to have power.

According to Roussopoulos *eco-feminism* has its origins in anti-militarism and links the environmental problems that the world is facing today to the system of patriarchy. Therefore, ecological destruction and the oppression of women are linked.

As for eco-socialism there is a broad range of differing political perspectives, including cultural eco-feminism, liberal eco-feminism, social eco-feminism, and socialist eco-feminism.

Political tension over sustainable development therefore underlies much of the debate about its interpretation. A fundamental division is between those for whom sustainability represents little more than improving technology and environmental accounting systems, whilst preserving the *status quo* of existing hierarchies and power structures in society, and those who have more radical political agendas involving changing the value systems and power structures of society.

SUSTAINABILITY AND TOURISM

In terms of the application of the concept of sustainable development to tourism, varying perspectives have been adopted, which are a reflection of the wider political debate about sustainable development outlined in the preceding section of this chapter.

A broad differentiation can be made between 'sustainable tourism', in which emphasis is placed on the customer and marketing considerations of tourism to sustain the tourism sector, and using tourism as a vehicle to achieve 'sustainable development', in which emphasis is placed on developing tourism as a means to achieve wider social and environmental goals.

Therefore 'sustainable tourism' will not necessarily equate with the aims and objectives of sustainable development. Both Coccossis and Parpairis and Hunter identify a form of sustainable tourism which is oriented toward the viability of the tourism industry. Coccossis refers to this as the 'economic sustainability of tourism' and Hunter as the 'tourism imperative'. The aim of development is primarily concerned with satisfying the needs of tourists and players in the industry.

The central justification of this approach is that tourism development is to be encouraged and seen as acceptable, if developing other economic sectors, such as logging and mining, are viewed as being more environmentally damaging than tourism.

However, this perspective fails to allow for the fact that the negative consequences of tourism development are incremental and cumulative, and that the prejudgement of the likely environmental impacts of tourism development through techniques such as environmental impact analysis are therefore difficult. Comparative impact analysis with other types of development alternatives therefore becomes meaningless and misleading.

Hunter's second position is when the environmental resources for tourism receive consideration, but is secondary to the growth of the tourism sector, an approach known as 'product-led tourism'.

Hence although environmental and social concerns may be more important than in the former scenario, their relevance is still largely equated with maintaining the existing tourism product. Hunter suggests this is a 'weak' interpretation of sustainable development, but that such a position is justified in communities already heavily economically dependent upon tourism, where placing a high priority on environmental concerns may mean the well-being of the community is threatened.

Development may have already led to extensive alteration of the natural environment and attention will therefore focus on environmental improvements to the existing development. Hunter's third scenario is termed 'environmentally led tourism', in which types of tourism would be promoted that are reliant upon a high-quality environment.

The main aim would be to make the link between the success of the tourism industry and environmental conservation so obvious to all the stakeholders that stewardship of the environment is a priority.

This is analogous to what Coccossis refers to as 'sustainable tourism development', where the protection of the environment is seen as a key component of the long-term economic viability of the industry.

The main difference compared to 'product-led tourism' is that the environment is prioritised and forms of tourism are developed that are not damaging to it. Tourism would therefore be centred upon attracting tourists who would wish to be educated about the natural environment and perhaps participate in its conservation.

The final scenario suggested by Hunter is 'neotenous tourism'. In some exceptionally sensitive areas, where the preservation of species is paramount because of their ecological significance, tourism should not be permitted at all. In other areas which are viewed as being ecologically significant tourism should be limited to very small numbers through policy control measures.

The focus of both Coccossis and Parpairis's and Hunter's work is the physical environment. However, the concept of sustainability should be broadened to include cultural, political and economic dimensions.

The ambiguousness of the concept of sustainability means that the political context, and especially the political values of those who have power and decision making, will be influential in determining the interpretation of sustainable tourism. Butler points out that it is not possible to separate sustainable tourism from the value systems of those involved and the societies in which they exist.

Concerning this latter point, Mowforth and Munt (1998:122) remark: 'If it remains a "buzzword" which can be so widely interpreted that people of very different outlooks on a given issue can use it to support their cause, then it will suffer the same distortions to which older-established words such as "freedom" and "democracy" are subjected.'

Mowforth and Munt continue to demand that if sustainable tourism is really to be achieved then there is a 'need to politicise the tourism industry in order to promote its movement towards sustainability and away from its tendency to dominate, corrupt and transform nature, culture and society' (1998:123).

House also infers a political dimension to the application of sustainability in tourism. She recognises two polarised positions or 'schools of thought' reflecting different ideologies on the employment of the concept.

At one end are the 'reformists', whose ideology and actions of implementation are preoccupied with the *status quo*, whilst 'structuralists' possess a much more radical view of tourism development, which challenges the paradigm on which economic, social and political development is based. Reformists are therefore 'reluctant to challenge the existing social, political and economic structures that underpin tourism development and behaviour' (1997:93).

Reformists do not challenge the values in society that create environmental and social problems but try to manage them.

House draws a distinction between those who modify existing models of tourism to make them more 'sustainable', and those who use tourism as a vehicle to experiment with 'alternative existence approaches' to achieve an alternative social order to the present one.

The structuralist model of tourism is therefore one which is radical, involving questioning the values of society, as much as those of tourism. The relationship between the ideas of 'reformists' and 'structuralists' and sustainable tourism is analogous with the differing positions taken on the meaning of sustainability within the field of political ecology, explained earlier in the chapter.

It is therefore necessary to realise that sustainable tourism is not merely connected with conservation or preservation of the physical environment but incorporates cultural, economic, and political dimensions.

As has been pointed out, the ambiguity of the term means that it can be interpreted and owned by so many different groups with opposing ideologies that trying to agree a common definition of the term is meaningless. Perhaps the most useful way of thinking about

Does 'sustainable tourism' mean the same thing as 'sustainable development'? sustainability is not necessarily to think of it as an end point, but to think of it more as a guiding philosophy which incorporates certain principles concerning our interaction with the environment.

The next section of this chapter considers the guiding principles that have been developed in connection with tourism.

SUSTAINABILITY IN ACTION

The concept of sustainability has been applied in the tourism sector in different ways, at both national and local levels, and in the public and private sectors. The last decade of the twentieth century saw an increased effort by some private sector tourism organisations to make it evident that they were placing the environment in a more central position to their operations and attempting to become more 'sustainable'.

The extent to which this is from a genuine concern for the environment, or a business ploy to attract more customers and an attempt to stave off regulation of the industry, is unsure. Butler (1998:27) suggests that the tourism industry has adopted sustainability for three reasons: 'economics, public relations and marketing'.

One of the first public strategies on tourism and sustainability emerged from the Globe '90 conference in Canada, which brought together government, non-governmental organisations (NGOs), the tourism industry, and academics to discuss the future relationship of tourism with the environment.

Five main goals of sustainable tourism were identified:

- To develop greater awareness and understanding of the significant contributions that tourism can make to the environment and economy;
- To promote equity and development;
- To improve the quality of life of the host community;

- To provide a high quality of experience for the visitor; and
- To maintain the quality of the environment on which the foregoing objectives depend'.

As with the concept of sustainability, the goals tend to be all encompassing, potentially conflicting and give little guidance on how tourism should be developed.

The first of these principles is significant because of its recognition that the environment has an intrinsic value, that is, that nature has a consciousness and value in its own right.

Notably, the recognition that this intrinsic value outweighs its value as a tourism asset may mean that the environment is excluded for use for tourism. The first principle also endorses the recommendations of the Brundtland Report by stressing the need for long-term planning considerations as opposed to short-termism.

The principles also stress other elements that are viewed as being essential to achieving sustainable development. The need for a balanced approach to development, respecting the character and nature of the place, is implicit to the principles. This involves the balancing of the needs of the physical environment with the needs of the community, and the needs of the tourist.

However, this principle tends to imply that the needs of the tourist as a distinctive group are homogeneous, and the needs of the local community as a distinctive group are also relatively homogeneous. In reality, this is too simplistic and unlikely to be the case, as there are different types of tourists, and communities can be divided on grounds of class, ethnicity, religion and gender.

Nevertheless, community control over development decision making has often been advocated by those who favour increased local democracy. Ecocentrics support development decision making at local level, not only on democratic principles, but also on the presumption that local people are more likely to act as stewards of the environment than external parties. However, community participation in planning and development may or may not be successful in encouraging people to favour less environmentally damaging development options, as attitudes to the physical environment are likely to reflect economic priorities.

Even when tourism is presented to a local community as a less environmentally damaging development option than other forms of economic activity it may not be favoured by the local community.

Burns and Holden comment upon the case of tourism development in the St Lucia Wetlands in Natal, South Africa, an area containing coral reefs, turtle beaches, high-afforested dunes, freshwater swamps, grasslands and estuaries. Rio Tinto Zinc (RTZ), the giant transnational mining corporation, wanted to mine the dunes for titanium dioxide slag.

Despite assurances from RTZ over redressive environmental restoration of the area when the mining had ceased, central government was opposed to the use of the area for this purpose on environmental grounds, and instead favoured the development of ecotourism. However, local people, mainly Zulus, favoured the development of mining on the basis that RTZ had a good track record of paying comparatively high wages and investing in schools, clinics and other facilities.

The Natal Parks Board, who run the surrounding game parks, were perceived by the local community as paying low wages, and having displaced local people from their lands to establish game reserves in the 1960s and 1970s.

Similarly, at Cairn Gorm, in the Scottish Highlands of Britain during the 1990s, there was a high level of controversy over the planned development of a funicular railway up the mountainside for the purposes of downhill skiing. Opposition to the scheme from major non-governmental organisations, such as the World Wildlife Fund (WWF) and the Royal Society for the Protection of Birds (RSPB), was based upon the possible environmental impacts on the arctic-alpine environment, which is unique within the British Isles. However, instead of receiving the support of the majority of local people, the two non-governmental organisations were largely seen as outsiders attempting to stop economic development to protect birdlife and flora, thereby denying local people employment and other economic opportunities.

To realistically encourage stewardship of the environment by local communities, forms of tourism will need to be developed that are not only sympathetic to the environment, but also offer economic benefits as is the case in Senegal described.

INTEGRATED RURAL TOURISM, LOWER CASAMANCE, SENEGAL

The development of tourism in the Lower Casamance is an example of how tourism can be used as a tool to enrich the livelihood and well-being of rural peoples. The aim of the scheme was to aid development, and also provide a more meaningful interchange between the local people and tourists than was being experienced on the coast, where hotels had largely been built with foreign capital and local people were excluded from tourist complexes by security guards and high walls.

In total, thirteen tourist camps have now been built, from an initial investment of US $7,000 each, provided by the l'Agence de Cooperation Culturelle et Technique. Tourists stay in simple lodges, built using traditional materials in the local architectural styles, so diminishing the differentiation between tourist and local facilities.

Tourist numbers are restricted to a maximum of 20-40 guests and lodges are only constructed in villages where the population is 1,000 or above. Tourists eat locally grown produce wherever possible following traditional recipes.

The scheme has proved to be a success, aiding development and social stability, improving health and educational facilities, and critically providing employment opportunities for the young which discourages them from migrating to larger towns to look for employment. Public expenditure of the revenues from tourism is controlled by village co-operatives.

In terms of a private sector led project aimed at encouraging sustainable tourism development, a notable project is the one developed by the International Federation of Tour Operators (IFTO), in the Balearic Isles, in the Mediterranean. Concerned with the problems that were being caused by tourism development in parts of Mallorca, the largest of the Balearic Isles, the ECOMOST ('Ecological Model of Sustainable Tourism') study was supported by IFTO, the European Community, and the Ministry of Tourism for the Balearics. The aim of the ECOMOST project was to attempt to develop a 'model of sustainable tourism'.

The researchers likened this model to tourism's stethoscope, the idea being that it could be used to gauge a destination's attainments against the ideal of sustainability, by using indicators of change.

Within the context of the study the adopted definition of sustainable tourism was 'the maintenance of a balance where tourism runs at a profit but not at the expense of the natural, cultural, or ecological resources' (IFTO, 1994:6). The report identifies four main requirements for the long-term maintenance of a tourism destination:

- The population should remain prosperous and keep its cultural identity;
- The place should remain attractive to tourists;
- Nothing is done to damage the ecology; and
- An effective political framework.

The study developed 'check lists of dangers to sustainable tourism', under four different subheadings of 'population', 'tourism', 'ecology', and 'politics'.

For each subsection, different components or targets were identified along with indicators of change, accompanied by 'critical values' which will determine if the indicator is positive or negative.

The idea of using indicators as an environmental management tool, to help achieve sustainable development, has gained pace since the adoption by the majority of the world governments of Agenda 21 in 1992. For example, the European Union is currently trying to establish relevant information systems, to ensure that socio-economic environments are developed in a way that respects the natural environment.

Eurostat, the Statistical Office of the European Communities, in 1997 produced a list of forty-six indicators covering areas of the economy, society, environment and institutions.

Examples of economic indicators that are relevant to the environment include the 'annual energy consumption per capita' and the level of 'environmental protection expenditure as a percentage of GDP'; examples of social indicators include the 'rate of growth of the urban population' and the 'per capita consumption of fossil fuel for motor vehicle transport'; examples of environmental indicators include the 'level of consumption of ozone depleting substances' and the 'quantity of fertiliser used in agriculture'; and an example of an institutional indicator is the level of 'expenditure on research and development as a percentage of GDP'. In 1998, the

British government announced a range of indicators to help assess changes in the quality of life of the population, which could be used alongside traditional measures, such as gross domestic product (GDP), that are used to assess economic progress.

Thirteen groups of indicators were decided upon covering the following areas: economic growth; social investment; employment; health; education and training; housing quality; climate change; air pollution; transport; water quality; wildlife; land use; and waste.

However, although these developments are encouraging and indicators have undoubted use as part of an environmental management system, both for the general environment and tourism, their usefulness in securing a more sustainable future will ultimately be determined by the political views and wills of those in power.

- Sustainable development encapsulates a way of thinking about economic development that is inclusive of the environment. Development cannot take place upon a deteriorating environmental resource base, neither can the environment be protected when development excludes the cost of its destruction. The main aim of sustainable development is poverty alleviation, that is satisfying the needs of the world's population but achieving this in a way that does not threaten the earth's resources, nor the ability of future generations to satisfy their own needs.

- It is an ambiguous term and subsequently can be interpreted in different ways by groups with opposing political and philosophical viewpoints. Some groups and ideologies believe sustainable development can only be achieved by a radical restructuring of society involving changes in political structures and value systems. Others believe sustainable development can be achieved through alterations of the market system and improvement in technology that does not threaten the *status quo* in society.
- The application of the concept of sustainable development to tourism has also led to different perspectives on its meaning. A major difference is between those who interpret 'sustainable tourism' as advocating the sustaining of tourism in a destination, and those who advocate tourism as a vehicle for achieving sustainable development, which encompasses much wider socially determined goals and priorities. To date, the principles for sustainable tourism that have emerged from the tourism sector emphasise the former interpretation rather than the latter.

It's a small world after all. At least, that's what the millions of tourists who take to the skies, roads, and paths each year to discover it are finding. Advances in technology and transportation and the emergence of a global economy are providing greater access for unprecedented numbers of travelers to explore the once-remote world around them. Directly and indirectly, however, tourism may often also be harming the very environment that lures so many people away from home in the first place.

Tourism is a key part of the economy in such biodiversity hot spots as the Caribbean, the Amazon basin, and countries such as Mexico, Thailand, and Kenya. Although tourism supplies badly needed income to such areas, there are environmental costs for every visit to the elephants in Kenya, the tortoises in the Galapagos, or the national park nearer to home.

The damage comes in the form of noise, air, and water pollution, the usurpation of productive land, natural habitat degradation, and the disruption of local cultures and economies.

According to The Ecotourism Society, a nonprofit membership group of outdoor travel entrepreneurs, researchers, and conservationists, there is currently an explosion of tourism based on nature, wildlife, and adventure travel. The society estimates that 40-60% of tourists are attracted to natural areas such as coral reefs, savannas, beaches, and forests.

In a September 1997 article in Parks and Recreation, Alan Ewert and John Shultis estimated the growth in this so-called resource-based tourism at 15-25% per year, compared to 2-4% for conventional tourism.

Tourism of all varieties, however, is on a half-century boom. Tourism is defined as voluntary travel to see and experience new sights, so its volume roughly equals the transportation and hospitality businesses, minus business and personal travel. Direct receipts from 613 million international tourists in 1997 were tallied at $448 billion, according to the World Tourism Organization.

Intranational tourism, although harder to measure, is a much larger business. The Travel Industry Association of America says tourism is America's third-largest retail sales industry, with $542 billion in total receipts and nearly 7.6 million direct employees.

According to the association, in 1998 tourists made 222 million air trips in the United States alone. The World Travel and Tourism Council estimated the global receipts of domestic and international tourism in 1998 at $4.4 trillion; during that same year, the industry employed 230 million people, about 10% of the formal global workforce. If that estimate is correct, the tourism economy is larger than the gross domestic product of every nation except the United States.

Where jobs and money are scarce, tourism's huge economic potential gives the industry considerable clout, even when it conflicts with environmental values. Because so many tourists are attracted to natural, unspoiled destinations, however, the environmental degradation caused by tourism also hurts the tourism industry.

Traffic-choked national parks and shorelines damaged by untreated sewage from tourist developments play a major role in the final stage of what tourism researchers call the life cycle of tourist destinations—discovery, development, maturity, and decline.

According to Jafar Jafari, editor-in-chief of the Annals of Tourism Research, in 50% of the studies published in his journal, environmental problems are the key to the decline of tourist destinations. Although some of the problems are cosmetic, such as beaches lined with high-rise hotels, Jafari says habitat degradation and air and water pollution also contribute to eventual avoidance of areas by tourists.

PLANES, TRAINS, AUTOMOBILES ... AND CRUISE SHIPS

It's not just what people do to their destination once they get there that harms the environment-getting there in the first place is also a major culprit, whether it's by air, sea, road, or even by foot. Airplane and car travel contributes to air and noise pollution, cruise ships may dump human and fuel wastes into the oceans, and people exploring fragile ecosystems may trample wildlife underfoot or collect natural souvenirs to take home.

Although it's difficult to estimate the tourist proportion of airplane travel, airplanes in general are a major source of air pollution. Michael Prather, an atmospheric scientist at the University of California at Irvine, evaluated the global warming impact of air travel for the Intergovernmental Panel on Climate Change, which analyzes the global warming issue for the United Nations.

Prather says aircraft produce 2-3% of the global emissions of carbon dioxide, the principal greenhouse gas. After adding in the warming effect of contrails (the clouds formed around jet exhaust) and other airplane impacts (such as the emission of sulfur oxides, which tend to reflect sunlight), he says, planes account for 6-7.5% of overall human-caused warming.

In addition to their warming effects, airports rank as high as smokestack industries in the amount of pollution they release into the environment, according to Flying Off Course, a 1996 study by the Natural Resources Defence Council.

For example, the report says, based on government statistics, airplanes at Los Angeles International Airport were the second largest stationary source of smog in Los Angeles (an oil refinery was the largest source).

And air pollution is not the only problem. The number of noise pollution complaints seems to be rising along with the volume of airplane travel. Flying Off Course states that "the [Federal Aviation Administration] reports that 60 of the largest 100 airports in this country are currently proposing to build new runways or runway extensions."

Expansions are encountering opposition—mainly based on the anticipated noise increase—in cities such as Los Angeles, Oakland, Atlanta, Chicago, Boston, and New York. Howard Beckman, a San Lorenzo, California, attorney who is active in airport regulation issues, says the issue has "erupted" in the past two years, fueled by increases in passenger and air cargo traffic.

Arline Bronzaft, a New York City psychologist who studies the effects of noise, admits that although noise cannot be unequivocally linked to health problems, the evidence is highly suggestive of a connection, particularly regarding hypertension. Studies have found that children exposed to aircraft and train noise in classrooms learn more slowly than their nonexposed peers. In 1997, Bronzaft surveyed residents of two communities in Staten Island, one within the flight path of Newark International Airport and one outside, as to their general health and noise. Bronzaft says questions were written in an open-ended manner to avoid biasing the results. For example, one of the few questions that mentioned noise was "Are there things that bother you, like noise?"

In the study, published in the January 1998 issue of Environment and Behaviour, 70% of respondents within the flight path complained about noise. These subjects rated their health as significantly poorer than did those outside the flight path.

Noise from airplanes carrying tourists has also become an annoyance at the Grand Canyon, which 800,000 people view from the air every year. According to a 21 July 1997 article by Michael Satchell in U.S. News & World Report, the aircraft create "a droning mantle of noise over a park whose views are already degraded by industrial haze."

Tom Robinson, director of government affairs for the Grand Canyon Trust, a public interest group, says overflights now total 100,000 each year. Although aircraft are not supposed to fly below the canyon's rim, the canyon funnels noise, and planes and helicopters are audible for 10 miles inside the normally quiet canyon.

Although the 1987 National Parks Overflights Act was supposed to control aircraft flying over the canyon, overflights have doubled since then, Robinson says. "It's still bad; there's been no significant improvement since the law was passed."

Ground travel also causes environmental problems, as floods of tourist cars and other vehicles inundate pristine environments.

In popular U.S. parks such as Yellowstone, the Grand Canyon, and Yosemite, roads are gridlocked for much of the summer by tourists eager to visit the natural wonders, producing plenty of exhaust as the cars sit idling.

And cars are not the only environmental culprits here. According to Satchell's article in U.S. News & World Report, "In wintertime, as many as 1,000 snowmobiles a day roar into Yellowstone, spewing nitrous oxide and hydrocarbons equivalent to 1.7 million cars."

Some observers say these "crown jewels" of the American landscape are in crisis, with visitation reaching 287 million tourists in 1998. According to the same article, "the snarl and whine of snowmobiles, personal watercraft like Jet Skis, all-terrain vehicles, and sightseeing overflights are destroying the solitude and marring the scenic beauty in dozens of [national] parks."

In sites that are new to tourism, roads cut for tourist transportation (and for logging and mining) can become pathways for the sprawl of human populations that colonize and disrupt sensitive habitats. Roads can also cause stream sedimentation in mountainous areas, leading to overflow and erosion.

In the United States, mounting highway noise has lead to the construction of barriers along roadways. Although it's impossible to separate out the tourist proportion of the traffic, a report by the Federal Highway Administration called Highway Traffic Noise in the United States: Problem and Response says that by 1995 the 10 states with the largest barrier programs had built 1,493 kilometers of barriers at a cost of $1.15 billion in 1995 dollars.

Even on the seas, the transportation of tourists creates environmental costs. Cruise ships have been implicated in ocean dumping of garbage, particularly plastics and human waste.

Currently, a coalition of 54 environmental groups has asked the U.S. Environmental Protection Agency (EPA) to develop tougher regulations for monitoring and controlling illegal cruise ship dumping.

A 23 March 2000 article in The New York Times says that "in a formal petition, the organizations called for tightening long-standing exemptions from the Clean Water Act that allow cruise ships to discharge untreated waste water from sinks, showers, laundries, and galleys, known as gray water, wherever they choose and for revising rules on other discharges."

While cruise ships can dump gray water anywhere, they must be more than three miles off shore to dump sewage and food waste. "Regulatory loopholes are allowing cruise ships to dump millions of gallons of pollutants directly into our nation's most sensitive waters," says Kira Schmidt, a campaign director with the Bluewater Network, one of the parties to the petition.

According to the article, the largest cruise companies adopted voluntary standards last year to improve waste treatment and reduce discharges from their ships. The International Council of Cruise Lines, which represents the major cruise companies that operate in U.S. waters, said the industry is discussing its practices and goals with the EPA and state environmental agencies.

MOUNTAINS OF WASTE

Tourism can cause large increases in the number of temporary residents of a tourist area and a resulting surge in sewage (which is often untreated) and garbage wastes. According to The Green Host Effect, a 1999 study of ecotourism by the nonprofit Washington, DC-based group Conservation International, only 10% of the sewage from 14 million visitors to the Caribbean in 1994 received any form of treatment.

Sewage damages surface and ground waters by odor, nutrient loading, and pathogens, according to the report. In addition, it states, "Poor sewage treatment can lead to pollution of ground and surface water, bacterial growth, the smothering of corals, the accumulation of toxins in aquatic and marine organisms, and algal blooms, which reduce oxygen available to other organisms and can cause biologically dead areas."

Garbage is another sore spot. Tourists often consume far more packaged and disposable goods than the average resident, and local disposal systems frequently can't handle all the extra trash.

In Zihuatanejo, on Mexico's Pacific coast, the evening air is often soured by the stench of burning plastic as restaurant owners torch their trash in open pits.

Island resorts, where land is inherently limited, are particularly prone to garbage disposal problems. For example, according to a report cited in The Green Host Effect, residents and hotel owners on the island of Lesbos, Greece, throw their trash into the water, exacerbating an existing pollution problem.

In the Himalayas, Mount Everest is visited by a growing number of climbers who have traditionally had more energy for packing in supplies than for packing out trash. The camp at 26,000 feet "has become known as the highest junkyard in the world," according to a 4 March 1996 article by Peter Ford in The Christian Science Monitor.

"Like camps farther down the mountain, it is littered with empty oxygen and cooking gas cylinders, tins, tents, sleeping bags, food, ropes, batteries, plastics, and the frozen corpses of climbers who have died on the mountain." The government of Nepal now requires climbing groups to submit a deposit that is refunded only after teams return with their trash.

A ROOM WITH A VIEW

Tourism development can drastically alter land use, particularly when large numbers of tourists descend on small, fragile environments such as often exist on coastlines. In the Philippines, the 2,500-acre island of Boracay had 2,000 residents in the 1980s; today, up to 20,000 tourists may crowd the island at once.

One-tenth of the land is now devoted to a golf course, and in 1997 environmental regulators noted dangerous levels of fecal coliform bacteria, an indicator of untreated sewage, in ocean waters where people were swimming. According to figures cited in The Green Host Effect, sprawl is further advanced in Cancun, on Mexico's Yucatan Peninsula, which grew from a tiny fishing village in the early 1970s into a tourist mecca with more than 20,000 hotel rooms and 2.6 million visitors annually.

Each day, the local landfill receives 450 tons of garbage. Many of the poor among Cancun's 300,000 residents live in shantytowns, and 75% of their sewage flows untreated into the lagoon behind the beach. Heading south toward Belize, shoreline destinations along modern highways are replacing pristine rainforest, and tourism in Playa del Carmen, Mexico, has been growing at 30% annually.

Coastal development can damage other marine resources. Anchoring and disturbance by scuba divers and their boats has damaged reefs in the Yucatan, the Caribbean, and elsewhere. Road building and development can cause siltation and destruction of harbors and sea life.

Tourist development can also cause problems inland. In Asia, for example, golf courses near tourist destinations are causing concern. Thailand bills itself as a "golfer's paradise," but densely populated tropical nations may be ill-suited to golf courses, which appropriate large tracts of land from agriculture.

Golf courses also reportedly use between 800,000 and 1.3 million gallons of water per day during the dry season. Oliver Hillel, director of the ecotourism programme at Conservation International, says, "In the Malay Peninsula of Thailand, a local government has opted to supply tourist facilities—golf courses—with water and energy before [serving] the local people."

The average golf course also receives 1,500 kilograms of fertilizer, herbicide, and pesticide each year, according to The Green Host Effect, which also notes that the chemicals "have been associated with pollution of water resources, the death of wildlife, and increased diseases, including cancer, among humans."

Tourism development and the visitation it occasions also contribute to habitat decline. In a 1997 survey of 44 U.S. national park superintendents titled Environmental Impacts of Tourism on U.S. National Parks, 37 parks reported vegetation problems related to tourism. Camping along streams in crowded parks causes trampling of stream banks and erosion into surface waters.

Laura Loomis, director of the visitor use and experience programme at the private National Parks Conservation Association, says the National Park Service has recently done a reasonably good job of moving campsites away from streams. The service has been less effective at dealing with damage due to new forms of recreation, she says.

For example, "sand boarding" is a dry version of surfing done on the sands of the Great Sand Dunes National Monument in Colorado.

Critics charge that the activity leads to erosion of the dunes and that regulations to protect the dunes are not being enforced. "They say it's only 10 people per year and that it's too expensive to send rangers out," says Loomis, "but that's the same head-in-the-sand attitude they took when snowmobiles were introduced into Yellowstone."

The effects of tourism development are perhaps most vividly evident in the Galapagos Islands, the volcanic islands in the Pacific Ocean where Charles Darwin gathered data before propounding his theory of evolution.

The Galapagos archipelago has long been a destination for tourists with an ecological or scientific bent, but the habitat is rapidly changing.

The islands and its wildlife are threatened by an onslaught of tourists and a surge in population among the people who serve them. The islands' population has reached 20,000, causing problems with sewage, trash, and habitat destruction due to such introduced species as goats and pigs.

BIODIVERSITY

It's not just geography that can be threatened by tourists. Animals may be affected by the presence of tourists as well. Much of the international concerns in this area originated in Kenya, where lions, cheetahs, elephants, and other wildlife at game parks are frequently surrounded by scores of tourist vans.

A 1990 survey by J. S. Akama published in Progress in Tourism and Hospitality Research found that 80% of tourists in Kenya were disturbed by animal harassment, off-road driving, and vehicle congestion.

Visitors may also affect animals in the fragile rainforests, according to research in the Ecuadorian Amazon basin by biologist Stella de la Torre, formerly at the University of Wisconsin at Madison.

After tracking howler monkeys at two locations, de la Torre found that noise from tourist boats was changing the way the monkeys used their habitat. "In the area with motorboats from 17 tour agencies, the monkeys seem to be retreating from the lake edge, where they would normally be spending most of their time," says University of Wisconsin researcher Charles Snowdon, who oversaw the research, which was published in the September 1999 issue of Neotropical Primates.

In a companion study of the pygmy marmoset scheduled for publication in Biological Conservation, de la Torre found that the five-ounce primate stayed higher in the trees and interacted less in areas with more tourists. The pygmy marmosets at the heavily traveled site produced only 31% of their potential offspring, compared to 86% in areas with low tourist numbers.

ECOTOURISM TO THE RESCUE

If today's trends continue, tourism and particularly travel to exotic natural destinations is expected to increase. Perhaps in response, the industry is looking at its environmental effects, says Jafari. "There's a huge debate and [environmental] concerns. There are programs alerting the industry to the fact that it will have to police itself, or somebody will police the industry."

Many of the suggestions for reducing environmental damage from tourism include proposals for alleviating the more generic human impact on the planet.

One popular proposal is to reduce energy use by substituting buses for cars. In California, however, plans to deliver tourists in buses to the crowded Yosemite Valley portion of Yosemite National Park have encountered opposition by local businesses, which fear that a reduction in tourism would ensue if people could not use their personal cars to get there.

Many of the solutions for reducing the environmental impact of tourism are lumped together under the label "ecotourism."

Ecotourism, sometimes called sustainable tourism, tends to overlap with adventure, wildlife, and nature travel, but true ecotourism should simultaneously benefit tourists, the environment, and the local society and economy.

According to a commonly used definition from The Ecotourism Society, ecotourism is "purposeful travel to natural areas to understand the culture and natural history of the environment, taking care not to alter the integrity of the ecosystem, while producing economic opportunities that make the conservation of natural resources beneficial to local people."

Ecotourism development proposals involve controlling construction in vulnerable locations and grouping resorts to leave some land undisturbed, as well as increasing the local benefits to make conserving habitat more profitable to local people, the idea being that the need to conserve land for tourism and the income it creates may become more valuable to the local economy than activities that deplete resources, such as logging.

In 1999, the Centre for International Forestry Research in Bogor, Indonesia, published an extensive study of ecotourism projects in the Ecuadorian Amazon titled Promoting Forest Conservation through Ecotourism Income?, which found benefits to local communities and the environment. "In all five study cases of tourism in Cuyabeno [Wildlife Reserve], local community members receive economic benefits that are significant and competitive, compared with other sources of monetary income," writes analyst Sven Wunder.

The tourism income to each community was between $15,000 and $50,000, much higher than previous estimates. The impacts on the forests were lessened by regulation, peer pressure to preserve animals that tourists like, and the fact that employed people had less time for hunting.

Wunder writes, "There are good reasons to believe that the rise of tourism and the stream of income ... have substantially helped to conserve the integrity of the reserve." In essence, tourism became a counterweight to profitable but destructive uses of the land such as plantation farming, logging, and drilling for oil.

Ecotourism is popular among conservation organizations, some of which promote ecotourism develop ment projects and sponsor ecotravel. Such development projects can provide a more environmentally friendly alternative to conventional tourism.

Lodges that use local materials and traditional architecture, for example, may need less material transported in during construction and use less air-conditioning during operation.

Similarly, buying local produce reduces the environmental effects of freight transportation such as air pollution and energy usage, and supports the local economy.

One well-known example of ecotourism development, Maho Bay in the U.S. Virgin Islands, was built largely with recycled materials.

Rather than houses, it uses tents that rest on platforms to reduce soil damage. Communal toilets, cold-water showers, and solar panels all reduce energy use. But while the site does offer so-called green lodging, critics charge that it falls short on local social and economic benefits such as community empowerment.

Such benefits have been more evident at a project near the Maya Biosphere Preserve in Guatemala, where more than half the local forest had been destroyed by logging and resin collection. There, Conservation International helped start a Spanish-language school.

By 1998, the school was run by a local cooperative and was attracting 500 students, each paying $50 per week for instruction, to an area that had seen little tourism. Local people also earn money at new tourist-associated businesses selling lodging, food, and guide and telephone services, which provide alternative income to logging.

Ecotourism projects may also be designed to attract internal tourism that is environmentally friendly. Andrew Smith, a professor of biology at Arizona State University, has consulted for such an effort outside Mexico City, the world's largest metropolis.

Smith says the Ejido (communal lands) Park at San Nicolas attracts city residents to its fenced, protected land. He expects the park to help stem a transformation of this rural highland into a suburb. "Three years ago, 90% of the people were getting their basic income from Mexico City," he says. "They'd given up the heritage of living on the land."

Now, on weekends, hundreds of Mexicans from the city pay parking and entrance fees to hike, bike, and camp in the area.

A fish hatchery and tree nurseries are helping restore the biological vitality, Smith adds, and now that standing pine trees are becoming profitable, "all the biodiversity in the area is protected."

In New Jersey, birdwatchers contribute $31 million annually to the Cape May economy. In a familiar type of industrial—environmental conflict, the shorebirds that attract the birdwatchers eat horseshoe crab eggs, which are also harvested for bait and as a raw material for a medicine. As a result of discussions between the birdwatchers and industry, the fishery was restricted but not banned.

"Hopefully it's a win-win situation," says Michael Weinstein, director of the New Jersey Sea Grant programme. "If the fishermen give up a little, the shorebirds gain and the ecotourism is sustained."

Yet, many ecotourism projects fail to meet the lofty standards of the comprehensive definition.

In her 1999 book Ecotourism and Sustainable Development: Who Owns Paradise?, Martha Honey, director of the peace and security programme at the Institute for Policy Studies in Washington, DC, writes, "While ... many projects around the world may be missing a few of the pillars of sound ecotourism, others amount to little more than green packaging."

For example, she writes, "In Costa Rica, a $3 billion megaresort project that will include shopping centers, two golf courses, and a polo field is officially called an `ecodevelopment.'"

In the long run, the debate over the environmental effects of tourism will likely gain significance if, as the World Tourism Organization predicts, over one billion people travel internationally in 2010, producing revenue totaling $1.55 trillion. Will tourism destroy the world? Probably not—there are plenty of other contenders for that dubious honour.

Will ecotourism save the world? Equally unlikely. But for its potential to deliver environmental, economic, and social benefits to places that could use plenty of both, tourism—and particularly the ecotourism variation—can be a boon.

Still, if tourism is to provide real benefits in a sustainable way without wreaking havoc on the environment, the multitudes of travelers who traverse the planet will need to learn to tread softly on the earth.

Chapter 5

Management Approaches

Up to this point this book has demonstrated that marine tourism is large and growing rapidly, and furthermore that this kind of tourism is causing many problems. It has also been pointed out that not all impacts resulting from marine tourism are detrimental—in some cases the impacts are beneficial. The question arises, therefore, of what it is that causes the impacts of marine tourism to be positive or negative. The answer is—it depends.

Sometimes the positive impacts are much greater than the negative simply because the tourism enterprise is very small, the resource large and consequently the use of the marine resource negligible. The benefits to the local community from the tourism may, however, be relatively large. Therefore, it may be concluded that the marine tourism operation is, on balance, beneficial.

This judgement does, of course, depend on your perspective. If you are a local person deriving income from, say, a new, small-scale charter fishing operation, inevitably your perspective is inclined to the positive. If, however, you are a person who has retired to the location for peace, quiet and relaxation, your perspective on the benefits of local charter fishing business bringing more tourists to the area may be quite different.

And, of course, if you take the extreme example, and put on not rose-coloured but marine-blue glasses and view things as a local reef fish, that perspective may view the small-scale fishing operation extremely negatively—especially if you are the fish that gets caught!

This simplistic illustration shows that judging the relative costs and benefits of tourism is extremely difficult, if not impossible. It is, however, possible to agree that a goal of maximising the positive and minimising the negative impacts of tourism is a worthy one. Thus, rather than trying to quantify costs and benefits it is better to concentrate on developing a management regime for marine tourism which maximises the good and minimises the bad.

There is a wide variety of strategies that can be utilised in developing such a regime. This chapter details some of them. It also discusses the concepts of 'sustainability' and 'ecotourism', two terms that have become widespread in the laws and literature.

These approaches seek to solve the tourism development dilemma of how to stop people destroying the very features which attract them to a location. This chapter also details a case for education as a management approach for marine tourism. Finally, some suggestions for measuring the impacts of tourism are made, and a conceptual model for its management is offered.

STRATEGIES USED TO MANAGE MARINE TOURISM

A number of well-established management regimes are utilised to manage tourists and their activities on the sea. These strategies range from no control whatsoever, to complex combinations of structures, technology, economics, regulation and education. In order to simplify this situation, Orams divided tourist management strategies into four main categories: regulatory, physical, economic and educational.

The first two control tourist behaviour through external manipulation and have dominated most approaches to managing marine tourism in the past.

More recently, economic strategies have been utilised. The fourth category has traditionally been incorporated in park management activities but has had limited application elsewhere. The following sections discuss each category in more detail.

REGULATORY MANAGEMENT STRATEGIES

Regulatory management practices are the traditional method of controlling tourist activities in marine settings. Rules and regulations are commonly utilised to restrict visitor actions, access, times and numbers, and are usually posted on signs, notices and written material. Enforcement is usually undertaken by police, park rangers or other agents of the management authority.

A system of progressively harsher punishment is most common; for example, a warning at the first offence, banning from the area at a second offence, and eventually fines and imprisonment in extreme cases of misconduct, such as harassment or killing of protected wildlife.

Examples of regulations commonly used to manage tourists are visitor number restrictions, limits on times and locations, types of visitor activity permitted, spatial and temporal zoning, restrictions on the types of equipment permitted, noise levels, speed limits, permits, lease and licence requirements, and codes of practice.

The purpose of regulatory practices is threefold: first, to protect the safety of the tourist; second, to reduce conflicts between tourists; and third, to protect the marine environment from negative impacts due to inappropriate tourist behaviour.

As a result of the increasing use of marine areas for recreation and the increasing demand for opportunities for commercial tourist operations, there has been a proliferation of regulations pertaining to marine activities.

These regulations often restrict the freedom of visitors to do as they wish and there is some evidence that this may reduce enjoyment of the experience.

Other difficulties can arise from the cost of enforcing rules, particularly in large and remote areas such as those that exist in marine locations. Nevertheless, regulation remains the most common management response to increasing pressure from tourism.

PHYSICAL MANAGEMENT STRATEGIES

'Physical' approaches to management are those human-made structures that control human activity by restricting the movement or type of activity which can be undertaken. A typical marine example is the construction of a boardwalk across a wetland.

This physical structure directs and facilitates the movement of tourists and reduces the negative impacts that could be caused by their walking through sensitive areas. Additional examples include underwater observatories, mooring buoys for vessels in coral reef areas, sea pens, tethered animals (sea turtles) and grandstands, such as those provided at the Phillip Island Penguin Colony in Victoria, Australia (personal observation).

Because of the difficulties involved with erecting structures in the marine environment, physical controls are not a particularly common system in controlling marine tourism. They are, however, very commonly used in terrestrial protected natural area management. In a number of situations physical structures have been successfully used to control tourists in the sea.

The use of mooring buoys to reduce anchor damage on coral reefs is a notable success story. Additional examples include the use of such things as glass-bottom boats, semi-submersibles, self-guided underwater trails and beach bicycle pathways. Human-made structures are also utilised to provide additional opportunities and services for tourists. Examples are marinas, wharves, boat ramps and observation platforms. Of particular relevance are vessels which tourists use to access the marine environment.

Regulations can be used to restrict the type of vessel permitted in an area; for example, by allowing only electrically powered boats in an area sensitive to noise disturbance. Thus, the negative impacts of an activity can be mitigated by a combination of regulatory and physical approaches.

ECONOMIC MANAGEMENT STRATEGIES

Economic strategies use prices as incentives or disincentives to modify people's behaviour. Although these techniques have received little explicit recognition, they have been used in many natural areas for many years. An example of this type of strategy is the use of higher entry fees to facilities during peak use times in an attempt to spread visiting. Permits that are auctioned to commercial tourist operators can restrict the number of operators.

Imposing fines for littering, taking undersize fish, or other inappropriate behaviour is another example of a regulation combined with an economic disincentive. Although the use of economic strategies has not been common in marine tourism situations, considerable potential exists.

For example, discounts on access fees to a marine park can be provided if groups undertake a clean-up project, or assist with research, during their visit. Fees could be more expensive during times when wildlife is more sensitive to disturbance, thus providing an incentive for tourists to visit at other times.

Most marine resources are managed by publicly funded government organisations. Given the increasing financial pressure under which many of these public management agencies find themselves, the opportunity to utilise economic techniques to generate additional funds, and accomplish management objectives, may be worthwhile.

EDUCATIONAL MANAGEMENT STRATEGIES

The goals of education-based management strategies are to reduce the incidence of inappropriate tourist behaviour by encouraging a voluntary behaviour change, and to increase visitor enjoyment and understanding.

Many authors, therefore, view education as a potential 'win-win' situation for both the marine environment and the tourist. However, the use of education as a management strategy in tourism situations has not been as common as the use of physical or regulatory techniques.

This is due to a number of factors that make the planning and implementation of an effective educational programme for tourists particularly difficult. These factors include the diverse characteristics of tourist groups such as different group size, age and educational attainment. As a result, the needs of each tourist are unique and are difficult to cater for in the design of an educational programme.

This is further complicated by the 'non-captive' nature of marine tourists; that is, tourists are usually free to come and go as they please and will often 'vote with their feet' and leave when educational programmes do not meet their needs or hold their interest.

In marine settings, the diverse locations and the mobility and geographical spread of tourists often make it difficult for an education programme to be scheduled at a time, or located at a place, where tourists will be exposed to it.

Lack of knowledge regarding the marine environment and a lack of suitably trained and qualified personnel can also complicate efforts to implement an effective education programme. These factors result in little use of education as a management strategy and the predominance of physical and regulatory approaches.

However, a number of authors argue that education is, or should be, a critical component of nature-based tourism experiences. This argument is further developed later in this chapter, where the role of 'interpretation' is discussed.

CASE STUDY: THE REEFS OF THE FLORIDA KEYS

The coral reefs of the Florida Keys are the only extensive coral reef tract in North America and the third largest reef system in the world. They contain many unique and endangered species, host intensive recreational use and support a significant commercial tourism industry producing an estimated $US1 billion per year for the local area.

The Keys' marine environment attracts more than three million visitors each year and there is widespread concern over the impact this high level of tourist use is having on the Keys' ecosystem. Ward's comments typify the reaction of many to the masses of tourists visiting the reefs:

Their boats pollute the water and everything in it with petroleum products and sewage. Incompetent operators crash into the reefs. They litter the sea with plastic foam cups, aluminum cans, glass, plastic bags, bottles, and miles of tangled fishing line. This debris does not go away—it is, for all practical purposes, indestructible. Thousands of swimmers routinely bump, scrape, and step on coral.

In 1990, as a result of an Act of the United States Congress, the Florida Keys were declared a national marine sanctuary. National marine sanctuaries in the US are administered by the National Oceanic and Atmospheric Administration, an agency of the federal government.

The central management tool for marine sanctuaries is a comprehensive management plan. The plan establishes the specific objectives, policies and guidelines for the sanctuary and helps to determine the regulations to be enforced.

These management plans, therefore, consider the range of management strategies outlined earlier in this chapter and adopt those which are considered most appropriate for protecting the resources of the area whilst allowing for traditional commercial activities, such as tourism, to continue.

The management plan for the Florida Keys National Marine Sanctuary (National Oceanic and Atmospheric Administration, 1995) outlines a wide variety of strategies to manage tourist use of the area.

Fundamental to these strategies is the establishment of a system of five types of geographic zone. This regulatory approach designates specific areas for specific uses. *Wildlife management areas* have restricted access and activities in order to protect endangered or threatened species and their habitats. *Replenishment reserves* protect spawning and nursery areas by minimising human influences and restricting extractive practices such as fishing. *Sanctuary preservation areas* protect areas for non-extractive recreational use. *Special use areas* designate areas for specific purposes such as scientific research. *Existing management areas* allow for activities to continue under current management restrictions.

Additional 'action plans' set out in the management plan include channel marking (physical approach), a mooring buoy action plan (physical approach), a regulatory action plan (regulatory approach), an enforcement action plan (regulatory and economic approaches), an education action plan (educational approach) and ones dealing with water quality, research and monitoring, submerged cultural resources and volunteers, each of which contains elements of all four management approaches.

The Florida Keys is a large area that is intensively used for tourism. A comprehensive management plan that sets out a variety of management strategies is a common technique used in marine resource management.

MARINE PARKS

One of the most popular and successful management regimes utilised both to protect resources and to facilitate recreational use of them is the establishment of marine parks. These locations are administered in many different forms. One extreme is the designation of a 'no-take' marine protected area where no disturbance or removal of marine life is permitted, such as the Cape Rodney to Okakari Point Marine Reserve at Leigh, New Zealand.

The other extreme is illustrated by the adjacent Hauraki Gulf Maritime Park, offshore from Auckland, which provides no special protection or management of marine resources but seeks to manage the publicly owned islands of the area.

Within these extremes there is a wide variety of institutional arrangements for managing marine resources and marine recreation. The most popular is the 'multi-use' marine protected area. These marine parks seek to manage recreational and commercial use of the marine resources whilst protecting them from unacceptable damage.

The most popular mechanism for doing this is establishing a range of geographic zones. This kind of management approach has received widespread support at both a scientific and a political level. In January 1992, then United States President George Bush declared that 'in the United States, marine sanctuaries and other protected areas offer one of the best methods of safeguarding the marine environment'.

Marine parks are, therefore, now seen by many as an important framework under which various management techniques can be applied to ensure that use of the marine environment, including tourist activities, is sustainable. The largest marine park in the world is the Great Barrier Reef Marine Park.

CASE STUDY: THE GREAT BARRIER REEF MARINE PARK

The Great Barrier Reef (GBR) is the world's largest coral reef system, stretching 2,000 km down the northeastern coast of Queensland, Australia. The reef is actually comprised of some 2,600 individual reefs that vary greatly in size. It supports a diverse range of marine species, including around 1,500 fish species, 350 species of hard corals and 240 species of birds.

Estimates in the early 1990s placed the number of visitors to the reef at 2.2 million per year. By the year 2000 this number is expected to have doubled. In 1975 the Australian government established the Great Barrier Reef Marine Park (GBRMP). The park is managed by the Great Barrier Reef Marine Park Authority (GBRMPA).

However, the GBRMPA shares responsibility for the management of the park area with the state of Queensland (Dinesen, 1995). The broad management tools used to control tourism and recreation in the park include zoning plans, management plans, regulations, special area designations, permits and education.

Zoning plans require considerable public consultation and establish permitted uses along each section of the reef. For example, some zones exclude permanent structures. Zoning plans also establish which tourist activities require permits.

Management plans are prepared for individual reefs or islands that are likely to receive significant use for tourism. Historically, the management of tourism impacts has been largely controlled with the use of permits for commercial tourist operators because management plans have been slow to develop.

In the early years of the park the relationship between use of the park's resources and impacts was not well understood. Permits were therefore favoured as a means of managing impacts because they allowed flexibility. Over time the number of permits being issued and their complexity increased dramatically.

The process of permit granting and renewal was also being slowed down with appeals. A further concern was the inequity of the process.

Commercial tourism operators were being prevented from offering activities in some areas where private individuals could undertake the same activities.

In high-use areas of the GBR, the GBRMPA has adopted a number of physical methods to reduce impacts. In 1989, four permanent large-vessel moorings and six small-boat moorings were erected in close proximity to dive sites. These were designed to prevent coral being damaged by boat anchors.

Fishing in the area was also restricted in order to protect the area's resident populations of potato cod. In 1992, it was estimated that this site, an area around 300 metres in length, received 30,000 dives.

A further management initiative for the GBR was taken by the commercial tourism operators themselves. In 1992, they grouped together to form a reef operators' association. With the help of the GBRMPA they instituted a degree of self-regulation. For example, they placed restrictions on boat sizes, on length of stay at particular reefs and on fish feeding.

This technique has proved an effective way of reducing the negative impacts associated with commercial tourist use of the reef. Educational approaches have also been emphasised by the GBRMPA. A number of studies have shown that these techniques have been effective; for example, research showed that educating scuba divers reduces the impact that they have on coral reefs.

The GBR is a large resource with rapidly growing use and associated impacts. However, through the establishment of a marine park it has an agency with a mandate to manage human use of that resource comprehensively. This organisational structure and the use of a wide variety of management techniques are seen as an important model of how tourism can be managed sustainably in marine environments.

MARINE TOURISM AND SUSTAINABILITY

The objective of sustainability in managing natural resources has become widespread in recent years (World Tourism Organisation, 1997c).

Derived from the influential Brundtland Report (United Nations World Commission on Environment and Development, 1987) and ratified by the Rio de Janeiro Environment Summit in 1992, the concept of sustainability has become a guiding principle in legislation, policies and approaches to a wide range of resource management topics (World Tourism Organisation, 1997c).

Sustainability is defined as 'a characteristic of a process or state that can be maintained indefinitely'. Sustainable use is defined as 'use of an organism, ecosystem or other renewable resource at a rate within its capacity for renewal'.

Tourism has also been considered in terms of the principle of sustainability and has been viewed as a potentially sustainable industry.

However, a number of authors question the ability of any tourism venture to be sustainable. For example, Zell states: 'Tourism creates more tourism, thc location becomes well known and thus desirable creating demand, more supply and ultimately destruction of the original reason for going there'.

Partly in response to the push for 'sustainability' in resource use and management, and partly as a result of the recognition that tourism can result in significant environmental impacts that are not 'sustainable' in the longer term, the concept of 'ecotourism' has arisen.

ECOTOURISM

Ecotourism has been hailed by some as the 'answer' to tourism development, and 'its supporters argue that ecotourism is the only tourism development that is sustainable in the long term'. The concept that tourism should contribute to the health and viability of the natural attraction upon which it is based is an appealing one.

However, these lofty aspirations and the rapid adoption of this label by many operators and nations have been greeted with cynicism by many, who view ecotourism as simply nature-based tourism 'dressed up' under a new, attractive label:

Ecotourism is big business. It can provide foreign exchange and economic reward for the preservation of natural systems and wildlife. But ecotourism also threatens to destroy the resources on which it depends. Tour boats dump garbage in the waters off Antarctica, shutterbugs harass wildlife in National Parks, hordes of us trample fragile areas. This frenzied activity threatens the viability of natural systems. At times we seem to be loving nature to death.

Berle's statement typifies the concerns of many regarding the increasing number of tourists who are visiting natural areas and who are having a detrimental impact on those areas. Others, such as Wight , caution that the ecotourism label is being utilised to take advantage of a 'greening' of the economic market place and to 'eco-sell' tourism and travel.

In some cases ecotourism may well be nothing more than a new marketing gimmick which dresses up existing tourism attractions in an attempt to increase market share:

There is no question that 'green' sells. Almost any terms prefixed with the term 'eco' will increase interest and sales. Thus, in the last few years there has been a proliferation of advertisements in the travel field with references such as ecotour, ecotravel, ecovacation, ecologically sensitive adventures, eco(ad)ventures, ecocruise, ecosafari, ecoexpedition and, of course, ecotourism.

Johnston agrees and states that: In some cases people have been blindly applying the buzzwords ecotourism, soft-path tourism and sustainable development to national and international development schemes, promoting and acquiring funding for these schemes because of the labels they wear.

Although many countries and agencies look towards ecotourism as an answer to both economic and conservation objectives, many remain unconvinced that such ventures are a panacea that both protects the environment and supports economic activity.

Considerable debate exists, therefore, over whether

ecotourism can be sustainable, and over what management regimes and strategies can be employed to minimise the negative impacts associated with anthropogenic influences on natural ecosystems.

As a result of the rapidly increasing use of resources and the desire to protect them, a number of leading authors in the field are arguing for research in the ecotourism area. For example, Boo states that: 'despite rising expectations regarding the value of nature tourism in many fields of expertise, there are great gaps in the information necessary to manage the nature tourism industry'.

The debate therefore centres upon the type of tourism that ecotourism is, or should be. A variety of management strategies, such as those outlined above, can be employed in an attempt to negate detrimental impacts. However, it is possible that educational approaches are best suited to the management of nature-based tourism.

THE CASE FOR EDUCATION AS A MANAGEMENT STRATEGY

Educational approaches to management have long been utilised in the park management field. In fact, the profession has coined the term 'interpretation' to describe the use of educational approaches to natural resource management.

Interpretation is a word traditionally used to describe the process of translating meaning from one spoken language into another. Interpretation of the natural environment in a park management context is a similar kind of communication.

Although the activity of interpretation has existed since pre-biblical times, the first explicit use of the term and discussion of its meaning were made by Freeman Tilden, who defined interpretation as: 'An educational activity which aims to reveal meanings and relationships through the use of original objects, by firsthand experience, and by illustrative media, rather than simply to communicate factual information'.

He suggests, therefore, that interpretation is a particular type of education that focuses on meanings and relationships.

It is not necessarily about the communication of facts, but about the communication and learning of ideas and concepts and the imparting of an appreciation for the natural environment involved.

What is not provided by Tilden's definition is an explanation of the practical management objectives of interpretation. Interpretation has, in fact, multiple roles which go beyond imparting an appreciation for nature. In particular, it can assist in achieving management objectives. For example, Beckmann, who conducted a review of interpretation activity in Australian parks, states:

Most Australian interpreters believe that interpretation has a real role to play in the management of parks (e.g. by reducing the need for regulation and enforcement, increasing visitor awareness of appropriate behaviour, enabling careful distribution of visitor pressure to minimize environmental impacts on fragile natural resources).

Despite widespread support of interpretation as a management strategy for natural areas, there has been little empirical research which has demonstrated the specific benefits of interpretation programmes.

'Unfortunately, very few applications of interpretation to management in Australia are fully documented, and the full potential of interpretation as "the public face of management" has still to be realized'.

This is most likely to be related to the difficulties in undertaking research in natural area settings and in determining such things as the incidence of visitor behaviour that is counter to agency management objectives, visitor enjoyment and visitor knowledge, attitudes and understanding.

There is, therefore, a case for assessing the effectiveness of education-based management strategies in managing marine tourism.

The objectives of such strategies are sound and the potential exists to protect the marine environment, increase visitor enjoyment and understanding, and prompt more environmentally responsible behaviour.

CREATING MORE RESPONSIBLE MARINE TOURISTS

At a basic level, the overall goal of management strategies designed to control marine tourism is twofold: first, to protect the marine environment from detrimental impacts, and second, to provide for and promote enjoyable tourist experiences. However, in order to accomplish this ambition tourists must somehow be prompted to do more than simply 'have a good time'.

Furthermore, and equally important, commercial operators must see their responsibilities as extending beyond making a profit. They must see their role as one of contributing to the health and viability of the resource upon which the livelihood of their business depends. If this can be achieved, the environment, upon which the tourism is based, would actually benefit from the tourism.

This view is contentious and certainly would be viewed with cynical contempt or, at the very least, as overly optimistic by some. However, in certain specific circumstances, nature is already benefiting from tourism.

For example, the Wildfowl Trust in Gloucestershire, England, has successfully assisted in the recovery of a number of endangered bird species, and now reintroduces many back into the wild to supplement threatened wild populations. These kinds of programme, largely funded by tourists, are becoming more common.

In addition, a number of habitats, which might have otherwise been lost, have been set aside as wildlife parks because of their tourism value, thereby benefiting the wildlife.

The fact is that many tourists are willing to give of their time, money and labour in order to assist with nature conservation. It may not, therefore, be overly optimistic to aim for marine-based tourism that is mutually beneficial. Given suitable management strategies, it may be possible.

The success of a management regime can, therefore, be measured in terms of its effectiveness in prompting the movement of the tourist experience towards these desired objectives.

The first of these is changing tourists' behaviour and lifestyle so that their actions become more environmentally responsible, both during the tourism experience and, longer-term, after the experience.

The second is promoting tourist actions that directly contribute to the environment while they are visiting it; for example, through assisting with research projects, becoming involved with habitat restoration programmes, removing litter, acting as volunteers for the management agency, or even helping to police the area so that other tourists' actions are not detrimental to the environment.

The categorisation of current management practices persented earlier in this chapter showed that a number of authors place significant emphasis upon educational techniques as a suitable mechanism for managing human impacts on the natural environment.

This optimism has seldom been empirically tested. The view that an effective interpretation programme for tourists will result in better tourism is, however, commonly held. The potential exists to prompt more desirable tourism through a management strategy that is based upon educational techniques.

One of the few pieces of research which has attempted to assess the effectiveness of an education-based management regime on marine tourism was conducted at Tangalooma, Queensland, Australia.

CASE STUDY: THE DOLPHINS OF TANGALOOMA

Tangalooma is a tourist resort in southeastern Queensland, Australia. Since 1992 a group of wild bottlenose dolphins have been regular visitors to the beach adjacent to this resort. The dolphins visit the area nightly to receive fish handouts from tourists in shallow water beside the resort's pier.

This opportunity has been promoted as an attraction and it has become increasingly popular since its inception. The dolphin feeding at Tangalooma was used as an opportunity to assess the effectiveness of an environmental education programme as a mechanism to promote environmentally desirable changes in tourists' attitudes and behaviour.

The study compared tourists who were exposed to the education programme (experiment group) with those who were not (control group). Indicators of changes in levels of enjoyment, knowledge, attitudes, intentions and behaviour were measured and compared between control and experiment groups in order to assess the impact of the education programme. The study showed that interacting with dolphins produced a desire in tourists to change their behaviour and become more environmentally responsible.

However, those tourists who were given the structured education programme seldom carried out these good intentions. In contrast, many of the tourists who were given the education programme became significantly more 'green' in their behaviour, by doing things such as joining environmental groups and getting involved in environmental issues.

MEASURING THE IMPACTS OF MANAGEMENT

In order to measure the success of management strategies in achieving a shift towards the objectives for tourism illustrated, a number of indicators need to be selected, for, as Pearce states:

Tourism impacts have been widely studied, but comparatively few attempts have been made to incorporate these impacts into tourism typologies. If this were more commonly done, it would facilitate bringing together cause and effect... In each case, specific measures of each variable used must be established, either in quantitative or qualitative terms.

These specific measures or 'outcome indicators' are shown. This figure shows the transition to the desirable form of ecotourism as a series of steps. As a first step, a management regime can be measured in terms of its impact on tourist satisfaction and enjoyment. However, this should not be viewed as the primary objective of such a strategy.

More complex educational and behavioural objectives

should be given equal weighting. The intermediate steps which assist in a transition from mere enjoyment to actual behaviour change that benefits the environment are, initially, the facilitation of education and learning, and subsequently, the changing of attitudes and beliefs to those that are more environmentally and ecologically sound.

The research instruments used to measure the achievement of these outcomes could include such things as participant observation, questionnaires and interviews. Of particular importance in assessing behaviour change are follow-up surveys which assess the impact of the experience some time after the tourists have returned home.

For this purpose, a follow-up interview or questionnaire needs to be conducted. It is well recognised that intentions to change behaviour do not necessarily result in actual behaviour change. The follow-up research should attempt to gather information on whether the desired behaviour change actually occurred.

The second set of steps shown is that of those that assist in measuring the impact of the tourists' behaviour on the marine environment. The objective is to encourage a transition from a passive position, where the tourist simply seeks to minimise detrimental impacts on the environment, to an active one, where the tourist actually contributes to the health and viability of the environment.

These three categories—minimising detrimental impacts, improving habitat quality and comprehensively contributing to the long-term health and viability of the ecosystem—are far more difficult to design measurement instruments for. Indices will need to be drawn up on a case-by-case basis; however, management regimes which are judged to fulfil the last criterion should be viewed as more desirable than those that merely seek to minimise detrimental impacts.

Each environment upon which tourism is based will be different and, therefore, indicators selected to monitor progress towards the desired state will need to be carefully chosen. However, for each setting, decisions should be made on, first, what types and levels of change in the natural ecosystem are acceptable; second, what critical indicators should be used to monitor this change; and third, what human actions are appropriate and inappropriate for that setting.

Various techniques can be used to make these decisions. For example, if adequate scientific knowledge is available for the resource, the most important indicators may already be known. In reality, however, this is seldom the case.

Processes such as those developed for environmental and strategic planning (including public participation) can be used, or an 'expert' panel can be developed to arrive at a consensus on the indicators. In this way hypotheses can be developed which allow testing of the level of disturbance to the natural environment.

Assessing whether tourists' actions improve habitat quality/protection is less difficult. If tourists provide financial support and/or labour which directly assists in the maintenance, protection or improvement of the natural resource they are visiting, they are meeting this objective.

The more desirable state occurs when a comprehensive and on-going programme exists where tourists can not only contribute during their visit but continue to support and contribute finance, labour and expertise to the resources on a long-term basis. Measurement of these indicators involves assessing the management regimes in place for specific tourism programmes to establish whether they facilitate this kind of tourist involvement.

A CONCEPTUAL MODEL FOR THE MANAGEMENT OF MARINE TOURISM

This chapter has attempted to review the range of strategies available for managing marine tourism. It has also proposed that management strategies should attempt to do more than simply minimise negative impacts. It argues that marine tourism can be managed to be, on balance, a positive thing for the marine environment. It is recognised that this is extremely ambitious and perhaps unrealistic given the rapid growth and intensity of use demonstrated in earlier chapters.

However, the alternative, namely to accept that our

enjoyment of the seas will result in their eventual destruction, is less palatable. Educational strategies in combination with other approaches show considerable potential for creating the sustainable 'ecotourism' that so many hope is attainable.

When considering the management of marine tourism activities this statement of Plimmer's is pertinent:

So, we have a wide range of management techniques. We can add to them as we realise the possibilities. It is essential that we look at all these possible techniques as a menu, and choose the one, or combination, best suited to the situation.

This pragmatic view is backed by the comments of Ceballos-Lascurain , who argues that managing tourism requires a multidisciplinary approach. This chapter attempts to provide a brief review of some of the approaches that may be a 'menu' from which specific strategies can be designed.

Earlier, the Spectrum of Marine Recreation Opportunities was outlined. This model, combined with ones of management techniques and outcome indicators, provides a conceptual framework for considering the management of marine tourism. This framework is useful in clarifying the marine recreational activity being discussed (the Spectrum of Marine Recreation Opportunities), the human intervention being undertaken (the management options available) and the outcomes that are being sought (outcome indicators). This model represents a conceptual framework that can be used as a basis for understanding and assessing the effectiveness of differing management regimes.

Chapter 6

From Policy to Professionalism

The discussion that follows is designed to act as a continuation of some of the many issues dealt with in the previous chapter (i.e. regulation, and planning). For example, Buckley and Pannell write that environmental impacts might be minimised through the use of a combination of factors including planning and regulation, incentives to encourage or discourage particular activities, hardening of sites receiving high levels of use, and through the use of education both on- and off-site.

Such policy-related actions are increasingly required, according to Goodwin , to ensure that tourism development is consistent with the needs of both local people and the environment.

Tourism and ecotourism policy encompasses a broad spectrum of concerns related to the implementation of tourism programmes around the world, including social, ecological, and economic relationships; but also how tourism affects or is affected by tourists, local people, operators, government, and so on.

In addition, much discussion has surrounded the notion of regulation as a means by which to provide a stronger element of control in how ecotourism products are shaped and implemented. Regulation, therefore, is also an integral part of this chapter. The final part of the chapter deals with certification and accreditation in the ecotourism industry. It is suggested that the industry is committing itself further to these programmes as a means by which to offer a higher standard of quality and professionalism in the field.

TOURISM POLICY

In a simplistic sense, tourism policy is the identification of a series of goals and objectives which help an agency—usually a governmental one—in the process of planning the tourism industry.

According to Akehurst , however, policy development is much more detailed. It is further defined as: a strategy for the development of the tourism sector...that establishes objectives and guidelines as a basis for what needs to be done.

This means identifying and agreeing objectives; establishing priorities; placing in a Community context the roles of national governments, national tourist organizations, local governments and private-sector businesses; establishing possible co-ordination and implementation of agreed programmes to solve identified problems, with monitoring and evaluation of these programmes.

In this sense it is the coordination of many organisations and agencies involved in the provision of tourism services, and the planning, development, and management of these groups. It is felt that all countries should endeavour to create tourism policy to guide their planning, management, and development of tourism consistently throughout a region and as a means by which to use resources in a wise and efficient manner.

The sector most responsible for the impetus to create policy is government, in either a passive (e.g. legislation is introduced but is not intended to discriminate in favour of the tourism industry) or an active manner, where government takes action to discriminate in favour of the tourism sector managerially (through the creation of objectives and legislative support) and/or developmentally (in the establishment and operation of tourism facilities).

In a similar context Lickorish suggests that governments have given low priority to the establishment of policy in tourism, particularly in the developed world (the first policy reports were established by the European Community in 1986).

The reason for this is that governments have traditionally viewed tourism development as lying within the realm of the private sector.

If centralised action has not been taken within a country, often regions or localities have taken responsibility but, according to Lickorish, with uneven results. In addition, policy-related problems are compounded by the fact that government policies related to tourism and the environment can be quite divergent.

Ministries of agriculture, the environment, tourism and industry, and transport may all vary in their approach to environmental policy.

Coccossis feels that there has not been a good understanding between the complex nature of the environment and tourism (e.g. the synergistic effects of tourism), coupled with a high degree of administrative fragmentation.

In addition, he writes that environmental conservation was perceived as a threat to social and economic development, a threat which has only recently subsided as a result of our efforts towards the clarification of sustainable development.

Without due regard to appropriate development guidelines, the integrity of public and private lands within communities has often been at risk owing to the sacrificing of socioecological values at the expense of profit.

A key point in Coccossis's argument is that environmental policies now are characterised by a more holistic, ecosystem based approach that relies less on specific issues and more on a regional integrated perspective.

This wider approach involves the following:

- Linking development policy with environmental management. As a first step, the review of projects, plans and programmes from an environmental point of view should be instituted;
- Regional-level environmental management schemes which would provide a framework for guiding local environmental management programmes;
- Integration of tourism development and environmental management policies at the local, regional, and national level; and

- Increasing local capacity to cope with environmental issues, particularly in rapidly developing tourist destination areas.

Priority areas identified by Coccossis in Europe for sustainable tourism development, utilising the aforementioned concepts, include coastal areas, rural areas, built environment and urban areas, and islands.

One of the best examples of policy related to hotel development was the implementation of measures to control the height of hotel development in Bali, Indonesia, and other places around the world in the 1980s. Hotels could not be built higher than the tallest palm trees to avoid the unsightly nature of these developments.

Hence, the development would fit into the landscape rather than dominate it. In support of what Coccossis illustrates above, Fayos-Solá writes that tourism policy has started to change in line with the evolving nature of the tourism industry.

Consistent with the paradigmatic shift in the 1980s away from mass tourism to alternative forms of tourism, the industry has given way to globalisation of markets, supersegmentation, new technologies, and an increased sense of social and ecological responsibility.

Competitiveness is a key function of the tourism industry and it is based on quality and efficiency rather than the quantity, which has been the *modus operandi* of mass tourism. Conversely, tourism policy objectives have undergone three distinct generations, according to Fayos-Solá .

The first generation was based on large numbers of visitors, the maximisation of revenues from tourism, and the creation of numbers of jobs, indicative of the mass tourism paradigm.

The second generation evolved from the economic difficulties of the 1970s, including growth-recession fluctuations.

In this stage, social, economic, and ecological impacts are better understood, while the economic and legal objectives are redefined in tourism's contribution to societal well-being. The final generation shows competitiveness as a key function of the vitality of the tourism industry.

In addition, both total quality management and the partnership between public, private, and not-for-profit agencies is underscored, leading to a more symbiotic relationship between sectors.

As such, the politics of policy-making for the twenty-first century will go beyond the conventional discussions related to marketing, promotion, tax incentives, accommodation, and transportation to more holistic-centred issues related to the environment, social impacts, issues of rational and equitable access (who gets what, when, and how), and the international regulation of health and safety issues.

Richter further illustrates that the political interest in policy is coming of age and that the democratisation of the electorate may prove to be formidable proponents in shaping key tourism decisions.

In a different line of thinking from the policy issues outlined above, Hjalager (1996a) argues that innovation must be the key to future policies and regulation designed to limit tourism's impact on the resource base.

She feels that policy, when it is considered, is hampered first by the fact that it is governed by ideology and personal sympathies rather than the need for balance, and second by the fact that cost is unlikely to be considered in implementation.

Her research touches on three policy control mechanisms: the market, bureaucracies, and clans (industry in cooperation with other stakeholders).

For example, Hjalager writes that bureaucracies regulate tourism in basically two fashions:

- By directing tourists, locals, and the industry through legislation, and
- Through the provision of tourism infrastructure. Central to Hjalager's thesis is the notion that regions must be open to alternative modes of regulation in addressing significant and challenging environmental issues.

Table. Innovation's Place in Tourism Policy and Regulation.

Instruments	How the environmental effect is achieved	Influence on innovation
Emission standards. Inspection in order to control	Industrial 'end of pipe' norms expressed according to carrying capacities. Development permissions with environmental standards	Control may raise standards, severe control may lead to the development of new techniques. No evidence that tourism will take the innovation lead
Compulsory use of specific energy resources or specific technologies (e.g. district heating or waste treatment systems)	Obtaining economies of scale in environmental management systems	Typically, innovation will not take place in tourist industries, but with specialised plants and suppliers
Zoning in order to limit or control opportunities for development Control of land use	Limiting the developer's activities according to carrying capacities or environmental objectives	Probably none
Zoning of tourists' access to vulnerable resources or areas	Visitor control systems and regulation of tourism by volumes Compulsory methods or training, motivation	Opportunities for development of IT instruments combined with communication/interpretation instruments

CASE STUDY: THE REGULATION OF WHALEWATCHING IN CANADA

The impact of ecotourism on the beluga whale population of the St Lawrence River, Canada, has prompted Blane and Jackson to call for stricter policies in the control of such vessels. The authors found that the high number of trips/vessels in the area of the whales was affecting their behaviour. They recommended that the number of operators should be restricted, that low speed limits should be spatially increased and enforced, and that boats should be required to travel around beluga pods in an appropriate fashion. Further, the authors suggested that policing should be accomplished by the Canadian government and informally by peers (i.e. operators). Such regulations have been addressed on the west coast of Canada by whalewatching operators, government, and other interested groups, and a set of guidelines for the industry to follow has been developed. A recent draft of a document by whale watching operators north west advocates the following:

- Stay approximately 100 metres away from the whales;
- Operators should be familiar with the Canadian Federal Fisheries Act;
- Slow down half a mile before arriving at the whales;
- Whales should be approached slowly at any time;
- When approaching whales from the front, STOP and allow whales to come to you;
- When approaching from behind, move to the outside of the nearest whales or boats, parallel to the direction of travel at a similar or slower speed;
- When travelling with the whales, do not alter speed or change course abruptly;
- Never make high-speed runs through the middle of a group of whales or boats;
- Avoid approaching whales that are feeding;
- Try to work with the whales in rotation; and
- Do not reposition your vessel by the leap-frog method.

ECOTOURISM AND POLICY

In many countries, ecotourism is presently at the policy consideration and initiation stage, with the recognition that further political and socio-economic coordination must exist for it to proceed. Policy development has only started to be initiated as a result of the lack of consensus as to what constitutes appropriate ecotourism development and activities. This has been the case in Hawaii, as identified by the Centre for Tourism Policy Studies .

This group has identified a number of policy recommendations to address in developing Hawaii's ecotourism industry, including:

- A state ecotourism policy and ecotourism development plan;
- Interagency coordination and cooperation with the private sector;
- Increased funding support through direct and indirect means; and
- Active community participation in planning and decision-making.

These recommendations are further broken down into integrated planning, public- and private-sector roles, research, land use, conservation, preservation, funding, marketing, operator concerns, socio-cultural concerns, regulation, monitoring, and education and training.

As a prime US destination, Hawaii is realising that apart from its extensive mass tourism industry, there is a definite market for ecotourists based on interests in whalewatching and the rainforest.

Although rough estimates indicate that ecotourism represents about 5 per cent of Hawaiian tourism revenue, there is the feeling that ecotourism is on the rise in this state, which is good news given the negligible tourism growth in Hawaii over the past decade.

Much like the Centre for Tourism Policy Studies cited above, Liu suggests that government policy is one of the keys to supporting the development of ecotourism. Her work on behalf of the American Affiliated Pacific Islands discusses the importance of government policy as a means by which to regulate and monitor the industry in a way that balances protection and restriction without hindering the individual operator.

This means a balance between development and conservation, supply versus demand, benefits versus costs, and people versus the environment.

In addition, Liu feels that government must play a leadership role in providing the necessary financing, management skills, and knowledge so the private sector can operate smoothly and efficiently.

This means government must:

- Facilitate efficient private-sector activity by minimising market interference and relying on competition as a means of control;
- Ensure a sound macro-economic environment;
- Guarantee law and order, and the just settlement of disputes;
- Ensure the provision of appropriate infrastructures;
- Ensure the development of human resources;
- Protect the public interest without obstructing private-sector activity with too many regulations;
- Promote private sector activity by not competing in the business arena with private enterprise; and
- Acknowledge the role of small business entrepreneurs and facilitate their activities.

Liu has developed a public-sector guide for the implementation of ecotourism. These are the points that should be considered for the purpose of implementing appropriate ecotourism policy.

Increasingly, planners and developers are realising that policy must involve the many stakeholders who stand to be impacted by ecotourism development, as suggested at the outset of this chapter.

According to Ceballos-Lascuráin, some of these groups include protected-area personnel, local communities, the tourism industry, NGOs, financial institutions, consumers, and national ecotourism councils. One of the finest examples of policy development involving stakeholder involvement in ecotourism can be found in the Australian National Ecotourism Strategy.

In this document an integrated approach to the development of ecotourism has been adopted with the belief that development and management of ecotourism is fundamental to optimising the benefits it offers.

This strategy is truly a national document in that it integrates the collective opinions of Australians through the implementation of a series of public consultation workshops involving government, industry, conservation groups, educational institutions, and community.

Policy implementation framework:

Development objectives: Establish economic, ecological, and socio-cultural objectives in consultation with local communities; designate specific areas for ecotourism development.

Inventories: Survey and analyse the region's ecology, history, culture, economy, resources, land use, and tenure; inventory and evaluate existing and potential ecotourist attractions, activities, accommodation, facilities, and transportation; construct or consolidate development policies and plans, especially tourism master plans.

Infrastructure and facilities: Provide the appropriate infrastructure and facilities, avoiding a reliance on foreign capital; establish means to assist the private sector in developing ecotourism enterprises in line with ecological and cultural standards.

Market: Analyse present and future domestic and international ecotourism markets and establish marketing goals; know and understand the market in achieving goals; assist the private sector in its development of marketing strategies.

Carrying capacity: Strive to understand the social and ecological limits of use of an area through appropriate management and research; establish social and ecological indicators of use and impact; implement an appropriate pre-formed planning and management framework.

Development: Establish a development policy giving consideration to balanced economic, ecological, and social factors; form a development plan on the basis of attractions, transportation, and ecotourism regions; assist developers to plan and build ecologically.

Economic: Consider ways to enhance economic benefits; conduct present and future economic analyses; ensure that profits are made, locals benefit, and public revenues are self-sustaining.

Environment: Consistently evaluate the impact of ecotourism on the resource base; link ecotourism with other resource conservation measures (e.g. parks and protected areas).

Culture: Evaluate the socio-cultural impact of ecotourism, prevent negative impacts, and reinforce positive outcomes; empower local people to become decision-makers; conduct a social audit of social impacts.

Standards: Apply development and design standards to facilities and accommodation; facilitate the adherence to standards by providing financial or tax incentives and access to specialists.

Human resources: Promote job creation and entrepreneurship; establish community awareness programmes; provide adequate education and training for local people.

Organisation: Establish a working relationship between public, private and not-for-profit organisations.

Regulations and monitoring: Establish legislation/ regulations to promote ecotourism development, through support for tourism organisations, tour operators, accommodation; establish facility standards.

Data system and implementation: Establish an integrated ecotourism data system for continuous operation that provides research and marketing information; identify ecotourism implementation techniques; and collaborate with private industry and educational institutions in implementation.

Groups: (The stakeholder approach used in this strategy has been outlined by Boo , who suggests that there are several stakeholder groups that must be involved in the development of ecotourism initiatives.)

The intent of the strategy is summarised as follows: 'to provide broad direction for the future of ecotourism by identifying priority issues for its sustainable development and recommending approaches for addressing these issues'. The bulk of the strategy concentrates on a variety of issues, objectives and actions which are essentially steps towards putting policy and planning initiatives into practice.

It is the ultimate aim of these directives to move

Australia to create an ecologically and culturally sustainable ecotourism industry in line with the ideals of sustainable development.

The development of this document was instrumental in demonstrating to the rest of the world the advanced state of ecotourism in Australia, and it is a model which other governments can follow. For example, the Ecotourism Task Force in association with Tourism Saskatchewan

Table. Australian National Ecotourism Strategy objectives

Strategy component	Objective
Ecological sustainability	Facilitate the application of ecologically sustainable principles and practices across the tourism industry
Integrated regional planning	Develop a strategic approach to integrated regional planning based on ecologically sustainable principles and practices and incorporating ecotourism
Natural resource management	Encourage a complementary and compatible approach between ecotourism activities and conservation in natural resource management
Regulation	Encourage industry self-regulation of ecotourism through the development and implementation of appropriate industry standards and accreditation
Infrastructure	Where appropriate, support the design and use of carefully sited and constructed infrastructure to minimise visitor impacts on natural resources and to provide for environmental education consistent with bioregional planning objectives
Impact monitoring	Undertake further study of the impacts of ecotourism to improve the information base for planning and decision-making

Table. Australian National Ecotourism Strategy objectives

Strategy component	Objective
Marketing	Encourage and promote the ethical delivery of ecotourism products to meet visitor expectations and match levels of supply and demand
Industry standards/ accreditation	Facilitate the establishment of high-quality industry standards and a national accreditation system for ecotourism
Education	Improve the level and delivery of ecotourism education for all target groups
Involve indigenous people	Enhance opportunities for self -determination, self-management and economic self-sufficiency in ecotourism for Aboriginals
Viability	Examine the business needs of operators and develop ways in which viability can be improved, either individually or through collective ventures
Equity considerations	Seek to ensure that opportunities for access to ecotourism experiences are equitable and that ecotourism activities benefit host communities and contribute to natural resource management and conservation.

(the government-private industry consortium that leads tourism development in this Canadian province) has developed a similar document which will be the basis of the ecotourism industry for the future.

Recommendations (among others) include the development of an accreditation process, the development of cooperative relationships with other land-users, and the construction of sustainable ecolodge facilities using state-of-the-art technologies and modelling.

As regions and countries make the decision to plan and develop an ecotourism industry, Ceballos-Lascuráin (1996a) advocates following a basic planning process such as the one identified below.

Policy may naturally evolve out of first identifying many of the catalysts and constraints to the development of the industry. In the case of ecotourism, this process must proceed out of government's general development policy and strategy (if such a strategy exists).

- *Study preparation*: Includes the assessment of the type of planning required and the preparation of terms of reference.
- *Determination of objectives*: Such objectives must reflect the national or regional government's general ecotourism policy/strategy, and include development priorities, temporal considerations, heritage, marketing, and annual growth.
- *Survey*: A complete evaluation and inventory of existing resources must be made, especially related to the attraction base. The ultimate aim of this inventory is to link attractions to various market segments and forms of development.
- *Analysis and synthesis*: This step involves studying the historical background of tourism in the region, analysing constraints to development, legal and risk management considerations, financing, tax incentives, protection of cultural and natural features, and other economic-related variables (e.g. contribution to GNP, and complementarity with other sectors of the economy).
- *Policy and plan formulation*: From an analysis of the synthesis, policies must be structured to reflect the economic, social, and ecological needs of the region. Alternative policies should be developed to assess how each fits with the country's overall development policy, from which final policies are derived in the areas of: infrastructure, human resources, transportation, intersectoral coordination, establishment of councils and

committees, tax incentives and subsidies, and the creation of tourism programmes.

- *Recommendations*: The result is a plan that indicates attractions, tourism development areas, transportation linkages, tour routes, and design and facility standards. Also, recommendations are made for implementation, zoning, land use plans for the future, economic benefits, education and training, ecological and social impacts, private industry incentives, and legislation.
- *Implementation and monitoring*: Prior to implementation, the policies and overall plan should be reviewed and ratified legally. Formal review periods should be established and committees or corporations should be developed to help implement or guide the implementation of the various developments.

The prime mandate of many state and provincial tourism authorities is to bolster tourism and ecotourism in their various regions, through the development of new product strategies to capture a larger travel market.

Given the marketing premise under which many of these regional bodies operate (they are designed primarily to generate profits through marketing and incentives), the social and ecological elements associated with sustainable tourism and ecotourism often take a back seat.

However, with increasing frequency subcommittees are being created within these agencies to deal specifically with ecotourism and sustainable development. For example, in 1990 the California legislature's Senate Select Committee on Tourism and Aviation convened to address the many problems facing the California tourist industry, including energy shortages, the inhospitality of cities, and development overkill in resorts.

From this committee's study of these and other dysfunctions, it was suggested that a strong ecotourism ethic be created that could be advantageous economically, socially, and ecologically, for the purpose of generating more positive tourism experiences in the state. In part because of some of these early examples of policy development at the regional level, in 1997 I sent out an E-mail to all North American provincial and state governments requesting information on ecotourism policy and accreditation (over 60 offices).

Although the response was rather limited, the overwhelming consensus among regional bodies was that policy and accreditation are 'on the table', meaning that while they have been thought about, little has been done in the way of legislation.

In some cases regions are in the process of stating recommendations to government on how to proceed in the ecotourism sector.

For example, Florida recently developed a report, based on the deliberations of an advisory committee, on how to protect and plan for its heritage and commercial assets (Ecotourism/ Heritage Tourism Advisory Committee 1997), with the mission of developing 'a blueprint that identifies goals, strategies and recommendations needed to create a statewide, regionally based plan to effectively protect and promote the natural, coastal, historical, and cultural assets of Florida, and to link these to commercial tourism in Florida'.

The plan focuses on forming strategic relationships with agencies in the community, developing inventories of sites, protection of the environment, education, and marketing.

REGULATION

According to Metelka , regulation refers to the efforts of an agency (government, international or trade) that has been given the authority to regulate the actions of businesses which fall within its jurisdiction. Historically, this has meant that government has seen fit to dictate the actions of, for example, the airline industry in terms of appropriate policies related to safety.

The fear, as always, is that if left unchecked, tourism will contribute to a diverse range of social and ecological impacts. More recently, though, the influence of alternative and sustainable forms of tourism has rekindled discussions related to the need to ensure that service and the provision of tourism products stem from appropriate business practices.

The belief that the tourism industry can operate without due regard to its short and long, and direct and indirect impacts is being challenged as more and more there is the recognition that business must be held accountable for its actions.

Goodall provides an excellent overview of regulation through the process of environmental auditing in the context of the British tourism industry. Citing the European Commission, Goodall writes that environmental auditing is essentially a mangement tool designed to evaluate how well organisations (their management and equipment) are performing towards the safeguarding of the environment through various environmental practices and policies.

Goodall suggests that this environmental tool has technical (e.g. noise reduction technology), legislative (e.g. the 'polluter pays' principle), and business (e.g. the costs and benefits associated with the will to undertake environmental audits) dimensions, which act as both catalysts and constraints to their implementation.

In Britain, Goodall writes, environmental auditing is voluntary and thus the responsibility lies within the agency, hence it is not likely to happen owing to the competitive, fragmented, small-scale nature of the industry.

Consequently, few tourism agencies have formal environmental policies and management systems, and 'Unless required to by law, such firms will only adopt best environmental practice where there is an incontrovertible commercial advantage'.

In reference to the UK outgoing tourism industry Forsyth discusses the link between sustainability and regulation.

His findings suggest that tourism businesses would be in favour of sustainability; however, he feels that because of the fragmented nature of the industry itself (i.e. hotels, tour operators, travel agents, carriers, associations), different industry sectors have separate aims and varied levels of power, and therefore may be unable to implement all forms of sustainable tourism consistently. Another main conclusion of his study was that host governments.

Summary of Policy and Environmental Audit Objectives.

Environmental policy objectives for firms:

- Compliance with relevant environmental legislation and indication of a willingness to develop reasonable and workable regulations.
- Reduction or elimination of any negative environmental impacts of current activities and avoidance of any negative impacts from proposed developments.
- Development of environmentally friendly products.
- Sustainable use of resources which include increasing efficiency of resource use, minimising waste, the use of environmentally benign inputs and equipment, and the safe disposal of wastes.
- The fostering among employees, and also customers and communities in which the firm functions, an understanding of environmental issues.

Key aims of an environmental audit:

- To judge whether the tourism firm's environmental management system is performing satisfactorily.
- To verify compliance with relevant environmental legislation.
- To verify compliance with the firm's stated policy.
- To minimise human exposure to risk from the environment and to ensure appropriate health and safety provision.
- To identify and assess the firm's risk resulting from environmental failure of its activities.
- To assess the impact on the environment, both local and global, of its plant, processes and products.
- To advise the firm on any environmental improvements it could make.
- To review the firm's internal procedures to help it to achieve its environmental objectives.

should be involved in the business of sustainable tourism (through regulation), not necessarily tourism businesses. The implication is that business practice occurs under the umbrella of regional and/or national policy schemes. The problem with such an approach is that such policies would probably be flexible to accommodate demand of the domestic tourism product and flexible in terms of accommodating multinational interest in the destination, which is usually driven by a profit motive.

One of the significant issues related to the imposition of regulatory measures for ecotourism operators is the perceived loss of control in the delivery of services and decision-making. In a discussion of the adventure and ecotourism industry in South Carolina, Tibbetts (1995-6) illustrates that many of the operators in this region favour self-regulation and voluntary guidelines.

There is a strong belief by such operators that since they are the ones out there working in the environment, they know how to manage their affairs without government help, how to solve their own problems, and how to take the lead in terms of planning and implementing an appropriate product. This may very well be true, but there are other, more broadly based concerns that may need to be considered. The operation of an ecotourism business involves an interaction with other tourism businesses, other land-users, local people, tourists, and so on.

The result is that the potential conflicts that may arise from these interactions (e.g. the overuse of trail systems, and the dumping of wastes in the Galápagos Islands) are not simply local and operator-specific, but rather have larger regional and socio-ecological implications. A key question to address is whether or not policy-makers can afford to provide the time for operators to distil out problems of complementarity and conflict, especially when it is the resource base that should be protected first over the needs of tourists and private industry.

We must consider that today, more than ever, businesses must be accountable to themselves, but, more importantly, to society. Given this axiom, it is appropriate that we continue to press the issue of whether or not the tourism industry and environment might better be served by regulation or self-regulation, or indeed both.

In addition, research needs to concentrate on the difference and/or similarities between ecotourism and more conventional forms of tourism with respect to regulation and self-regulation, in an attempt to discern whether ecotourism businesses are in fact more ecologically minded than mass tourism firms.

CERTIFICATION, ACCREDITATION, AND PROFESSIONALISM

Along with regulation, there has been an increased focus on the relevance of certification, accreditation, and professionalism in the tourism industry over the past few years. Certification and accreditation programmes act as the basis for the education and the provision of skills of those working in the industry.

The heightened level of attention afforded to certification and accreditation is discussed by Morrison *et al.*, who identify a number of existing programmes in North America, including programmes for the posts of Certified Travel Counsellor, Certified Hotel Administrator (the two longest-standing programmes), Certified Tour Professional, Certified Meeting Professional, Certified Hotel Sales Executive, Certified Festival Executive, Certified Incentive Travel Executive, Certified Travel Marketing Executive, and Certified Exhibit Manager.

According to Morrison *et al.*, the two terms 'certification' and 'accreditation' may be differentiated on the following basis:

- *Certification*: A process by which an individual is tested and evaluated in order to determine his or her mastery of a specific body of knowledge, or some portion of a body of knowledge.
- *Accreditation*: A process by which an association or agency evaluates and recognises a programme of study or an institution as meeting certain predetermined standards or qualifications. It applies only to institutions and their programmes of study or their services.

As Morrison *et al.* point out, certification deals with the individual professional, while accreditation is concerned with programmes and institutions. An interesting conclusion of their research is that certification programmes have grown to replace the university as a means by which to gain expertise and professionalism in the tourism industry.

They caution, however, that although certification will indeed increase in the future, it should not be a substitute for travel and tourism degrees. In addition, whereas universities are able to offer a good grounding in the theoretical aspects of tourism, they may also diversify into offering certification options to their graduates through their programme offerings.

Outside tourism, the relevance of accreditation has been debated in several other disciplines. Scalet and Adelman , for example, discuss the pros and cons of accreditation in fisheries and wildlife programmes, while Silverman examines accreditation of undergraduate programmes in environmental health science.

In the realm of adventure recreation, there has been significant debate on how best to certify certain aspects of the adventure programme experience, including standards of programme quality, professional behaviour, professional conduct, and risk management.

Similarly, these have revolved around the certification of leaders and guides through organisations such as the American Mountain Guides Association and the Wilderness Education Association, while the American Camping Association and the National Recreation and Parks Association have implemented accreditation programmes to meet their own specific needs.

Two studies found overwhelming support for accreditation over individual certification as it (accreditation) provided an umbrella to ensure a higher degree of professional credibility and less reliance on individual operators.

These findings were considered in the recent development of a US national accreditation process that focuses on programming in the adventure recreation field by the AEE, which is designed to consider the technical skills of adventure recreation, but also the teaching and ethical elements that need to be consistent from the programme side of the experience.

This document provides a means by which to systematically evaluate operations in areas related to ethics, risk management, staff qualifications, transportation, and technical skills. For example, with respect to the environmental aspects of river rafting, code 43.B.01 suggests that 'Staff are familiar with the operating sites for rafting.

Explanation: A pre-site investigation is conducted to understand the conditions as well as the education/ therapeutic possibilities. This includes locating appropriate takeout areas and access to safe transportation sites'.

According to Gass and Williamson (1995:25), this national programme maintains the following accreditation procedure:

- *Self-assessment and documentation stage*: Operators must compare their programme against the AEE programme guidelines.
- *Verification stage*: A team of between two and four reviewers visit the operator and conduct interviews, inspect equipment, and observe activities as necessary. A standards report card is used to determine whether a component of the programme 'passes', 'fails', is 'conditional' based on the need to remedy the situation, or 'does not apply' in the case where an activity is not associated with a programme.
- *Follow-up stage*: Findings from the verification stage are forwarded to the Programme Accreditation Services committee, who send a recommendation to the AEE Executive Board, who in turn decide whether the programme should receive accreditation.

In further support for the idea of accreditation, Gass and Williamson (1995:23) offer the following:

- Accreditation provides adventure programmes with the ability to achieve standards without losing the flexibility to decide and design how these standards are met.
- Accreditation takes a 'systematic view' of the process

of adventure programming rather than dividing it into individualised categories.

- Accreditation encourages ongoing improvement through internal and external review.
- Accreditation assures clients, agencies, and resource managers that a programme has clearly defined and appropriate objectives and maintains conditions under which their achievement can be met reasonably.

As suggested, ecotourism shares some aspects of adventure recreation/tourism, more from the context of setting than in programming.

This element of setting (e.g. tropical rainforests) may provide a component of risk that is absent from other, more conventional forms of tourism.

To a lesser extent than adventure travel, ecotourism may be seen as bridging a gap between various forms of adventure recreation and tourism. In comparison to outdoor recreation, however—in particular, outdoor guides and leaders—tourism lags far behind, and as in adventure recreation, programming in ecotourism will be a key issue in the future.

Recently the topic of accreditation and certification has been debated in ecotourism, consistent with this trend in the adventure pursuits industry.

For example, Wearing (1995:34) suggests that professionalisation and accreditation in ecotourism will continue to be at the forefront of discussions related to regulation and control, as a means by which to provide focus to an industry that is almost impossible to limit (in terms of expansion). He feels that accreditation affords the opportunity to improve tourism industry standards while at the same time ensuring high-quality services and programmes in a very competitive marketplace.

Wearing identifies a series of advantages and disadvantages of accreditation as they relate to ecotourism, as follows:

Advantages of accreditation:

- The ecotourist has the knowledge of what will be

taught, and the approaches used will be the best and the safest.

- The ecotour operator has a recognised and accepted methodology and thus increased social status.
- The employer of ecotourism guides has knowledge of an accepted industry standard.
- The government has the knowledge that new operators have been taught to a minimum standard.

Disadvantages of accreditation:

- The idea that one needs a service which is best provided by an expert creates a relationship of mutual dependency and creates a social distance between the ecotourist, the operator, the host community, and the natural environment.
- Ecotour operators are assessed on their accomplish - ments rather than their human characteristics to the effect of depersonalising the human-natural environment relationship.
- Professionals can tend to rationalise and focus on facts, objective data, and procedures, thus potentially losing the intrinsic, intuitive association so often formed through ecotourism.
- Through commodification, the operator may come to view the natural and cultural environments as a means to an end and so become alienated from the natural world and hence unable to encourage the ecotourist or encourage environmental awareness.
- Loss of perceived freedom by the individual ecotourist, who feels he or she must do as the operator says; this restricts the ecotourism experience.
- The imposed structure that is required to assess or measure the ecotour operator entails limitations.

The message put forward by Wearing is that although accreditation would certainly reduce risk, increase standards, and increase status, there is a danger of restricting innovation and accessibility within the ecotourism industry.

One of the significant dilemmas, therefore, is the degree to which the industry can afford to emphasise innovation and accessibility at the expense of ensuring that proper standards are being upheld. The issue is one that clearly requires more time and education to be provided for operators in the field.

In addition, it is a normative concern as the likelihood for compliance is directly related to how operators feel individually, but also collectively, about the process of accreditation. If it is imposed upon them, only time will tell how operators will react to the imposition. However, in time accreditation may be fully accepted as proper or appropriate business practice.

A good example of the accreditation process in action can be found in Australia, where those working in the field, i.e. operators, submit to a standardised procedure. At present, operators are given a core level of accreditation if they satisfy the programme's basic criteria; however, the system encourages operators to implement measures beyond the standards of the core criteria in earning advanced standing.

Eligibility for accreditation is based on eight criteria. According to these criteria, ecotourism:

- Focuses on personally experiencing natural areas in ways that lead to greater understanding and appreciation;
- Integrates into each experience opportunities to understand natural areas;
- Represents best practice for ecologically sustainable tourism;
- Productively contributes to the conservation of natural areas;
- Provides constructive, ongoing contributions to local communities;
- Interprets, involves, and is sensitive to different cultures (particularly indigenous ones);
- Consistently meets client expectations; and
- Its marketing is accurate and leads to realistic expectations.

In Australia there was resounding support for the idea of ecotourism accreditation in the mid-1990s which culminated in the launching of the National Ecotourism Accreditation

Programme at Australia's 1996 national meeting. Accreditation is offered to those operators working in the accommodation, tour operations, and attractions sectors, and operators are accredited by first completing an application (through a nomination process involving three referees), and by paying a one-off application fee and an annual fee.

One of the key features of the Australian accreditation initiative is the level and style of enforcement employed in the programme.

Each of the applicants is monitored in four ways:

- The applicant's honesty in completing application documents;
- Feedback from clients;
- Feedback from referees (random selection of operators); and
- Through random audits.

PROFESSIONALISM

A typical end-product of the acceditation and certification debate in the tourism industry, and more particularly ecotourism, is the link to professionalism. This has been the general pattern in other, related fields, including the recreation and leisure field, where debate has continued in the United States, according to Sessoms , since the 1930s.

Professionalism is viewed in essentially two ways. In one sense, the term implies only that one is paid for a service, as if, for example, a professional football player. It is, however, the stricter sense of 'profession' regarding conceptions surrounding occupations, such as lawyers and doctors, that is more difficult to define, and the focus of this section.

Foremost in the minds of professional groups and the lay public, the word 'professional' seems to be represented by two main themes, as suggested by Wilensky: '(1) the job of the professional is technical—based on systematic knowledge or doctrine acquired only through long prescribed training; and (2) the professional man adheres to a set of *professional norms*'.

In recreation, researchers and practitioners, historically, found it difficult to agree on a set of professional criteria to guide accepted practice. Professions therefore need to satisfy, and be consistent with, broad criteria in bonding the discipline together, as evident in the following work by Weschler .

- The profession has a body of specialised knowledge.
- The profession sets its own standards.
- The profession requires extensive preparation.
- Specialised knowledge is communicable.
- Service is placed over personal gain.
- The profession has a strong professional organisation.

In recent years, university and college programmes in Canada have shown interest in addressing the issue of professionalism in the adventure tourism and ecotourism fields. The adventure Travel Guide Diploma programme of the University College of the Cariboo (UCC) in Kamloops, British Columbia, is one such programme that has been developed to prepare a more highly trained labour force in this area.

These authors rely on projections that suggest that the demand for highly trained personnel in the adventure tourism industry will grow at 3.6 per cent (compounded rate), which, comparatively, far exceeds the anticipated 1.6 per cent yearly growth rates of the entire British Columbian labour force.

This programme recognises the integral relationship between industry and government (and government-sponsored institutions) in certifying highly trained instructors, guides, and operators. The UCC programme emphasises the following five main themes as being critical to the success of the programme:

- Technical skills (e.g. wilderness first aid training),
- Business skills,
- Hospitality and service skills,
- Environmental skills, and
- Intimate involvement in industry associations (e.g. student networks with potential employers).

The tourism field will have to come to grips with the notion of professionalism (whichever form this takes), given the tremendous interest in this area of late. One of the key elements to overcome is enabling the tourism worker to feel personally competent and confident in his or her work; as Wright (1987:17) points out, 'it is preferable to establish credibility through capability, competency, efficiency and a professional attitude. One earns respect, one does not establish respect through a glossy diploma on the wall.'

This chapter has illustrated that sound planning and management related to policy, regulation, and accreditation, certification, and professionalism are necessary considerations for the future viability of the ecotourism industry. While some governmental bodies have recognised early the importance of government leadership in the ecotourism industry, others have not been so quick to act.

There must be both leadership and partnership between government and industry in the development of mechanisms to control the impact of ecotourism on the environment, and to ensure that operators are providing safe and enriching programmes to their clientele. Such mechanisms will most likely include policy, regulation, accreditation, and professionalism in their various forms.

Chapter 7

Management of Ecotourism

In this broadly based chapter the economics, marketing, and management of ecotourism are discussed using a variety of examples and research studies in the literature. The section on economics examines the current predisposition of researchers to predict the global economic impact of ecotourism, in addition to a discussion of leakages and the multiplier effect, revenues in parks, and the economic value of land.

The section on marketing evaluates the potential of marketing in the ecotourism field, but also addresses the need for such studies to be accurate in their projections of the market, now and in the future. The final section on management issues in ecotourism discusses a number of issues thought to be relevant to the field, including privatisation, not-for-profit organisations and NGOs, agents and operators, and interpretation.

THE ECONOMICS OF ECOTOURISM

The World Tourism Organization projects that international tourism arrivals will grow from 593 million in 1996 to 702 million by the year 2000, and over 1 billion by 2010. At the same time earnings from international tourism are expected to climb from US$423 billion in 1996 to US$621 billion by 2000, and US$1.5 trillion in 2010.

Such is the magnitude of the tourism industry, which by many accounts is reported to be the world's largest. With continued growth at the rate identified above, the general trend does not appear to be faltering.

In a review of the literature on the economic impact of the global ecotourism industry, there is the feeling among some researchers that ecotourism is expanding even faster than the tourism industry as a whole, with upwards of 20 per cent of the world travel market as ecotourism.

Others, however, are more sceptical and feel that it is more logical to view ecotourism's growth in a site-specific manner than as a general overview. Jenner and Smith estimate that ecotourism had a global value of $4 billion in 1980, $5 billion in 1985, and $10 billion in 1989.

They forecast ecotourism's value to be $25 billion in 1995, and $50 billion by the year 2000; whereas Tibbetts (1995-6) illustrates that of the $2 trillion that tourism generates annually, $17.5 billion is from ecotourism. Such statistics indicate the disparate views that exist on the economic impact of ecotourism. One of the main reasons for such a discrepancy in quantifying ecotourism is the lack of a clear-cut definition of the term.

THE FLOW OF LOCAL MONEY

Foremost in the minds of many local, regional, and national bodies charged with the responsibility of tourism development is the importance of earning money. However, all such regions are not created equal in terms of their ability to generate and keep money within the economy.

Simply stated, although tourism will always create an infusion of money into local economies, the amount of money that stays in that economy is subject to a number of factors. In evaluating the impact of money on the economy, economists must understand the multiplier effect and the associated concept of leakage.

In general, as new money from tourism enters a local economy it changes hands many times, resulting in a cumulative economic impact that is greater than the initial amount of tourist expenditure. This is referred to as the multiplier effect.

More specifically, direct income or first-round income is the amount of that spent money that is left over after taxes, profits and wages are paid outside the area and after imports are purchased. The money that remains, after these leakages, is referred to as secondary income, which circulates successively through the economy creating indirect income and induced income, again with various amounts of leakage occurring.

National multipliers tend to be highest and, according to Bull , have ranged from 2.5 in Canada to 0.8 in Bermuda and the Bahamas. Most of the less developed economies, especially those island economies, tend to be lower because of the high level of leakage. It follows that even in the developed world, the multipliers of small towns and counties are typically low (in the neighbourhood of 0.25) because of the higher leakage rates.

Leakage rates can be determined by assessing the percentage of money that flows out of the economy. Clearly, those regions or localities that can minimise the amount of money leaving their economy will have more of the initial expenditures left to circulate through the economy.

Those regions or localities that rely upon resources from outside the region or country—human, physical, and monetary—will no doubt suffer by having to pay for their services. The reverse also holds true in that those regions that can sustain a tourism industry based on the resources that they have at hand will potentially be able to prosper under these conditions.

This form of leakage is referred to as import substitution. It is an important concept in the context of ecotourism and sustainable tourism because there is much evidence pointing to the fact that tourism, for example in the less developed countries (LDCs), has been hampered by the fact that management control of the industry lies in the hands of external, multinational interests.

Hotels, car rental agencies, restaurants, and airlines, all the big money-makers in the tourism industry, are quite often owned by companies that reside outside the destination region, and the destination region relies upon these to export its product through tourism.

REVENUE AND PARKS

Tourism is inherently a private-sector activity that capitalises on a market for the purpose of making a profit. A conflict emerges when a profit-motivated enterprise relies on the provision of supply that does not necessarily advocate the same market philosophies. Parks and protected areas, as public entities, provide the cornerstone for the ecotourism industry. In many cases there is debate over whether parks should be operated more as a business in response to shrinking public budgets.

Conventionally the management of parks has *not* been subject to the same market principles and philosophies as the private sector.

While it is generally accepted that ecotourism in protected areas has positive economic spin-offs (e.g. direct employment, both on- and off-site, the diversification of the local economy, the earning of foreign exchange, and the improvement to transportation and communication systems), there are also some associated negatives, including the lack of sufficient demand for ecotourism, which could result in the draining of badly needed funds; the fact that ecotourism may not generate local employment opportunities; the fact that leakages may be quite high, as they are in many small and developing regions; and the fact that it may not be socially and economically acceptable to charge fees in parks.

The preceding discussion alludes to the fact that one of the most significant issues facing parks and protected areas today is the means of attaining funds for their operation—indeed, in many countries, for their survival.

Many parks agencies that have historically relied on certain specific means by which to support their parks and park services have had to consider diversifying in order to maintain good-quality programmes and infrastructure. Sherman and Dixon illustrate five main ways in which to gain revenue from nature tourism.

These include:

- *User fees*: These are usually a reflection of the public's willingness to pay, and in recent years have altered

into more of a two-tiered or multi-tiered system with a differential scale of fees, the fee varying according to whether the visitor is a resident or a foreigner.
- *Concession fees*: In the case of government, fees are charged to private firms who provide tourists with goods and services (guiding, food, etc.).
- *Royalties*: Souvenir and T-shirt sales provide a good basis of this type of revenue, which is given to the agency as a percentage of the revenue made on the items.
- *Taxation*: Sales tax, hotel tax, and airport tax are examples.
- *Donations*: Tourists can be prompted to contribute money in an attempt to address a local problem (lack of resources or money for endangered species) and, in the process, aid in the management of a protected area.

In the case of the Monteverde Cloud Forest Reserve of Costa Rica, the issue of park entrance fees has been widely discussed in the context of the viability of this reserve. According to Aylward *et al.* , in the early 1970s visitors, regardless of their origins, were asked to pay a fee of approximately US$2.30 to gain entrance to the reserve.

However, owing to the increasing levels of visitation, and the demands placed on the reserve, a new fee structure had to be developed. In 1995 fees were restructured as follows: <$1 for Costa Rican students; $1.50 for Costa Rican residents; $4 for foreign students; $8 for non-package tour foreigners; and $16 for foreigners on tours (ibid.). Such fees have been instrumental in enabling this private reserve to become more economically self-sufficient.

Tisdell , however, suggests that there are some inherent limitations to the implementation of fees in financing ecotourism developments, including the possibility that few people may visit the site and/or if the park is located in peripheral areas. As alternatives, managers might elect to make visitors purchase permits from park offices, require tourist operators to pay visitor fees (as is the case in many destinations), or erect automatic ticket machines in car parks and trail heads—an approach that has worked well in Pacific Rim National Park, Canada. Laarman and Gregersen and Steele concur that pricing holds tremendous power in providing greater efficiency and sustainability in ecotourism, but is seriously neglected in public policy.

These authors identify pricing objectives, pricing strategies, and categories of fees in arguing that the user-pays principle and the removal of free access to public lands are perfectly logical today as a means by which to recover costs and, indeed, make money.

While it is not necessarily the goal of publicly run natural areas to 'make money', it is for community-run organisations and of course private enterprises. Laarman and Gregersen offer some guiding principles for fee policies in nature-based tourism.

Laarman and Gregersen argue that pricing objectives can be many-sided, and administrators are constantly challenged to set fees in accordance with the resource conditions of the park, the needs of the park staff, and the needs of visitors. The guiding principles are varied and range from a relationship of fees to general sources of revenue, fees for certain sites, fees only for certain sites, and the management and accounting of fee systems.

In some park systems fees that are generated in each of the individual parks go back into a general operational account. The positive spinoff of this is that the money that is generated for this account aids in the maintenance of parks in the entire system. The negative element is that those parks doing the best job (either because they have better administrators or because the park simply generates more visitation) do not get the opportunity to utilise directly for their own purposes, the money that they generate.

This type of fee philosophy may further decrease the motivation of those working in the money-generating parks, so that they become less conscientious, and may lead those in the money-losing parks chronically to rely on the money generated in other areas.

Steele illustrates that a policy allowing for open accessibility to ecotourism sites leads to certain economic and

Table: Guiding Principles for Fee Policy in Nature-based Tourism.

Principle	Rationale
Fees supplement but do not replace general sources of revenue	Even for heavily visited sites, fee revenue rarely covers total costs, especially capital costs. Heavy dependence on fee revenue reduces visitor diversity and the scope of attractions that can be offered. Yearly fluctuations in fee revenue make fees an unstable income source
At least a portion of fee revenues should be set aside ('earmarked') for sites that generate them	Earmarking increases management's incentives to set and collect fees efficiently. Visitors may be more willing to pay fees if they know that fees are used on-site
Fees should be set on a site-specific basis	National guidelines specify fee objectives and policies, yet management goals and visitor patterns vary across nature-based tourism sites, requiring local flexibility in assessing the type and amount of fee
Fee collection is not justified at all sites	Fees are not cost-effective at places with low visitation demand and high collection costs
Fee systems work best when supported by reliable accounting and management	Administrative decisions about fees require acceptable data on costs and revenues of providing NBT for different sites and activities

ecological inefficiencies. Economic inefficiencies occur in the sense that if sites allow free entry they lose the rental value of the resource. Agencies must also be wary of excess demand where sites are left vacant during certain seasons of the year, and also of costs related to congestion where tourists impact on each other owing to overcrowding (congestion costs are found to reduce the profit per tourist by lowering tourist demand and raising marginal costs for the supplier).

Ecological inefficiencies include consideration of carrying capacities and an analysis of the total volume of tourists and the damage done per tourist. By distributing tourists appropriately in space and time, some natural areas, according to Steele, have been able to increase the numbers to the natural area and reduce the overall impact of these tourists.

Also of importance to Steele is the choices that land managers have with respect to pricing controls and quantity controls (limits on numbers of users, which are employed more often than pricing controls). This author suggests that the use of variable tariffs or tiered pricing is an efficient way to increase revenue, where foreigners are charged a higher entrance fee than locals. The most oft-quoted example of this is the Galápagos Islands, where foreign tourists are charged the equivalent of US$40 and local tourists US$6.

McFarlane and Boxall write that, historically, many public wildlife agencies get their funds from hunting and fishing licences and general tax revenues. However, owing to the recent decline in many consumptive forms of outdoor recreation (e.g. hunting), and budgets, financial resources for conservation initiatives are dwindling.

Their research of 787 birdwatchers indicated that this group shows great promise in supporting conservation efforts in a number of ways. While committed and experienced birders could help to identify wildlife management issues and participate in fieldwork with various agencies, the less specialised birders could aid by improving bird habitat in their backyards and through the contribution of funds.

The research demonstrates that conservation agencies must diversify and include innovative schemes to capture the interest and support of the birding population.

THE VALUE OF LAND

In determining the appropriate use of a resource area,

government and other decision-makers must determine the most financially and socially acceptable use of the land. Decisions must be made whether or not (and how) to develop land such as dams, parks and protected areas, mining, or forestry, all of which have certain associated costs and benefits which will most certainly differ in different settings.

Land planners and developers have begun to recognise that destinations are increasingly demanding business ventures that will add value to raw materials, instead of taking it away. While many of the large tourism developments of the 1950s, 1960s, and 1970s occurred with only the financial motivations in mind, these days, in most cases, such large endeavours are undertaken with both ecological and socio-cultural impacts in mind.

Given ecotourism's attractiveness as a sustainable tourism option, it is critical to have development ideas accompanied by appropriate social and ecological measures. One of the most effective ways in which to decide on how best to develop or not develop an area of land is through the implementation of a cost-benefit analysis, which includes easily quantifiable costs and benefits (such as start-up and operating costs) and those which are not easily quantified, such as impact assessments.

Despite the difficulty in doing so, researchers have endeavoured to place values on ecological and social settings and situations. In the case of the environment, Munasinghe has categorised economic values attributed to ecological resources by examining the use and non-use values of assets. He suggests that the total economic value (TEV) of a resource is based on its use value (UV) and non-use value (NUV), which are further broken down.

In the figure, Munasinghe shaded the option values (an individual's willingness to pay for the option of preserving the asset for future use), the bequest values (the value that people derive from knowing that other people will benefit from the resource in the future), and the existence values (the perceived value of the asset) as a caution to the fact that they are all quite difficult to define. From here, analysts may use a number of non-market valuation techniques to quantify the above values, including the travel cost method and the contingent valuation method.

The travel cost method, for example, has been employed by Menkhaus and Lober in Costa Rica as a means by which to estimate the values of ecotourism to tropical rainforests, based on a sample of US travellers. This valuation method, according to the authors, 'estimates ecotourism benefits of a protected area based upon observed travel expenses by visitors to an area'.

These estimates are then used by decision-makers to address issues related to entrance fees, competing land uses, and so on. The argument for the use of such a method is that certain goods such as parks are not effectively valued on the basis of entrance fees alone; individuals, it is felt, would be willing to pay much more to experience the good.

The measure of the value of a good such as ecotourism to a protected area is represented by the consumer surplus. In their study Menkhaus and Lober estimated the consumer surplus to be approximately $1,150, which represents the average annual per person valuation of the ecotourism value of protected areas in Costa Rica for the sample. These authors estimated the annual ecotourism value to Costa Rica's rainforests by this population at $68 million, which is determined by multiplying overall US ecotourist visitation to Costa Rica by the per person consumer surplus.

An example of the contingent valuation method is found in the work of Echeverría *et al.* in their evaluation of the Monteverde Cloud Forest Reserve of Costa Rica.

This technique, otherwise known as the direct or survey method, is an approach 'in which individuals are asked directly about their willingness to pay for some improvement in a resource or for additional use of a resource'. This can take the form of an assessment of the willingness of tourists to pay for habitat protection. Echeverría *et al.* sought to address these non-market values of the visitors to Monteverde in demonstrating that, on average, foreigners were willing to pay $118 of their own income to secure reserves such as Monteverde.

This figure is comparable to the willingness of British Columbia residents to pay money to increase the scope of the protected areas in that province. In valuing places like parks and protected areas (and tourism within such areas), it must be realised that there is a significant degree of grey area between the ideologies of business and those of conservation. Profit and preservation, therefore, are often construed as a partnership, according to Carey (in Giannecchini 1993), that is analogous to an arranged marriage, not one based on love. For example, Giannecchini notes that:

Their [the tourism industry's] customary goal of quick optimum profits is in direct conflict with long-range goals of protection and conservation. This does not mean that the only, or even primary, relationship between the tourism industry and conservationists must be adversarial.

But it does mean that whatever laudable, environmentally sound policies and goals the industry articulates, they will remain subsidiary to the demand for profit. Therefore, if the tourism industry becomes the principal force in the development of ecotourism, it will almost certainly be detrimental to long-range environmental concerns.

A key means by which to prove the value of ecotourism (in economic terms) to those advocating other land uses has been economics. Researchers have looked at this type of tourism as a means by which to demonstrate that in light of other competing types of land use, ecotourism presents itself as an effective form of land use.

For example, McNeely estimated the economic worth of specific animal species in Amboseli National Park in Africa. He figured that each lion is worth about $27,000 per year, and each elephant herd at $610,000 per year, which far exceeded the amount of money that could be gained through hunting these animals.

Western and Thresher wrote that in Amboseli tourism could be much more environmentally desirable than agriculture, and in addition earn vastly more per unit hectare of land ($40 per hectare from tourism and $0.80 per hectare from agriculture).

This form of analysis brings to mind the ways in which people value objects such as wildlife. Clearly there is the economic focus, yet examples of this to some degree are required as a means by which to rationalise the existence or occupance of something, like ecotourism as a new land use.

Kellert suggests that attitudes towards wildlife as a commodity or utilitarian object became less widespread in American society between 1900 and 1975. He believes, however, that this attitude change has occurred in only some parts of society. Those who are elderly, rural, in a lower socio-economic category, and who live and work in resource-dependent occupations still harbour negative perceptions of wildlife.

It is often difficult for those who are not in one of the aforementioned categories to conceive of such perceptions. Although the point is not made in Kellert's research, one wonders about the impact that urbanisation, education, and wealth have in shaping the more positive attitudes towards wildlife.

Ecotourism is, or has been, conventionally considered an activity pursued by those who are better educated and wealthier than the 'average tourist', which would, according to the work of Kellert, lead one to believe that these individuals have a better chance of appreciating wildlife.

Those who are providers of the ecotourism experience in the least developed countries—assuming that they are not part of the privileged elite of that country—must acquire a 'personal conviction that land managed for wildlife is land ultimately more satisfying, attractive and enjoyable for people'.

MARKETING

Mahoney has suggested that tourism marketing fundamentally differs from the marketing of other types of products in three important ways:

- Tourism is primarily a service industry, where services are intangible, and quality control and evaluation of experiences are more difficult to envision;

- Instead of moving the product to the customer, the customer must travel to the product or resource; and
- People usually participate in and visit more than one activity and facility while travelling.

Therefore, tourism-related businesses and organisations need to cooperate to package and promote the tourism opportunities available in their areas. The marketing of tourism products is strongly based on a firm understanding of the fact that the overall travel market is partitioned into selected market segments.

Travel firms do not have the resources to tap the overall travel market, nor the inclination, owing to the magnitude of domestic and international travel. Instead, businesses target certain segments based on the product that they are selling and the needs and expectations of the group to which they wish to sell. Target marketing can occur in four main ways:

- Geographically, on the basis of geographical space;
- Demographically, based on age, gender, religion, race, etc.;
- Psychographically, based on individuals' lifestyles, attitudes, values, and personalities; and
- Benefits, which include an analysis of the benefits sought by tourists and the costs they avoid.

Marketers typically follow a systematic planning approach that enables them to focus on their organisational goals, and the specific needs of their clientele in association with various tourism products.

A typical plan, based on the work of Lovelock and Weinberg , is outlined. The first stage of the marketing plan involves the identification of the direction of the agency or organisation and the associated priorities that must be followed. This is followed by the definition of markets that will allow the organisation to achieve its chosen goals.

Upon the completion of this stage, the organisation endeavours to examine fully the behaviour, needs, and characteristics of the market. Once the markets have been segmented, the organisation can develop specific strategies which must be tailored to each segment. There follows the implementation of a monitoring and evaluation component, with subsequent modification in the future.

Demand is very much an integral part of the relationship between the tourism product and the market, and hence Krippendorf feels that in the future tourism marketers must be more sensitive to the changing composition of the tourist population.

He suggests that owing to the changing lifestyles, economic conditions, and demographic structure of travellers, 'the market is shifting from manipulated, uncritical "old tourists" to mature, critical and emancipated "new tourists"'. Eleven years on, this trend has certainly taken shape.

As is the case with the conventional travel markets, marketing research in the area of ecotourism has begun to flourish. The work of Ingram and Durst stands out as one of the earliest studies in this area, through their development of a bibliography on marketing nature-oriented travel in developing countries, and a subsequent publication that looked specifically at promotion of nature tourism in developing countries.

From their research they concluded that there was a need to improve the operations of tourism offices in the developing world. They also found that although marketing is common in the developing world, countries that are not promoting their natural attractions are likely to miss the opportunity to capitalise on the growing ecotourism market.

Ryel and Grasse suggest that the two cornerstones to effective marketing in ecotourism are the attraction for tourists (which includes biodiversity, unique geography, and cultural history), and tourism infrastructure to support the industry.

Given these criteria, agencies are free to undertake the necessary marketing requirements to attract tourists. These authors imply that it is important to attract or market to the 'right' clientele.

This includes 'born' ecotourists (those who have a built-in predisposition towards nature and nature travel), and 'made' ecotourists, who can be identified as representing latent demand or those who are unfamiliar with this form of tourism but who can be attracted through effective marketing. Ryel and Grasse suggest that a basic approach to marketing the ecotourism product is through (1) the identification of the characteristics of a desired group, (2) appropriate advertising, (3) careful crafting of the advertising message, and (4) the development of a mailing-list.

These further suggest that there is a definitive need to classify ecotourists on the basis of demographic, psychographic, and geographical variables, for, as Mayo has suggested, demographics alone are not an effective means by which to segment the market.

This fact has been further identified by Silverberg *et al.*, who undertook an investigation into the psychographics of nature-based travellers.

After identifying six factor dimensions on the basis of their survey of 334 travellers to the southeastern United States (education/ history, camping/tenting, socialising, relaxation, viewing nature, information), they concluded that psychographic research is an effective way for marketers to understand the nature-based traveller better.

In Australia, the Office of National Tourism undertook a market study of ecotourists in an attempt to understand the ecotourist market better and target ecotourism products more effectively. This research involved a number of focus groups involving ecotourists (actual and potential) from across the country. In general, the study found that ecotourists are seeking the following;

- Areas/attractions of natural beauty;
- Small groups away from crowds;
- Some level of interaction with the environment;
- Interaction with like-minded people;
- Some degree of information and learning; and
- Fun and enjoyment. More specifically, the research uncovered three broad ecotourism market segments.

These are as follows:

- *Impulse*: Characterised by nature-based day trips away from the main tourist destinations and mainly booked locally by both domestic and international tourists. The level of activity on these tours varies widely.

- *Active*: Characterised by younger and middle-aged professionals who generally book in advance. There is a skew to domestic tourists, although there could well be potential for growth through international marketing, infrastructure, and product development.
- *Personalised*: Essentially older professionals (or retired) who expect to be well looked after by the operator. This segment is skewed to international tourists who book overnight ecotours before arriving in Australia.

In 1994, the Canadian provinces of Alberta and British Columbia published a comprehensive marketing study (ARA Consultants 1994) which focused on assessing current and future demand for ecotourism in these regions.

The report sought information from a variety of sources in formulating their study, including a literature review of ecotourism, a travel trade survey, a general consumer survey of the residents of seven major metropolitan cities in Canada and the United States, and a survey of experienced North American ecotourists.

Ecotourism was defined as 'vacations where the traveller would experience nature, adventure, or cultural experiences in the countryside', and hence treated cultural tourism, adventure tourism, and ecotourism as being synonymous. One of the main conclusions from this research was that 'the ecotourism market is definitely expanding to encompass not only those with specialist skills seeking strenuous adventure, but also clients seeking activities supported by amenities, a higher level of services, and requiring lower levels of specialist skills'.

This finding is no doubt a result of the methodology employed in the study. Other conclusions of the study are as follows: For the general consumer group, 77 per cent said they had an ecotourism vacation, with the remaining 23 per cent expressing interest in ecotourism travel.

This led the researchers to conclude that from the general

consumers of the seven cities surveyed, the actual market ranges from 1.6 to 3.2 million visitors, and the potential market is approximately 13.2 million ecotravellers.

To two of Canada's most beautiful and 'natural' provinces, it is not inconceivable that travellers would involve themselves in any type of natural, adventure, or cultural experience. This probably extends to hard-path ecotourism trips right along the spectrum to bus tours of the city of Victoria.

The point to be made from this example is that researchers and practitioners must proceed cautiously in making inferences on the size and scope of the ecotourism market. Past research has concluded that ecotourism is a very small part of the overall tourism continuum.

Although it is certainly growing, so are the ways in which to classify and define ecotourism, many of which are based on convenience and less on a thorough review of ecotourism and ecotourism types. Thus the main fault of the research lies in the fact that it makes the assumption that, apart from the involvement of cultural and adventure tourism types, experienced and inexperienced ecotourists are one and the same. In substantiating this point, Wight (1996:3) reports that, with respect to the experienced North American ecotourist sample,

Because client lists were volunteered, it is not known to what degree those firms volunteering names are representative of the ecotourism travel trade. Consequently, it is also not known how representative the respondents are of all ecotourists. However, the sample does represent a large number of experienced North American ecotourism travelers.

In this case the softest of the soft-path ecotourists (or culture and adventure tourists) are grouped with the hardest of the hard-path ecotourists, groups which are perhaps worlds apart in their attitudes, motivations, and benefits sought. This ambiguity is indicative of the activity packages offered by the tour operators from which the 'experienced ecotourism' sample was drawn. Ranked in order of number of packages offered, hiking was first, followed by rafting, canoeing, cycling, kayaking, horseback riding, and then wildlife viewing—

activities which are more skill oriented and less learning oriented in nature.

Consequently, it was found that water-based activities were important, but particularly important to the experienced ecotourist (not surprising, and due most likely to the types of ecotourism packages offered); virtually all ages of adults are interested in ecotourism; and interest in ecotourism is spreading to less educated groups.

The results of this study have an element of inclusiveness, indicative of the rather loose methodology employed. Accordingly, the usage of the term 'ecotourism' has spun out of proportion and been misused as an industry label to capture a larger percentage of the travel market, with the main implication of misrepresenting or 'watering down' the ecotourism market.

For example, Thompson writes that a cruise aboard luxury liners, scuba diving, and helicopter sightseeing trips over Hollywood are all being touted as ecotourism. Clearly, in such cases ecotourism has been modified, repackaged, and 'mass' produced to the point where the line between what ecotourism is and is not, is quite blurred.

If this is the approach by the industry, and if ecotourism is to become successful by conventional industry standards, it will have undermined exactly what it set out to accomplish in the first place. Referred to as ecolabelling, this issue has been the source of recent debate over the TRINET (the tourism research international computer link organised out of Hawaii). For example, Iverson writes that:

When I sought to 'dive with the seals' in Kaikoura NZ I was attracted to a nice glossy brochure with eco-labelling. My accommodation host saw my interest and recommended another company, a fellow who 'started it here'.

When I met the fellow with this beat-up 4 wheeler hauling his van of dive gear I was wondering if I made the right choice. I had a great time and discovered later that the company with the glossy brochure had been in trouble with the Dept of Conservation for exceeding their permits and was told that they would take 24 people out with 12 permits and put half of them in the water at one time. Ryan follows up on this discussion by making similar observations on the state of affairs in New Zealand. He suggests that there are basically two types of ecotour operators: one that constructs a glossy pseudo front, and the other that is small in scale and that happily accepts size restrictions.

Continuing the discussion, Oppermann felt that too many tourists are subsumed under the ecotourism label—a stance adopted in this book—and that researchers need to be wary of studies that use wide-ranging definitions of the term. In order to avoid the misrepresentation of the ecotourism 'industry', Mason suggests that a system based on self-regulation is suspect and fraught with abuse.

He would rather see a form of policing and/or monitoring to avoid the unacceptable behaviour of those operating under free-market conditions. The problem to many marketers, operators, and agents has become so bad that they are refusing to use the ecotourism label because it has gained a poor image and means very different things to different people.

A further problem for regions in the development and marketing of an ecotourism product is the fact that there seems to be a feeling of unlimited assurance that ecotourism will ultimately resolve any tourism dysfunctions within a region.

Tourism decision-makers and planners, perhaps on the basis of overly optimistic forecasts of management consultants, often inherently believe that their jurisdictions will be competitive in a highly competitive global ecotourism market.

This has currently become an issue in Canada, where provinces that cannot hope to compete at the scale of other provinces—owing to their geological and natural features — have unbridled optimism for the sector. There is no question that ecotourism can and will exist in these regions, but regions must be realistic about the success of ecotourism initiatives. The size and extent of the sector will be a function of the demand, but it does not restrict them from creating innovative schemes to attract ecotourists given the attraction base from which they have to work. As a case in point, the province of Saskatchewan, in association with Industry Canada, has recently commissioned a study on the market potential of ecotourism in the province. The research was designed to gather valuable information from the travel trade (companies currently operating adventure, culture, nature, and ecotour trips) on the potential for Saskatchewan as an ecotourism destination.

One of the survey questions sought industry response on nine potential ecotour packages to be offered in the province. In only one case did over 50 per cent of the tour companies sampled feel that they could sell the package to their clients.

One of the most significant ecotour attractions in the province is the migratory and resident bird populations. However, in the case of the 'Birding in Saskatchewan' tour, only 43 per cent of the operators said that this tour appealed to them, and only 48 per cent said they could sell the package to their clients. The reasons cited for the lack of interest included 'wrong fit', 'too expensive', and 'not stunning enough'.

Other findings of the study indicated that a lack of information on the province and lack of demand for Saskatchewan ecotourism products were two most frequently cited barriers confronting the ecotourism industry in Saskatchewan.

A report on the ecotourism opportunities for Hawaii's tourism industry put ecotourism and Hawaii into perspective by acknowledging the fact that Hawaii faces some stiff competition from already well-established global ecotourism destinations (i.e. Latin America, Africa, and Asia).

They found that the main considerations constraining ecotourism in Hawaii could be summarised as follows:

- *Hawaii's physical characteristics*: Hawaii's isolation, limited size, and fragile natural environments create conditions which can lead to irreversible environmental harm from the overuse of its natural resources.
- *Hawaii's culture and local lifestyles*: Native Hawaiian issues and the preservation of community values have become increasingly sensitive to land use decision-making.

- *Hawaii's competition abroad*: Hawaii faces competition from a number of well-established ecotourism destinations including countries in Central and Latin America, Africa, Asia, and the Pacific. Island destination areas include the Caribbean, Mexico, the Galápagos, and the South Pacific.
- *Hawaii's dependence on a mass tourism economy*: Ecotourism's contribution to Hawaii's economy will be modest in comparison to Hawaii's mass tourism industry and should be viewed in terms of diversification, not substitution.
- *Hawaii's popular image*: As an ecotourist destination, Hawaii will have to overcome its sun, sand, and surf reputation and the impression that it is too overdeveloped to appeal to outdoor enthusiasts seeking back-to-nature experiences.
- *Private-sector investment*: Owing to the relatively low-return/ high-risk nature of the ecotourism industry, venture capital and investment support for small business enterprise development are limited while liability costs (i.e. insurance) for landowners remain high.
- *Public policy considerations*: There is presently a lack of policy which formally addresses ecotourism issues, resulting in inadequate support for the development and maintenance of ecotourism resources.

These barriers nicely encapsulate the constraints that Hawaii will probably encounter in its planning and delivery of ecotourism in the state. Other regions should be equally wary in the development of their ecotourism product. Substantiating ecotourism through inaccurate research methods is as disruptive as the development of an ecotourism industry on the basis of other related, and less ecologically sensitive, forms of tourism.

MANAGEMENT ISSUES IN ECOTOURISM

PRIVATISATION

The idea behind the partnering of public and private

sectors is not a new one. Adams reports that in the realm of community development, such endeavours came into being during the early 1970s. He further illustrates that a number of trends have emerged that help define the scope of such public-private interactions, which include the fact that:

- Local governments are becoming increasingly concerned with maximising efficiency through improving management and streamlining service systems.
- New ways of leveraging existing public resources are being explored.
- Local governments are beginning to alter their delivery systems to use existing resources in new ways.
- Cities and counties increasingly are having to consider almost completely devolving certain responsibilities back to citizens.

In general, privatisation, in the sense used here, refers to an arrangement entered into by an employer and an outside firm whereby production or service work which was or could have been done by their own employees and equipment is to be performed by the outside firm.

Privatisation is, in most cases, synonymous with the contracting out of services, but emphasises the *private sector's* role in fulfilling or winning these contracts (it is important to note that contracts may also be given to those in the not-for-profit sector).

Similar in nature to the aforementioned definition is one by Courchene, who wrote that privatisation is the private provision of a publicly financed service; while Heald suggests that privatisation is the strengthening of the market at the expense of the state.

As a result of the increasing pressure on governments to be more accountable with fewer resources, and in the absence of any change in this trend in the foreseeable future, public service providers are caught in the dilemma of how best in light of the changing socio-economic conditions, to accomplish traditional goals such as service provision and accessibility.

Given these changes, it is safe to say that in all probability there are few communities that have not endeavoured to privatise in one way or another. This assertion is best summed up by Beres (1986:4), who illustrates that good managers have always looked to the private sector when it did not make sense to employ people on a full-time basis.

In an extensive overview of the topic of recreation policy in Canada from the municipal perspective, Smale and Reid suggested that the decision to privatise, or not, is really a reflection of the perceptions and interpretations of what is a public good.

On the one hand, these authors feel that partnerships with the volunteer and private sectors may be necessary in order to deliver as much as possible to the entire community. On the other hand, they felt that in the debate on privatisation, policy-makers must consider what they value in providing for the community: privatisation may be interpreted as a public good in today's ideological world which places an emphasis on the *profitability* rather than the *accessibility* of leisure opportunities.

If the service can be provided through the market place, then it may very well end up there without great concern for its value as a public good. Consequently, even though the service may become 'successful', it would likely only serve a certain segment of the population, and hence, would no longer be available to the entire community; in other words, the principle of equal opportunity would be compromised.

Mintzberg is a firm believer in the notion that capitalism driven by the private sector is throwing the societies of the Western world out of balance. He would rather see a move to the incorporation of normative control, or values, beliefs, and human dedication in the provision of goods and services (the Japanese have been successful using this approach).

He continues by suggesting that 'we all value private goods, but they are worthless without public goods—such as policing and economic policies—to protect them'. Mintzberg substantiates his claims by referencing the current preoccupation with privatisation of public services in today's economy. He suggests that in some cases privatisation is warranted, but in most other cases we are too prone to scrutinising what does not belong in government when we should be equally diligent in assessing what does not belong in the realm of private business.

In areas more central to tourism, privatisation has generated much debate in the realm of destination promotion at the state and national levels. Bonham and Mak provide a good overview of the history of private and public financing of Hawaii as a destination, which they use to put the private/public promotion debate into context:

Faced with growing voter opposition to public financing of tourism promotion, governments are increasingly asking the tourist industry to assume a larger share of the burden of financing destination promotion.

However, asking the industry to make greater voluntary contributions will not succeed without some form of government intervention. Because destination promotion is a public good, individual beneficiaries have the incentive not to contribute and instead to free-ride on the contribution of others.

From a philosophical standpoint, there needs to be some clarity established in better understanding the role that privatisation could play in developing and less developed countries, and in the mass tourism and the ecotourism industries. For example, Jenkins has illustrated that privatisation will become more prevalent in the Third World as a pragmatic shift in policy—slowly over time.

He further acknowledges that such commercialisation would enable the industry to become more sensitive to market trends and forces. The private sector's role is one that is concerned with profitability. When ecotourism is involved, caution must be employed from a marketing perspective for the simple reason that preservation of ecosystems and just social and economic practices may be compromised in an all-out assault on profit.

Tisdell writes that investment in ecotourism takes the form of private firms and public agencies intent on making a profit or surplus from the development of ecotourism. In the case of the public agencies, investment usually occurs in an attempt:

- To make a profit or surplus from ecotourism to supplement its funds for conservation management;
- To add to political support for the conservation body, or avert political hostility or lack of political support; and
- To improve the working conditions and salaries of employees.

Eagles feels that private reserves have a role to play in the provision of ecotourism services in Canada. Notwithstanding, he feels that parks services (i.e. Ontario Provincial Parks and Parks Canada) should be flexible enough to do a better job at financing their parks.

He cites the fact that such parks will be ill prepared to accommodate visitation in the future as they increase in number with continued decreases in funding. Eagles feels that in order for parks to be more business-like, they will have to look closely at revenue retention, willingness to pay, and fees for service as means by which to balance their books, visitor satisfaction, and resource protection.

In a review of ecotourism, less developed countries, and parks and protected areas, Fowkes and Fowkes identify four different goods in relationship to the element of privatisation. They feel that both common goods, such as air, rain, and fish (individually consumed, and difficult to control), and collective or jointly consumed goods, such as national health services, should not be privatised. On the other hand, toll goods (e.g. telephone systems) and private goods (e.g. foodstuffs), where consumption can be controlled by the supplier, ought to be in private hands. These feel that parks and protected areas, or collective goods, should not be transferred to private interests. It is only when toll goods and private goods (accommodation) are provided in parks that privatisation should be considered as a strong option. In most cases involving support services (e.g. computers), retail activities (e.g. restaurants), tourist buildings, and infrastructure (e.g. roads), private intervention should be considered from the perspective of management, maintenance, control of access, marketing, and construction. Private involvement in aspects of the land or those that inhabit the land (plants and animals) is not appropriate.

NOT-FOR-PROFIT ORGANISATIONS AND NGOS

Depending on the perspective from which one approaches the concept and delivery of ecotourism, there may or may not be a natural linkage between ecotourism and the not-for-profit sector. In many cases the link that does exist between the two (parks and not-for-profits) is based on the vested interest in how such parks should be preserved in the face of competing usage.

Although one should not assume that not-for-profit organisations with environmental mandates are not conscious of the value of money in the administration of their operations, their motives can be thought of as being more park- or education- or ecology-centred than profit-centred when compared to the private sector.

While not-for-profit agencies are typically bound by the demands of a board of directors whose responsibility is to effectively direct programme and operational policy and decision-making within the agency, earnings that are made beyond operational costs (including salaries) are poured back into the programmes, rather than into the pockets of management/employees.

Gardner (1993:19) illustrates that an environmental non-government organisation (ENGO) is a citizens' group whose activities include efforts for environmental conservation. Generally these coalitions have the following characteristics:

- Voluntary membership in the group;
- The group is not profit motivated;
- It is autonomous, in that it makes its own decisions;
- It is service driven; and
- It seeks change on behalf of its membership, society, and the environment.

However, NGOs are simply defined as 'not government',

and can take the form of not-for-profit status or profit status. There appears to be an interesting dilemma evolving on this front. In many cases not-for-profit agencies (e.g. museums, universities) are heavily involved in the delivery of ecotourism programmes *for profit,* which, in theory, is inconsistent with their overall mandates as institutions.

Ziffer has suggested that not-for-profit sector agencies often sponsor ecotourism trips for a number of reasons, including member service, donor trips, a source of funding, and for education and research. Citing Ashton, a former not-for-profit trip provider, Ziffer comments that many not-for-profit agencies are making a significant amount of money from their trips.

CASE STUDY: HIGHLIGHTING THE NOT-FOR-PROFIT SECTOR: CONSERVATION INTERNATIONAL

Conservation International (CI) is a not-for-profit organisation that strives to conserve the earth's biodiversity along with demonstrating that human beings are able to live harmoniously with nature. One of CI's most significant hallmarks is the creation of the Dept-for-Nature Swap, which gives debt-poor nations a chance to make smart conservation choices.

CI negotiates to buy their foreign debt in exchange for national conservation initiatives. Native habitats that were in danger of disappearing are now safe havens for thousands of threatened species.

CI's mission in ecotourism is to develop and support ecotourism enterprises that contribute to conservation; and influence the broader tourism industry towards greater ecological sustainability.

In order to accomplish these ends, CI is involved in a number of national and regional ecotourism development initiatives around the world in countries such as Bolivia, Brazil, Guatemala, Peru, Botswana, Madagascar, Indonesia, and Papua New Guinea. CI uses a 'capacity-building' approach in these regions to ensure that ecotourism benefits communities and merges with traditional practices and conservation, through the training of local people via ecotourism workshops within the region.

Recently, CI has developed an Ecotravel Centre designed to provide information on ecotourism destinations, tour operators and lodgings, and relevant publications and information.

In a recent survey of US-based nature tour companies, Higgins illustrated that the not-for-profit sector has a firm stake in the delivery of ecotourism opportunities. Eleven tour operators (17 per cent of the sample total) were not-for-profit, serving some 20,215 clients.

Forty-two per cent of their client trips were offered in North America, which compared to 7 per cent of the rest of the sample, which were commercial in nature. Also, it was suggested by Higgins that the not-for-profit sector was quite active in securing its share of the market by using 'sophisticated marketing campaigns, including direct mail, advertising in tourism publications, and the development of glossy nature-tour brochures'.

In other research, Weiler found that on the basis of a content analysis of 55 tour operators' brochures involving 402 tour descriptions, 336 were private-sector tours and 66 were not-for-profit or university-run tours. Universities are given the status of not-for-profit, yet they sponsored and ran programmes designed to make money.

The jury appears to be still out on the relationship between the not-for-profit agencies in ecotourism. One of the main issues related to the profit and not-for-profit sectors is the quality of the tours that they run. Although no data were found in order to elaborate the point, it is nevertheless an issue of great concern for ecotourists and members of host communities.

Given ecotourism's local development mandate one could argue that the not-for-profit agencies (all things considered equal) would be the more legitimate tour operators. This is supported by Ziffer , who feels that the not-for-profit sector is a small but growing segment of the ecotourism industry with plenty of potential in establishing appropriate ecotourism development models for the future.

AGENTS AND OPERATORS

Travel agents and tour operators are key stakeholders in the relationship that exists between the destination and the tourist. Both have a tremendous influence on tourists relative to the choices made and types of experiences gained from travel. To destinations eager to capture part of the tourism market, agents, although not the only means by which travellers learn about various destinations, must be familiar with the broad spectrum of opportunities available to the travelling public.

Milne and Grekin and Wilkinson report that at least for some peripheral destinations, or those just starting to develop a tourism product, travel agents can play a critical role in counselling 'destination-naive' tourists. The information profile of a destination—how firmly entrenched it is as a travel option—especially to the travel agent, therefore, places each destination in a position of competitive advantage or disadvantage.

Tourism opportunities have historically been offered through operators, whom Metelka (1990:110) defined as owners or managers of a place of business. Recent evolution in the terminology has included the 'outfitter', which is representative of the fact that ecotourism is spilling over into the realm of the outdoor recreation, where such operators have been providing adventure (e.g. hunting and fishing) experiences for tourists for some time (at least in North America).

The types of experiences of interest to natural resource-based tourists (e.g. adventure tourists and ecotourists) have necessitated the inclusion of businesses that are prepared to offer equipment and other specialised services for tourists. Outfitters, then, are those 'commercial businesses that provide a person with the equipment necessary for an activity or experience'.

As Tims implies, outfitting traces its roots back to the

early explorers who provided a service to people, usually in a manner that placed humans against nature. More recently, outfitting has progressed to the point where it has taken on professional status through America Outdoors and the Professional Guide Institute (PGI).

The PGI provides training for people in the areas of wildlands heritage, back-country leadership, interpretation, and outfitter operations; with the mission to 'identify, enhance and disseminate the natural interpretive and educational resource of the outfitting industry so that outfitters and guides can offer the highest quality of experience to the public'. Clearly, the PGI operates with a mandate that involves guides as a natural ingredient to providing effective back-country experiences.

On a more practical note, an excellent presentation of a hands-on approach to ecotourism operation and outfitting is provided by Mitchell .

Although this is too detailed to present in its entirety here, he identifies the following main programme-related aspects in structuring and running ecotours: professional tour guiding, a survey of personal assets, a survey of recreational assets, balancing demand, environmental education, tour planning, pricing, preparing the client for the trip, questions clients ask, packing lists, client medical information, cooking and food, conflict resolution, camp and camp cleanliness, first aid, legal considerations, on-the-trail sitings, and evaluation.

For those more interested in actually organising and conducting tours, this document is a must. In addition, more specific guides related to first aid, risk management, leadership, interpretation, recreational programming, marketing and finance, and so on are recommended to prepare the operator for the task of leading successful ventures in the field.

CASE STUDY: WILDERNESS TOURISM AND OUTFITTING IN THE YUKON, CANADA

The interpretation of ecotourism takes a more general form in the Yukon Territory of Canada. The territory's selection of 'wilderness tourism' as an umbrella term for a variety of different back-country experiences is very much a function of geography (the remote wilderness setting of the territory) and the existing products and resources operating in the region.

The undeveloped wilderness setting is thus a key factor in the delivery of tourism products in the region. Wilderness tourism is defined as 'tourism related to nature, adventure, and culture, which takes place in the "backcountry" and is primarily associated with multi-day trips, although it also includes day trips'. Wilderness tourism is divided into.

- Hunting,'
- Fishing, and
- Adventure.

This latter category is very much a reflection of the adventure tourism definition and activities of the Canadian Tourism Commission. Such activities include nature and wildlife observation, land adventure products, water adventure products, winter adventure products, air adventure products, and native tourism.

RELATED RESEARCH ON OPERATORS

One of the earliest papers to emerge on the operation of nature tour companies was written by Ingram and Durst , who designed a study to document empirically the promotion and activities of such companies in the United States.

These authors used the Specialty Travel Index to identify 78 tour operators, of which 32 agreed to take part in the study. They concluded that firm size ranged from 20 to 3,000 clients, with three serving over 1,000 clients each.

The majority of their client base was described as 'outdoor enthusiasts, retired couples or students, equally male and female, over 30 years old, and usually travelling as individuals in late summer'. The companies had been in operation for seven years, on average. In other research, Eagles and Wind employed a content analysis methodology in analysing the advertising of 347 guide-led ecotours in 50 different countries, most of which were Canadian based. They found that on average the tours had a guide to participant ratio of about 1:13.

This statistic seems to be consistent with the outdoor recreation literature, which recommends guide to participant ratios of approximately 1:12 for hiking.

It should be noted that in most cases ecotourism is dependent upon parks and protected areas and those areas' specific guidelines and policies. As such, many parks restrict party sizes to manageable numbers, which means approximately 10 or 12 individuals to a party. The reason for this is not only ecologically based (too much impact on certain areas), but also sociological, in that large groups often contribute to crowding, noise, and other disturbances. Ecotour operators must be sensitive to such policies, and act accordingly.

These potential impacts are well documented in the work of Hendee *et al.* and Hammitt and Cole. For example, the latter authors suggest that 'large parties are typically defined in wilderness areas as groups larger than 8 to 10 members'.

Hendee *et al.* suggest that in most regions, parties with more than 10 individuals account for only about 5 per cent of all groups, and illustrate that party sizes are declining owing to park restrictions and the 'larger, organized groups have generally become smaller as both managers and organization leaders have become concerned about the impact of large groups on the environment and on other visitors'.

In a survey of 24 North American ecotour operators, Yee developed a profile of the content and philosophical orientation of such operations. While most (63 per cent) had been in business for 2 to 15 years, 17 per cent had been operating between 15 and 20 years, many suggesting that they were offering ecotours long before the term originated.

Ninety-two per cent of respondents followed a code of ethics, and 38 per cent considered ethical conduct in pre-trip orientation; 29 per cent addressed ethics in printed information packs; 13 per cent of those surveyed used videos or slides on ethics; while 33 per cent used lecture formats.

The use of trained interpreters and naturalists was also addressed in Yee's research, where it was found that 75 per cent of the respondents had 'ecologists, naturalists or other experts on staff to aid in conducting their tours'. Researchers have also analysed the degree to which ecotour operators promote and perceive themselves as being environmentally friendly.

In this study, described as being exploratory, it was found that about 40 per cent of operators were promoted as being environmentally friendly; 66 per cent of operators felt that their tours were either beneficial or very beneficial for the environment (only one was said to be harmful or very harmful); 70 per cent said that their tour educated tourists about impacts; and only 7 per cent said that their tour enhanced the environment through, for example, removing others' rubbish.

A companion study investigated the roles of nature-based tour leaders, and discovered that the main roles of the tour leader on a five-point scale (five being most important), on the basis of the responses of the operators, were organiser (mean=4.6), group leader (4.5), environmental interpreter (4.3), motivator (4.2), teacher (4.0), and entertainer (3.4). As Weiler and Davis suggest, in reference to the leader:

S/he must be an organizer, a group leader, a teacher, and even an entertainer. In nature-based tourism, the tour leader must also be responsible for maintaining environmental quality, by motivating visitors to behave in an environmentally responsible way during the tour, and by interpreting the environment in such a way as to promote long-term attitude and behavioural change.

Owing to the nature of the ecotourism experience, tour operators and resource managers have been forced into much closer proximity to each other, which, according to the research of Moore and Carter , has not been a compatible relationship.

In an interview of 16 nature-tour operators in Australia, the authors found that from the operators' perspectives, resource managers did not understand aspects of their business, including the profit motive, costs associated with marketing, costs of operations, the motivations and needs of tourists, and the need for minimal infrastructure in remote areas.

Conversely, the operators had concerns related to the managers, including the fact that managers did not have a conservation ethic, failed to provide visitors with appropriate information, had little understanding of the need to control visitors, and did not understand resource fragility. These are fundamental differences that exist between the philosophies of the two camps. In particular, the profit motive is one that has not historically been of concern to parks, given park managers' concern for preservation over use.

Although not considered in the paper by Moore and Carter, research needs to examine the relationship that exists between the ecotour participant (i.e. the individuals associated with a tour group) and the non-tour participant, especially from the perspective of the park manager. It would be interesting to understand how park managers view tour participants relative to the smaller group or individualised travellers.

These authors suggest that a close working relationship must be developed between these two parties in order to meet the objectives of each group. In a more comprehensive analysis, Higgins provides an overview of the structure of the nature tourism industry in the United States. In particular, he states that ecotourism is based on the existence of.

- Outbound nature tour operators, located in large key cities in industrialised countries;
- Inbound nature tour operators, who are centred in non-industrialised countries and usually provide services in one country; and local nature tour businesses, which include hotels, restaurants, ecolodges, souvenirs, guides, and so on. It is the outbound nature tour operators that play the greatest role, according to Higgins, in linking clients with other businesses and destinations around the world, particularly those in non-industrialised countries.

In a survey of 82 US nature tour operators, Higgins found that such operations have increased in number by 820 per cent between 1970 and 1994 (from seven to 83). Higgins also discovered that client lists for nature tour operators ranged from 25 to 15,000, with an average of 1,674-35 of which served over 1,000 clients in 1986—with the largest five serving 40 per cent of the total market.

ROLE OF INTERPRETATION

While interpretation is often thought of solely in the context of persons working within parks and protected areas (interpreting the landscape), according to Barrow interpretation is far more elaborate, and based on three types of planning:

- Town and country,
- Marketing, and
- Education.

In the town and country approach, appropriate land use philosophies and techniques are used to protect valuable land from development, provide access to the public, and to help create an affective tie with the resource base. Marketing interpretation, on the other hand, deals with how best to understand various user groups and their particular wants and needs.

The marketing approach to interpretation is often product oriented, but must temper this with other concerns of the site (e.g. resource protection). Finally, Barrow suggests that interpretation employs educational theory in its plan development in order to understand how people learn, and what to teach them.

In order to manage effectively, interpretive planners must be sensitive to the learning, behavioural, and emotional sides of interpretation. Veverka uses the following example of an archaeological site to illustrate the relationship between these three objectives in interpretation:

The Learning Objectives are designed to provide basic topic information or understanding such as: 'The majority of the visitors will be able to describe three reasons why protecting archaeological sites benefits all visitors'. But the real—or most important—aim the manager may have in mind for interpretation to accomplish is to prevent visitors from picking up 'souvenirs' such as pottery shards at archaeological sites. So the Behavioural Objective might be: 'All visitors will leave alone any artifacts that they may find at the site and not to take them home'. It is the job of the Emotional Objectives for the interpreter to get the visitors to appreciate the value of artifacts left in place, and feel that they are doing a good thing by not removing anything. So an objective of this kind might be: 'The majority of visitors will feel a sense of responsibility for not touching any artifacts they may find on the ground'.

The behaviour is the action that the interpreter would like to occur as a result of the interpretive programme; whereas the emotional objective prompts the interpreter to strive to realise how best to get the visitor to feel as though he or she is behaving in the appropriate manner at the site and beyond; that is, that the behaviour is something that they should want to do.

Veverka illustrates that the same philosophy is used by advertisers today, in that they make you feel as though you want or need a particular product. The behavioural response is to actually go out and purchase a product.

Interpretation, as identified earlier by Weiler and Davis , plays a significant role in the delivery of ecotourism services. For example, on Great Barrier Reef Marine Park in Australia Hockings examined the tour operator's role in marine park interpretation. While staff-recreationist interactions are not very high as a consequence of the level of use and size of the park, tourists have come to rely on the various tour operators in securing information.

Of a sample of 170 operators, 72 per cent of respondents indicated offering interpretation as part of their programme. A higher proportion of this number were found to be day reef trip, diving, and sailing operators; while a lower percentage of fishing operators provided interpretation. A significant finding of the study was that 56 per cent of staff involved in interpretation had no relevant formal qualifications, while only 4 per cent of all staff had formal qualifications.

It was suggested that this overall lack of training could not be linked to type of activity offered (types of activities included scenic flights, fishing, camping, day reef trip, seaplane rides, dive trips, and so on), as those indicated as having the appropriate interpretive qualifications were evenly spread across operator types and sizes.

Operators, according to Hockings, relied more on practical experience as a means by which to inform clients. Forestell has developed a unique model of interpretation and environmental education that he operationalised in his work in whalewatching.

This suggests that tourists experience different cognitive states during a whalewatching excursion that require the naturalist/interpreter to articulate information in three distinct periods: pre-contact with whales, contact, and post-contact. Pre-contact information involves learning on how participants should interact with the whales.

This may be supplemented with geographical information and marine environmental education. In the second, or contact, stage, interpreters focus on the need for participants to seek answers to a variety of questions related to the observation of the animals. Questions typically relate to whale identification, whale behaviour, verification of knowledge, and safety.

The goal of this stage is to 'generate motivation to learn by creating or uncovering and imbalance between an individual's initial knowledge base, and some current perception of the world ... [and] provide sound knowledge to allow the participant to regain cognitive balance'.

The final stage, post-contact, is characterised by the participants' need to make pre- and post-trip comparisons of whales and the marine world, and in addition to consider broader environmental issues (including active and financial support for conservation programmes or issues). Clients also question leaders about the well-being of the whales. Forestell suggests that ecotourism experience has the ability to empower people to synthesise unscientific observation with scientific fact, which he feels is not an inferior substitute for hard data, but rather one that is experiential and practical. This model demonstrates the need for interpreters to be sensitive to the different stages of an ecotourism experience.

In situations where guides are providing more personal

knowledge of a setting only, Forestell perhaps would argue for more of a trained approach to the delivery of the interpretive product, which would ultimately enable the tourist to benefit further from the experience.

This chapter has taken a broad-based look at how economics, marketing, and a series of other management issues relate to ecotourism. Ecotourism has blossomed into a rich array of programmes and opportunities in the public, private, and not-for-profit sectors.

Often a relationship must exist between public agencies (those who manage parks and protected areas) and private operators (those who run programmes in these public spaces). Good coordination must exist between these stakeholders such that the appropriate values (economic and emotional) are attached to the ecotourism experience.

A significant finding of the chapter is that marketing must better reflect the needs not only of the consumer but also of the industry, which by many accounts is being diluted by ecolabelling, or the misrepresentation of ecotourism by operators who at best are only peripherally ecotourism oriented in their product offerings.

Finally, the chapter emphasised the need to examine how privatisation, not-for-profit agencies and NGOs, agents and operators, and interpretation affect the delivery of ecotourism products.

Chapter 8

International, Community and Site Perspectives

This chapter focuses on tourism from three perspectives: international tourism development, including development theory, tourism in underdeveloped countries, and the core-periphery concept; community development; and site development. Each of the three offers frames of reference different from both the general tourism literature and ecotourism.

While the international development literature provides a clear indication of where we have been in terms of tourism development, the community development or community-based ecotourism initiatives provide a contrasting view in support of where ecotourism should go in the future. The ecolodge phenomenon is included as an example of how site development can occur using sustainable development design principles and local decision-making.

INTERNATIONAL ISSUES

I sit on a man's back, choking him and making him carry me, and yet assure myself and others that I am very sorry for him and wish to ease his lot by any means possible, except getting off his back.—Tolstoy

Development theory explores the economic and psychological link that exists between rich and poor countries. The relationship continues to be one that often contrasts meaning and value with respect to the use of natural resources and capital. Tourism is a sector of the world's economy that has tended to underscore and exacerbate the inequalities that exist between core metropolitan nations and peripheral, marginalised economies, and in doing so perpetuates the division between those who have access to resources and those who do not.

To Vogeler and DeSouza , this division has conjured up images of distorted human beings and grotesque folklorism, where the underdeveloped are like children unable to fend for themselves and with little capacity to make decisions.

Dependent countries were not considered economic entities until the late 1890s, when a new, 'lofty' responsibility regarding dependent peoples emerged (British Africa encouraged participation in the cash economy). This lofty purpose was coupled with a crude, hypocritical view of natives and administration, with the recognition that external power had a responsibility to develop the resources of dependent countries for the benefit of the whole world. Some saw the acquisition of overseas dominions as motivated by strategic reasons, while others sought only economic incentives.

In measuring development, past research has used a variety of means to define it, including number of hospital beds, daily intake of calories, daily intake of animal protein, percentage of population in agriculture, food as a percentage of total imports, export economy, infant mortality, death rate, and aid per capita.

Many of these have been criticised owing to the fact that the sociocultural, environment, and economic landscapes of each country are different. For example, food requirements are a cultural phenomenon, where countless generations have formed the habits of food intake seen today. Comparing the daily intake of calories between North Americans and Southeast Asians is pointless. Their physiological requirements are quite different.

Resources have also been used to gauge the development status of nations, where an abundance of resources is thought to be an indicator of development.

However, Mountjoy points out that even though Brazil has an abundance of resources and Denmark few, Denmark is considerably the more developed. Thus, development should be based not upon potential, but on existing levels of material welfare. Switzerland is a further case in point, where capital is a substitute for natural resource endowment.

The progression of development, according to Brookfield , occurred as a result of capitalist countries broadening or diversifying production into new sectors. This was to be achieved internationally through a widening of resource exploitation of less developed countries (LDCs). Brookfield maintains that the most aggressive industrial and trading nations (e.g. Britain) benefited most.

They put pressure on other countries to open their trade. Adam Smith's *laissez-faire* philosophy was the true avenue of growth unfettered; it would work towards optimal production.

In recent years there has occurred a major paradigmatic revision in development thinking that is presenting a fundamental challenge to the conventional consensus on economic development. This new approach emphasises the basic needs of the poor, and advocates a sensitivity for development at the ground level. Real improvement cannot, therefore, occur in LDCs unless the strategies that are being formulated and implemented are environmentally sustainable.

Brookfield emphasises support of this contention: the study of development joins directly with the study of all change in human use of the environment, and provides elements of empirical evidence for infusion with other theories in the task of generating a dynamic human-environment paradigm.

Mountjoy stipulates that the most important factors in gauging development are people; their number, age, enterprise, initiative, inventiveness, knowledge, and willingness to sacrifice. It is not the responses themselves (which are passive), but the way in which they are to be utilised that is deterministic of development.

The Western nations' concern for invention is not shared by all societies. Technologically inferior societies exploit single landscapes, within the framework of their social structures, while the Westerner is said to exploit all environments.

This is most clearly emphasised by the recent international debates on the implications of global warming for the future viability of the planet. LDCs make a strong case against the more industrialised developed nations for their role in the creation of the pollution (e.g. nitrogen oxide and sulphur dioxide emissions) that has contributed to global warming and ozone depletion.

TOURISM IN THE UNDERDEVELOPED WORLD

LDCs suffer from a history of colonial domination and what has been referred to as dependent development. A review of tourism literature reinforces the notion that there is a set evolutionary pattern of multinational interests in the tourism sector of the underdeveloped.

Dependency, therefore, can be conceptualised as a process of historical conditioning which alters the internal functioning of economic and social subsystems within a less developed country. This dependency occurs not from processes within the LDC's economy, but rather from demand from overseas tourists and new foreign company investment in the LDC.

For example, after a potential tourist destination has been identified (on the basis of unique biophysical or cultural conditions), the involvement of the multinationals increases. Foreign companies greatly influence the image of a destination country through development and promotion. Such efforts lead tourists to perceive the host country in terms of this image and the nature of hotel accommodation, attractions, and other tourist services as publicised.

Domination of the tourism sector in an LDC is most outwardly represented by the foreign ownership of airlines and hotels. However, the grip on the destination region often goes much deeper.

Because of the inability of agricultural and manufacturing producers in most underdeveloped economies to guarantee a good-quality supply of goods and services for international luxury-standard tourist facilities, there is a strong reliance on imported supplies for both the construction and the operation of tourist facilities. Also, as Winpenny writes, middle and senior management levels of tourism developments in underdeveloped countries are often occupied by expatriates. The following scenario of metropolitan dominance serves as an example:

On arrival in a Caribbean island between plane and hotel, the tourists could well have passed through a terminal building presented by the people of Canada and have been driven along a road either built or improved 'thanks' to Canadian aid, on behalf of the expected Canadian tourists of course.

At the hotel you will likely be greeted with rum punches the first of the few local products to be encompassed by the package. At your first meal, a menu, perhaps designed in Toronto, Chicago or Miami will provide you with a selection of food imported for the greater part from North America—good familiar, homogenized, taste-free food, dressed up with a touch of local colour.

The question therefore is as follows: who owns and controls the various components of a holiday package? It has been found that where tour packages consist of a foreign air carrier, but include local hotel and other group services, destination countries receive on average only 40-45 per cent of the inclusive tour retail prices paid by the tourists in their home country.

If both the airline and hotels are owned by foreign companies, a mere 22-25 per cent of the retail tour price stays in the destination country.

While Rajotte feels that tourism is less environmentally destructive than other forms of development that exist in tropical islands, there are still many significant effects that may be attributed to tourism. Many of these impacts are universal, but their intensity and severity are more noticeable in island environments (much of the past research on dependency and development has been linked to island environments).

Important is the notion that often with size comes ecological diversity. Nation states of the Caribbean, because of their small size, have tenuous floral and faunal vitality. Tourism can stress these systems through yearly visitation levels that exceed the local population of an island; for example, Hayward *et al.* write that in 1979, more than 600,000 tourists visited Bermuda, some ten times the population of the island.

A key area of research for the future is the need to document whether or not developing countries such as Brazil, Costa Rica, Dominica, the countries of Eastern Africa, and Ecuador undergo the same social, ecological, and economic dysfunctions from ecotourism as outlined above from the perspective of mass tourism.

For example, Kusler writes that ecotourism in the LDCs is marked by limited dollars, government-directed financing, foreign visitation, foreign ownership of hotels and other facilities, and non-existent land use planning. In this sense, ecotourism as an intervention may or may not improve the socio-economic conditions of a country from the example of mass tourism outlined above.

It is important to realise, as outlined by Kusler, that the LDCs and their developed-country counterparts are separated by a number of key structural differences. These include finances, the political climate of a country, accessibility to opportunities, discretionary income, and resources for the acquisition and planning of land.

CORE-PERIPHERY CONCEPT

One of the main theoretical approaches used to explain development is the concept of core and periphery, which Freidmann and Alonso describe as characterised by a dynamic, growing central region, and a slower-growing or stagnating periphery.

The core is marked by high-growth potential whereas peripheral areas are often marked by declining rural economies with low agricultural production (loss of primary resource). Shields (1991:3) refers to peripheralised regions as marginal places, regions that 'are not necessarily on geographical peripheries but, first and foremost, they have been placed on the periphery of cultural systems of space in which places are ranked relative to each other'. Important in his discussion is the fact that margins, from social, political, economic, and perceptual perspectives, are systems of centres and peripheries and are, therefore, locationally oriented.

These spatial systems are established in a series of binary relationships (economic, society, and so on) of centre and periphery, so that margins signify everything that the centre denies or represses. Our socio-economic paradigm is constantly exercising this binary relationship, and it reaches to the furthest outposts of physical space and humanity.

In a touristic sense, a classic example of the core-periphery idea can be found in Christaller's analysis of tourism location in Europe. Christaller wrote that tourism avoids central places and is drawn to the periphery, reaching the natural resource base not found in cities.

This idea has been further developed by a number of authors. In particular, Battisti reflected on the principles established by Christaller on tourist space organisation, noting that tourism is part of the continual process carried out by humankind in order to specialise and to diversify the exploitation of the soil.

Battisti made reference to the distinction between peripheral regions and peripheral places. The first represents a wide range of possibilities in choosing a recreational place. The second indicates real destinations of tourist flows, where the 'fruition of space for recreational purposes is accomplished'. The core-periphery concept has also been applied more recently to the analysis of adventure travel regions from a spatial context.

Zurick suggested that the movement of adventure travellers in Nepal takes place through a complicated hierarchy of gateways. Tourists from the core move through an international gateway (semi-periphery), to a national gateway (periphery), and further to a regional gateway (periphery frontier), said to be the adventure region.

In this latter region there is often a clash between traditional interests and national development goals. As frontier regions succumb to further intrusions, the uniqueness of these areas diminishes, as does the potential for travel to untouched areas in the future as these areas become fewer in number.

One of the key defining elements of travellers to outward peripheries is the need to experience something different in a remote setting. Along with this, perhaps, is the need to escape the mainstream of tourism, which can only be achieved by taking the road less travelled.

Although there are few data at hand to support this idea, the traveller's mind-set may alter upon reaching successive outward peripheries of a destination. Fennell thought that the following factors contributed to this feeling:

- *Familiarity with the destination*: A lack of knowledge or familiarity with a region's environment/culture may add to the uniqueness of such an area and therefore represent a perceived periphery.
- *Unscheduled change*: Movement that occurs spontaneously or that is not pre-planned (e.g. from a core region to a peripheral region).
- *Psychological and/or physiological change*: Personal adaptations that have to be made in order to feel comfortable or maximise feelings of satisfaction/pleasure, including culture, language, personal hygiene, food, and shelter.
- *Distance from amenities*: This factor reinforces the notion that a particular peripheral region does not, cannot, or will not offer goods and services that can be found at regions closer to the core.
- *Adaptation*: As tourists move out to a new periphery, the accompanying shortage of goods and services such as shops and facilities—found at regions closer to the core—becomes more accepted. The state of the infrastructure, therefore, plays less of a role in satisfying the tourist. Poor weather may also not pose a problem because a more 'frontier-like' attitude is adopted.
- *Population density*: Regions with a lower tourist and local population density may provide an indication that the periphery has been, or is being, reached.

- *Authenticity*: As population density decreases, the authenticity and/or incidence of natural and cultural attractions may increase in relation to the characteristics of the region. The character of the region is important, as Costa Rica may have a higher species diversity in urban areas than Shetland has at the periphery.
- *Symbolism*: The periphery may be represented by experiential, environmental, or cultural phenomena (symbols). Such phenomena may include lochs, mountains, wind, solitude, barrenness, a rainforest, or lack of banking machines. Consequently, the more these symbols are experienced, the greater might be the feeling of reaching the perimeter. Fear may also act as a symbol, as may the realisation that there is a lack of knowledge of a region and its characteristics. Fear or anxiety of the unknown is an important feature of adventure tourism (characteristics that Csikszentmihalyi has reported on regarding risk-taking in rock climbers).
- *Scale of attraction*: It is the region itself that may take on characteristics of 'attraction' in the outer periphery. For example, while cities have many attractions and goods and services to offer tourists and locals alike, small, peripheral islands may have comparatively few or no structural attractions, and because of this the nature of the island's limited infrastructure, small size, and distance from the mainland may be the attraction itself.
- *Distance from home*: This factor occurs in combination with other factors. For example, travel to Sydney, Australia, from rural Canada represents a large distance, but may not necessarily represent a mental change from core to periphery.

Thus the relationship between core and periphery has not only a psychological component but, as discussed earlier, a spatial one. This spatial component occurs at a variety of scales. Examples include small islands of the South controlled by the

North, and huge territories of the North controlled politically, economically, and socially by decision-makers of the core.

The Northwest Territories of Canada has been identified by Keller as an example of a peripheral region caught in transition regarding the development of its tourism industry. To Keller, differing authorities in control of development in this region become important actors in both decision-making and implementation of a viable tourist industry. These hierarchies of control occur at local, regional, national, and international levels.

As the sphere of tourism development becomes international, Keller suggests, the more the periphery has become 'a playground for exogenous investors, and the peripheral government an observer of its own fate' (ibid.: 25). It is stated by Keller that to avoid a transgression of the above scenario, the periphery (Northwest Territories) must act to control the decision-making in the development of a tourist industry, and limit the development to a scale of growth in tune with the resources, capital, manpower, and culture within the periphery.

The implications of the core-periphery concept to ecotourism are that, often, remote travel regions are dependent on national and international markets, inbound and outbound tour operators, as well as externally based transport modes and schedules.

With the inability and lack of resources fully to plan and implement ecotourism on their own, the cycle of tourism dependency continues for peripheral regions. This lack of an ability to link directly with the market in the developed world is one of the main reasons why the benefits of ecotourism do not percolate down to the community level; and it is precisely why those who are able to coordinate ecotourism activities—whether they be expatriates or local—between the LDCs and the developed world stand greatly to gain economically.

In such a case the power to make ecotourism happen in a developing country lies in the hands of a few, and perpetuates the phenomenon of a typical LDC economic situation, with much of the money and resources lying in the hands of a few, and the majority of the population, in the absence of a prominent middle class, living in impoverished conditions.

While the preceding discussion has emphasised the significance and impact of externally based control in the development of tourism and ecotourism enterprises at a macro level, the discussion of community development to follow offers an alternative to many of the tourism development concerns outlined above.

Community development, then, may be considered as a viable means by which to offset the conventional tourism development models of the past and redistribute control and decision-making among the individuals within the community, not to those from outside.

COMMUNITY DEVELOPMENT

Community development, as described by Smith (1990a), originated in the self-help programmes that were developed during the depression years in Canada, the United States, and the United Kingdom. A defining characteristic of community development is that it is based on local initiatives, in that it advocates a site-specific approach to finding solutions to community problems using community members and community resources.

Bujold (1995:5) defines it as 'the process by which the efforts of the people themselves are united with those of governmental authorities to improve economic, social, and cultural conditions of communities'. Typical community development encompasses all aspects of the community and focuses on the best quality of life possible for its members, and may involve creating new business and employment, increasing cultural awareness, or providing a range of opportunities for all members of the community.

However, Joppe alludes to the fact that it is important to understand that there exists a fundamental division between conventional community development and community economic development (CED) models. While conventional economic development focuses on the attraction of new businesses to the community (seen as an outward-directed approach to development), conversely a CED focus is on being small, green, and social, and is more inward in its orientation by striving to 'help consumers become producers, users become providers, and employees become owners of enterprise' (Joppe 1996:476), through the principles of economic self-reliance, ecological sustainability, community control, meeting individual needs, and building a community culture.

Tourism is increasingly seen as a key community development tool in the 1990s, with the recognition of its economic contribution in bolstering stagnating economies and diversifying existing sectors, and its ability to unify community members.

Such is the case in the Shetland Islands, Scotland, where tourism is being relied upon to sustain an economy that was once dominated by North Sea oil development, or the Finnish island of Åland, where all tourism initiatives are owned or controlled by local people.

With this realisation, researchers have begun to explore community development as it relates to tourism and ecotourism from many different perspectives.

As an example, Christensen examines the role that tourism can play in securing quality of life within the community. At the foundation of any tourism development strategy is the realisation that

> If tourism development is to be viable as a long-term economic strategy, these concerns [social and ecological] must be addressed, and the resource base must be protected in the process. The host community is the economic, social, cultural, and infrastructural resource base for most tourism activity, and resident quality of life is a measure of the condition of the resource.

Christensen proposes a community quality of life framework that addresses both objective and subjective indicators, at the individual and community scale. A tourism development project is said to affect change in the quality of life of members of the community, which in turn cause impacts at different social scales. Such impacts need to be evaluated both by individuals and by the community, depending on the scale of reference to the individual.

There is a deliberate hierarchy established with respect to agents of change, suggesting that appropriate solutions need to be implemented at the individual social scale first, followed by neighbourhood groups, coalitions, responsible industry, policy, and governmental regulation.

The tactical approaches used by regions (local or national governing bodies) will make or break how ecotourism is perceived by local people, according to MacKinnon . She sites a number of examples of communities in Mexico which have adopted or been identified to develop ecotourism in the country. One such community is Tres Garantías in the Yucatán peninsula.

This region was initially set out as a hunting reserve by an international development team, but the area's residents found that non-consumptive recreation was more attractive to tourists than consumptive forms.

The project, however, was conceived using a top-end approach, and even though there have been isolated benefits derived from ecotourism, MacKinnon suggests that social integration within the community is not complete, and will not be complete until benefits are more widespread and the perception of ownership is given to the community.

MacKinnon further uses the example of Los Tuxtlas, Veracruz, to illustrate that ecotourism has been successfully integrated into a community through more of a grassroots approach (initiated through the efforts of a local woman who set out to build empowerment slowly and deliberately). In this latter case, the community has been more quickly able to realise benefits which have been spreading on a more regional scale.

According to MacKinnon, the traditional mass tourism development model perpetuates the widening gap between rich and poor in countries like Mexico. Conversely, community-based tourism 'lends itself to being environmentally sustainable. Locals are the first to recognize the benefits of conserving their natural-resource base—much more so than large developers who don't live in the area'. While the interests of the community from a social standpoint are certainly paramount in the development of small-scale ecotourism, Williams feels that all factions within the community need to cooperate effectively in ensuring that a high-quality product is delivered without diminishing the ecology of the resource base.

He advocates the development of an institutional structures strategy with the capacity to respond to tourism development before such development runs out of control.

This strategy includes the following:

- Development of a grassroots planning process, driven by local interests and including aboriginal involvement;
- Understanding and appreciation of ecotourism market requirements;
- An inventory of the region's resources to determine areas that are suitable for ecotourism and ones that are not;
- The establishment of goals and objectives in line with concerns related to the cultural and natural impacts of ecotourism, with the creation of a vision statement to act as a control mechanism for the future; and
- The establishment of a formal Tourism Management Board, to work with both the operators and the public, with the responsibility of monitoring change, communication, local benefits, etc.

Despite the fact that there will be direct and indirect beneficiaries and participants in the ecotourism industry, it is important to recognise that the entire community should be involved to some level.

Participation therefore plays a key role in the initiative, as it empowers people to play a role in the decision-making process, where in many cases it is only those who are politically connected or affluent who are involved in the control and management of the enterprise. Such involvement can take the form of community representatives who speak for various elements of the population.

This 'management committee' is very much like the proposed Tourism Management Board outlined by Williams. The community ecotourism initiative needs to be founded on the notion of trust and transparency. Actions and decisions need to be communicated to the community through bulletin boards or other means. Money and finances are identified by Sproule as critical elements in dividing a community. To be open about expenditures and to share information in an attempt to dispel feelings of mismanagement or corruption is to be transparent in one's approach to management. Specifically, Sproule's community-based ecotourism (CBE) refers to ecotourism enterprises that are owned and managed by the community.

Furthermore, community-based ecotourism implies that a community is taking care of their natural resources in order to gain income through operating a tourism enterprise and using that income to better their lives. It involves conservation, business enterprise and community development.

A final example of how management may be used to control the development of ecotourism initiatives within a community is outlined by Drake. She defines local participation as 'the ability of local communities to influence the outcome of development projects such as ecotourism that have an impact on them'.

Important in this process is the demonstrated benefit to the community both through community members' participation and through their realisation that some aspect of their community has been treated or protected (e.g. natural resources). The following is proposed as a model of local participation in the development of ecotourism projects:

- *Phase: Determine the role of local participation in project*: This includes an assessment of how local people can help achieve set goals through efficiency, increasing project effectiveness, building beneficiary capacity, and sharing project costs.
- *Phase: Choose research team*: The team should include a broad multidisciplinary approach and include people in the social sciences and those within the media.

- *Phase: Conduct preliminary studies*: Political, economic, and social conditions of the community should be studied in the context of the environment, from existing documents, and by other survey-related work. Identification and assessment of the following is important: needs, key local leaders, media, the community's commitment to the project, intersectoral involvement, traditional uses of the land, the type of people interested in the project and why, the role of women, who will manage and finance the project, land ownership, and cultural values.
- *Phase: Determine the level of local involvement*: Local involvement occurs along a continuum from low-intensity to high-intensity involvement. This must be determined in addition to when the involvement is to occur. In cases where government is not supportive of local government, intermediaries (e.g. NGOs) can be used to facilitate local participation.
- *Phase : Determine an appropriate participation mechanism*: This is affected by the level of intensity of the participation, the nature of existing institutions (e.g. government, NGOs, citizens' groups), and the characteristics of the local people (how vociferous they may or may not be). This phase may include information sharing and consultation, which usually takes the form of a citizen advisory committee with representatives from many groups within the community. The committee is charged with the task of commenting on goals and objectives or other project-related aspects.
- *Phase: Initiating dialogue and educational efforts*: The use of the press is important in this phase as a means by which to build consensus through public awareness. Key community representatives can be used in this process. The ecotourism team should explain the goals and objectives of the project, how the project will affect the community, the values of the area, any history of threats, and the benefits of the project.

Various audiovisual techniques should be used to emphasise these points. Workshops or public meetings could be organised to identify strengths and weaknesses of the project.

- *Phase: Collective decision-making*: This is a critical stage that synthesises all research and information from the local population. The ecotourism project team present the findings of their research to the community, together with an action plan. Community members are asked to react to the plan, with the possible end result being a forum through which the team and local people negotiate to reach a final consensus based on the impacts of the project.
- *Phase : Development of an action plan and implementation scheme*: In this phase, the team and community develop an action plan for implementing solutions to identified problems. For example, if members of the community express the need to increase the community's standard of living, the team may respond by purchasing agricultural produce from local people at market rates or on a contractual basis. They may also develop a variety of positions to be occupied by local people including gift shops, research positions, park management positions, and private outfitting companies for the local people. This local action plan must then be integrated into the broader master plan of the project.
- *Phase: Monitoring and evaluation*: Monitoring and evaluation, although often neglected, should occur frequently and over the long term. The key to evaluation is to discover whether goals and objectives set out early in the project's life cycle have been accomplished or not.

Community development initiatives have a better chance of being accepted by local people if developers begin to acknowledge the fact that different groups within the community want different things, depending on their role in, affinity within, and utilisation of the community.

This perspective is discussed by Jurowski , who feels that because the impacts of tourism are not the same for all residents, residents' individual values need to be recognised by tourism developers in order for their projects to be successful. The first unique group identified by Jurowski is the 'attached resident'. Such a person is likely to be a long-term resident or an older individual who loves living in the community because of its social and physical benefits.

To these people, control over the form and function of their community is important. In general, tourism developers can gain support for their projects from this group by involving citizens in the planning process, establishing a focal point and common theme, developing projects that emphasise heritage themes, and showing that the project has social and ecological benefits for the community.

The second type established by Jurowski, the 'resource user', typically includes people like anglers and other recreationists who, although ambivalent about the economic impacts of tourism, can be won over by developers.

The developers can gain their support by providing skill opportunities for youth, involving this group in events related to their interests (e.g. bike races), protecting 'their' sites for participation, and allocating tourism funds for the development of facilities and services they desire.

The final group outlined by Jurowski is the 'environmentalist'. Although this group is the most likely to focus on the negative aspects of the development, it is in the best interests of development teams to do the following:

- Provide information on how the project will protect the environment;
- Incorporate ecological education programmes;
- Encourage the participation of environmentalists in development; and
- Prompt citizens to develop their own educational programmes for tourists. Projects that reflect the interests and concerns of the community, therefore, are said generally to stimulate volunteer activity and minimise conflict.

This research is attractive because it acknowledges that people residing in the local community are indeed different from one another. This is in contrast to much tourism research which considers the local community as one homogeneous group.

A key principle underlying the process of community development is the element of leadership. Mabey suggests that unlike the older model of leadership, seen as an individual influencing a group towards an end, newer leadership paradigms involve collaboration and partnerships between community individuals, groups, and organisations.

This means devolving power to the followers, according to Mabey, and being fluid in the connection of people and resources. Belasco and Stayer (1993:18) likened this new style of leadership to what happens in a flight of geese:

I could see the geese flying in their 'V' formation, the leadership changing frequently, with different geese taking the lead. I saw every goose being responsible for getting itself wherever the gaggle was going, changing roles whenever necessary, alternating as a leader, a follower or a scout.... I could see each goose being a leader.

This example illustrates the importance of a common purpose in removing obstacles and establishing responsibility within the community ecotourism initiative. In essence the process of empowerment—holding the will, resources, and opportunity to make decisions within the community—allows people, either internal or external to the community, to step in and provide assistance in a respectful manner, while allowing local people to shape and control the pace of tourism development within their communities.

Where this is especially relevant is in marginal places where there exists a tremendous void between those who can and those who cannot access information and resources. As such, education must play a key role in this empowerment process of revitalisation through ecotourism (e.g. providing the needed means to enable people to be informed of certain choices).

An excellent example of education's role in empowerment

lies in the Community Baboon Sanctuary project of Belize. Through education and partnerships, local farmers have stopped their conventional practice of clearing and denuding the land for agriculture purposes in favour of a land management strategy that is more environmentally sound.

In so doing they have been able to attract international tourists fascinated by the ecological and cultural diversity of this part of the world. Education, therefore, helps to rekindle people's love and appreciation of the land, which is indeed important for both community-building and nation-building.

A similar case study involves the Havasupai reservation adjacent to the Grand Canyon National Park in northern Arizona, where education and tourism have played a significant role in diversifying the local economy.

PARTNERSHIPS

A partnership, as defined by Uhlik is 'an on-going arrangement between two or more parties, based upon satisfying specifically identified, mutual needs. Such partnerships are characterized by durability over time, inclusiveness, cooperation, and flexibility.'

More specifically, Uhlik developed a six-stage model of partnership development that concentrates on the conditions that will lead to a successful partnership agreement.

These include:

- Education of self and others;
- Needs assessment and resource inventory;
- Identifying prospective partners and investigating their needs and inventories;
- Comparing and contrasting needs and resources;
- Developing a partnership proposal; and
- Proposing a partnership.

Clements *et al*. suggest that because tourism is starting to be recognised as a community development tool, development must be sensitive to the requirements of many stakeholder groups, including tourism providers (e.g. hotels), public providers (e.g. recreation and park providers), and residents.

Their view is that partnerships must be struck to ensure

that a high-quality product is delivered, and is based on the notion that tourism experiences rely on all aspects of the community. The overall effectiveness of the delivery system is only as strong as its weakest link, and communities intent on the development of a tourism industry will increasingly rely on the positive benefits of partnerships in being accountable to the local and non-local public.

The partnerships developed for ecotourism, according to Sproule, must also fit into systems that have been developed at regional and national levels. There are potentially many partnerships that can be struck to facilitate an atmosphere of cooperation and trust.

Potential partners include:

- Organisations within the established tourism industry, particularly tour operators;
- The government tourism bureau and natural resource agencies, especially the park service;
- Non-governmental organisations (NGOs), especially those involved with environmental issues, small business management, and traditional community development;
- Universities and other research organisations;
- Other communities, including those with a history of tourism and also those that are just beginning; and
- Other international organisations, public and private funding institutions, national cultural committees, and many others; the tourism industry literature is replete with examples of stakeholder groups that have conventionally been at odds.

In Canada, the United States, Australia, and many other countries around the world, there exists a significant degree of incompatibility between parks and aboriginal peoples. McNeely feels that despite what has occurred in the past, partnerships must be forged between these two groups in order that both may prosper in the late twentieth century and beyond. He feels that the following ten principles must be followed in order to help the cooperative efforts of these stakeholder groups:

- Build on the foundations of local culture.
- Give responsibility to local people.
- Consider returning ownership of at least some protected areas to indigenous people.
- Hire local people.
- Link government development programmes with protected areas.
- Give priority to small-scale local development.
- Involve local people in preparing management plans.
- Have the courage to enforce restrictions.
- Build conservation into the evolving new national cultures.
- Support diversity as a value.

Rather than emphasise what has not worked in the past, the partnership ideal must embrace the present and future needs of the groups involved in any transaction.

For those in the realm of parks it may be biodiversity and the establishment of more protected areas. From the perspective of aboriginal people, decision-making and culture may be issues that top the list.

ABORIGINAL INTERESTS

As outlined above, the relationship between parks and aboriginal people has often been one based on conflict, and stems from the physical displacement and socio-economic fragmentation of aboriginal people.

In Canada, the relationship has been one of mistrust, where peripheral lands (occupied by aboriginals) have been run outside the control and sphere of influence of local native authority. This in itself is a perpetuation of the rift that has existed between Ottawa in the south and those living in the 'north'.

Part of the problem exists because the concept of 'park' never existed in aboriginal languages, at least in North America, and the fundamentals of our Western view of park management (i.e. balancing recreational use with preservation) are completely alien to aboriginal culture, as oulined by Notzke:

The distinction between work and leisure is largely an artifact of industrial society. The fragmentation and compartmentalization of life and environment which is part and parcel of western culture, is totally alien to aboriginal cosmologies, which view the world in an essentially holistic and unified manner.

This view is supported by Sadler, who suggests that aboriginals think of space primarily from a holistic perspective, which is contrary to the dichotomous Western perspective associated with conservation. Park management therefore proceeded to exclude Aboriginals entirely from the park planning process.

This has led to an indifferent, even hostile, attitude towards the existence of parks close to or adjacent to aboriginal lands. The Clearwater River Provincial Park in northwestern Saskatchewan is an example of this indifference. Even though there is an abundant population of indigenous people in the vicinity of the park, there is little use of park resources (e.g. fish, game) by such people, in large part because of the park's political status.

In order for parks to become accepted by the aboriginal population, therefore, some feel that a revision must be made to the preservation mandate that currently exists in some types of parks, changing it to one that is conservation oriented, which will be more consistent with the social, economic, and ecological requirements of the First Nations people in Canada.

CASE STUDY: THE STRUGGLE FOR KAKADU

According to Fox, territories rich in resources provide more options for their use. This is the case with Kakadu National Park in the Northern Territory of Australia, which is a World Heritage Site and a place of immense ecological and cultural significance. Kakadu is owned by the Aborigines of the region, who lease it to the National Park Service. Legally, mismanagement of the resource may lead to the tenure being terminated.

Ecotourism is thriving in the park, so much so that according to the Aborigines, there is no longer a distinction being made between the effects of mining and tourism; both are contributing to the degradation of the park. Some Aboriginal people, according to Fox, recognise that while mining will ultimately end, tourism will continue to grow and grow, and has manifested itself in the form of planned multi-million dollar tourism projects for the park.

The issue of most concern to Aborigines is that their fundamental values are not consistent with current development philosophies in the park. According to Elliot, the example of mining and tourism in Kakadu is a perfect example of the competing and overlapping environmental values that various stakeholders have.

For example, would it matter if our actions caused a species to become extinct? Would it matter if our actions caused the death of individual animals? Would it matter if we caused widespread erosion in the park? Is the extinction of a species an acceptable price to pay for increased employment opportunities? One would imagine that miners, the tourism industry, Aborigines, the park service, and other interests would all differ along these fundamental lines.

The element of control is critical in analysing any relationship between the ecotourism industry and indigenous people. For tourism development to be successful, aboriginal people must be allowed to take control of it despite the social and political forces that often work against them.

This has been a problem in the restructuring of South Africa, where there remains a legacy of poor education and lack of training for black people. The result is that the whole touristic experience is one that is inherently foreign to the poor in South African society.

Given that part of the government's tourism vision relates to addressing the need to improve the quality of life of every South African, Swart and Saayman recognise the need for significant changes in legislation to benefit all people.

Keller, as discussed earlier, recognised that the Northwest Territories (NWT) has struggled with the development of its tourism industry, largely owing to the real lack of control of the industry at the local and regional levels.

Keller's conclusions imply that the people of this peripheral region must have decision-making control and act to limit development to a scale of growth in tune with the social, ecological, and economic climate of the region. However, at least in some places in the NWT, Inuit, Indians, and Metis people have started to realise that their varying social, ecological, and economic needs can best be met through cooperative action with other agencies.

The vehicle that is enabling them to do this is national parks, territorial parks, heritage rivers, and the tourism opportunities that emerge from such areas.

For example, Scale suggests that two rivers, the Thelon and the Kazan, were easily designated as within the Canadian Heritage Rivers System owing to the fact that the project planner lived within the community with his family for 18 months, in an attempt to educate and work closely with local organisations such as the Hunters and Trappers Association and the Elders' Society.

Scale believes that continued success will be contingent upon recognising the importance of conservation, tourism, and the needs of aboriginal people in Canada's north. In particular the following factors need to be considered:

Community involvement:

- Involvement of First Nations people in all aspects of tourism and conservation planning.

Community benefits:

- Continued and/or exclusive access to biophysical resources of the protected area for subsistence purposes.
- Provision of technical and professional training opportunities relating to positions in tourism and in conservation agencies.
- Priority status in hiring programmes undertaken by tourism interests and conservation agencies.
- Priority status in the licensing of businesses to be operated in the park or protected area.
- Compilation of traditional knowledge and heritage values of the aboriginal societies by the conservation

jurisdiction, for use both by the communities themselves in strengthening their societal traditions, and by the conservation agency in managing the protected area and in giving to its visitors a heightened appreciation of the traditional society.

Scale:

- Ecotourism and adventure tourism can be accommodated much more readily than mass tourism, where control of such tourists (numbers and use patterns) will be in the communities' best interests socially and ecologically.

Land ownership:

- Tourism and protected areas will be accepted much more readily by aboriginal societies if the legal status of the land in question is first settled to their satisfaction.

Sensitivity to needs of area residents and visitors:

- Ecotourists must be informed as to what is and what is not acceptable behaviour in the north, in recognising that the quality of their experience depends in part on their compliance to accepted norms.
- Traditional societies and conservation organisations need to come together to establish patterns in which visitors and locals can meet in circumstances of mutual respect.

Increasingly, however, examples in the literature are emerging that demonstrate the positive signs of local indigenous control in the ecotourism industry. For example, Hitchcock illustrates that the semi-nomadic pastoralist people of Purros in Namibia have been able to develop a successful ecotourism industry. Ecotourists are asked to pay the equivalent of about US$12 to enter their tribal area, with all the money generated from tourism being divided equally among members of the community.

Other aspects of the ecotourism initiative include:

- The fact that tourists must abide by structured guidelines (developed by the local people);

- Tour guiding and handicraft prices are set, so as to avoid undercutting; and
- Programmes to educate tourists on resource use in the area have been set up. Such community action, according to Hitchcock, is definitely on the rise in the developing world. Following point 1

Code for the indigenous-sensitive ecotourist:

- Who operates the programme. Is it indigenous-run? If so, is it operated communally or do only a few individuals or families profit?
- If not indigenous-run, do local communities receive an equitable share of the profits or any other direct benefits, such as training? Or do only a few individuals/families benefit?
- Learn as much as you can about the local culture and customs. Visit local indigenous federation offices for information and materials with an indigenous perspective.
- Do not take photographs without asking permission.
- If you want to give a gift, make it a useful gift to the community rather than to an individual (e.g. gift to a school). Most indigenous communities function communally.
- Refrain from tipping individuals. If you are with a group, everyone can contribute to a gift to the community.
- Be aware of the boundaries of individual homes and gardens. Never enter or photograph without permission.
- Bring your own water purification tablets. Don't rely on boiling water exclusively as it depletes fuelwood and contributes to forest destruction.
- Pack out what you take in, and use biodegradable soaps.
- Be sensitive to those around you.
- Don't make promises you cannot or will not keep—for example, sending back photos to local people.
- Do not collect plants or plant products without permission.

- Wear appropriate and discreet clothing (e.g. many cultures are offended by women in shorts even though they may go topless).
- Respect local residents' privacy and customs. Treat people with the respect you would expect from visitors to your own home.

above, Colvin proposes a code of ethics for the indigenous-sensitive ecotourist.

The issue of control in the development of ecotourism was at the centre of an incident between the Kuna Indians of Panama and the Panama national government. Chapin writes that in the 1970s the government of Panama had the specific aim of working with multinational corporations in the development of a tourism product in the region of the Kuna (around Carti on the Caribbean side of the country): 'In return for their services as tourist attractions, the Kuna were to be given employment as service staff'.

According to Chapin, the Kuna were unwilling to comply with the feasibility team and collectively forced the tourism industry influence out of the region. While plans for the development of casinos had to be discarded, one operator had his boat confiscated, and another individual had to endure being shot, set on fire, a hanging attempt, and a pummelling at the hands of many Kuna youth.

Conversely, the small hotels of the region that currently exist in the area are all run by Kuna and cater to a small and manageable number of tourists on the basis of Kuna ownership and Kuna law.

Communities are therefore cognisant of the importance of sustainable development and are striving to achieve it, but under the following conditions:

- They must have control of the industry;
- Projects must be small in size and therefore manageable; and
- There must be equity and dialogue among the various stakeholders.

The importance of training and education appears to be a common thread that links the literature on ecotourism and indigenous development. Wearing emphasises that at any level of hierarchy, 'ordinary' people are perfectly able to solve their own problems if given the chance.

Through an analysis of ecotourism and local indigenous communities, Wearing believes that experiential education and training are crucial in allowing such communities to develop ecotourism so that it is not just another commodified product where benefits are exported and natural resources are abused. 'Concrete experiences' are important in acting as cornerstones to teaching and learning in many indigenous communities.

Aboriginal people can contrast this with the 'formation of abstract concepts and generalisations' attitude, which is more akin to the Western approach, and provides the means by which to bring a more conceptual foundation to the learning process.

'Observations and reflections' and 'testing implications of concepts in new situations,' represent the integration of Western and local traditions that may be desired of an ecotourism experience, with the former representing a traditional method of learning in aboriginal cultures and the latter representing more of a Western scientific approach to problem-solving.

A significant body of research has surfaced in Australia on parks and Aboriginal involvement, where despite many years of agreements and talks, there still exists uncertainty regarding the role that Aboriginals must play within protected areas. In Kakadu, Cobourg, and Uluru national parks, reported to be the model of Aboriginal-national parks relations in Australia, co-management strategies have not been successful in integrating and protecting indigenous values and rights, despite the fact that land in these areas has been given back to Aboriginals as freehold title.

Davey reports that the models break down by failing to involve the aboriginal landowners in policy and planning, by not having majority Aboriginal representation on park boards, and by the lack of training and skills to enable Aboriginal people better to understand their role within the park setting.

Notwithstanding these failures, Australians have

endeavoured to overcome some of these problems through research initiatives designed to develop Aboriginal skills and training. Baker *et al.* suggest that Aboriginal people can contribute equally to park management by applying Aboriginal ecological knowledge—which is based on generations of accumulated knowledge—with conventional biological surveys to overcome the time and finance constraints normally associated with research.

In addressing the need to enhance Aboriginal skill levels, De Lacy discusses the development of a number of Aboriginal employment programmes in Australia in the 1980s, including the initiation of many courses and skills that are currently available at selected universities within the Australian system.

Similar training opportunities have been reported by Liu in the American Affiliated Pacific Islands, where support of indigenous écotourism entrepreneurs is thought to be critical in achieving sustainable economic growth. Liu suggests that government needs to take the lead in providing financing, development and operational support, and training programmes to develop appropriate marketing and business skills for this population.

This is supported by King and Stewart, who feel that national level controls are needed, in concert with local involvement, as a means by which to coordinate ecotourism development with the aim of reducing the effects of commodification of local indigenous cultures.

SITE DEVELOPMENT

The tourism industry has long been recognised as a formidable agent of social and ecological change, some say in a positive context through increased education, renewed pride in culture, the conservation of heritage, and of course economics, while others say in a negative sense, at the expense of people and the resource base.

For example, hotel developments in Spain and Turkey have been identified as being excessive in their impacts on beach environments.

In other cases, improper development and the lack of sewerage systems hamper the tourism industry to such an extent in places in Mexico and Brazil that tourists are told not to swim in the ocean owing to the pollution. In such cases tourism development is strongly affected by what does not exist (i.e. no sewerage systems) or because such systems are unable to keep pace with the ongoing increase in tourism visitation and associated development.

The style and extent of tourism development in the 1990s has been tempered by the trend towards the increase in the recent past, in mega-development projects designed to cater to a growing market of travellers looking for self-contained, hassle-free vacations.

Fennell writes that this mega-resort boom began in the mid-1980s, and includes sites such as the 31,000-acre resort community of Waikoloa in Hawaii and the 1,200-acre Sanctuary Cove mixed-use resort between Brisbane and the Gold Coast.

Yet while most of the development has been centred in what have been politically stable democracies, management consultants have been looking to the untapped markets of the Far East.

In the midst of this mega-development push there has emerged the move towards more responsible travel and development, in response to the green movement (pressure from various groups including academics, ENGOs, and the general public), and in keeping one step ahead of the competition.

The response to the changing emphasis has meant that even some of the major hotel chains have endeavoured to experiment with ecologically sound rooms through recycling, washing sheets only at the request of visitors, cutting down on the use of electricity, and so on.

However, where this changing focus has become the most noticeable is through the variety of small-scale initiatives that have developed in urban (bed-and-breakfasts), rural (farm tourism) and back-country (ecotourism developments) settings.

SUSTAINABLE DESIGN AND ECOLODGES

Over the past few years, several documents have emerged that analyse the development of ecolodges and ecotourism facilities on the basis of principles of sustainability. However, there appears to be some confusion on the scale and magnitude of development of such areas according to Epler Wood, who reports that ecotourism continues to be misunderstood in resort advertising schemes, while the term 'ecoresort' has yet to be appropriately defined.

For instance, a tourism industry trade publication recently wrote that 'Another recent and perhaps surprising region for ecoresort development is India.... There is interest in genuine cultural experiences within the country.

One man has proposed a historical tour of India by rail.' Interest in sustainable ecotourism design took flight in the early 1990s in part as a result of a US national park service publication dedicated to the principles of sustainable design.

Two events took place in the United States that prompted the development of this book. The first was the National Park Service Vail Symposium in October 1991 which discussed, among other things, the severity of environmental stresses within parks; while the second was the Virgin Islands National Park initiative in November 1991, which specifically dealt with issues related to sustainable design in parks and protected areas.

The latter publication explores interpretation, natural and cultural resources, site design, building design, energy management, water supply, waste prevention, and facility and maintenance operations in its overview of sustainable design. Of particular importance is its extensive checklist for sustainable building design that emphasises and respects the many interrelationships of all parts of the natural and cultural aspects of the site.

However, these were not the first attempts to integrate the developments of humankind with the natural world (especially parks), as evident in the seminal work of Miller (1976, 1989) on ecodevelopment.

Although the US Department of the Interior book is

devoted to facility design and construction *in parks,* there is a more generic section that deals specifically with sustainable tourism development.

Here the authors advocate using the principles of Aesculapia, which is the Greek place of healing. From this perspective, 'nature is respected for its restorative qualities. The human experience is set in harmony with the environment, and an opportunity is created to allow a reconnection of human needs to the natural systems on which all life is based'.

This type of design principle would then strive to meet the following criteria, according to the authors:

- Provide education for visitors on wildlife, native cultural resources, historic features, or natural features;
- Involve indigenous populations in operations and interpretation to foster local pride and visitor exposure to traditional values and techniques;
- Accomplish environmental restoration;
- Provide research and development on, and/or demonstration projects of, ways to minimise human impacts on the environment;
- Provide spiritual or emotional recuperation;
- Provide relaxation and recreation; and
- Educate visitors to realise that knowledge of our local and global environment is valuable and will empower their ability to make informed decisions.

Russell *et al.* (1995:x) define an ecolodge as 'a nature-dependent tourist lodge that meets the philosophy and principles of ecotourism'. Although they underscore the importance of the ecolodge concept from an educational and experiential perspective, they suggest that it is the philosophical tie with ecological sensitivity that must define these operations.

The importance of ecology is also underscored by the Ecotourism Society, which feels that such lodges promote an educational and participatory experience while at the same time being developed and managed in regard to the local environment in which it exists.

Table: Traditional Lodge Versus Ecolodge.

Traditional	Ecolodge
Luxury	Comfortable basic needs
Generic style	Unique character style
Relaxation focus	Activity/educational focus
Activities are facility based (e.g. golf, tennis)	Activities are nature based (e.g. hiking, diving)
Enclave development	Integrated development with local environment
Group/consortium ownership common	Individual ownership common
Profit maximisation based on high guest capacity, services, prices	Profit maximisation based on strategic design, location, low capacity, services, price
High investment	Moderate/low investment
Key attractions are facility and surroundings	Key attractions are surroundings and facility
Gourmet meals, service, and presentation	Good/hearty meals and service -cultural influence
Market within chain	Market normally independent
Guides and nature interpreters non-existent or minor feature of operation	Guides and nature interpreters focus of operation

Russell *et al.* distinguish between traditional lodges and ecolodges using the 12 points shown. They further distinguish between the ecolodge and the nature-based lodge, with the latter being associated with fishing, skiing, and luxury retreats.

The philosophical issue related to ecolodges identified above is one considered by Andersen (1993, 1994), who feels that along with environmental codes of ethics, a low-impact approach to the design of ecotourism facilities needs to be employed for such facilities to be truly sustainable—an approach that he suggests would entail a complete reworking of the conventional design of architects.

Andersen's work is well publicised in the field of ecotourism, especially his advocacy of a number of principles which, broadly defined, include organisational issues (e.g. has an analysis been done of the area's ecological sensitivity?), site planning issues (e.g. minimise trail crossing points at rivers and streams), building design issues (e.g. maintenance of the ecosystem should take priority over view or dramatic design statements), energy resource and utility infrastructure issues (e.g. consider the use of passive or active solar or wind energy sources wherever practical), waste management issues (e.g. provide facilities for recycling), and evaluation (e.g. whether accommodation is made for older guests and physically disabled individuals).

Andersen has been able to operationalise many of these design features in his Lapa Rios Resort development on the Osa Peninsula of Costa Rica's Pacific coast. This development has a main lodge in addition to 14 private bungalows which were built by local engineers with the removal of only one tree.

Given the low-capacity and low-impact philosophies of ecotourism development, a logical question is: at what scale does the ecolodge model *not* apply? That is, when is a development considered too big? This question, at least peripherally, has been addressed by Ayala .

As an international ecoresort developer, she believes both that ecotourism is becoming a segment of mass tourism, and that it is not incompatible with beach tourism. She supports this view by suggesting that there is the need to diversify the vast number of sea, sun, and sand products through the addition of ecotourism (but not at the exclusion of other hard-path experiences).

Ayala feels that the line between ecotourists and conventional tourists is least detectable in long-haul travel, citing similarities in their levels of education, household income, and their occupations. Interesting is the fact that the ability to travel long distances is directly related to one's wealth, and wealth is directly related to education and occupation. Ayala fails to discuss other factors (e.g. psychographics) that determine differences in travel types.

For example, the assumption being made is either that all long-haul tourists are ecotourists, or that all ecotourists are simply long-haul travellers. Ayala further writes that many of the mega-resort chains in Africa and Central America go so far as to donate money to conservation efforts.

However, if the link is being made to ecotourism, which is the focus of her article, then one wonders what percentage of the revenue from the hotels stays within the local communities and what percentage flows back to North America or Europe. Could such an initiative by the big companies be an appeasement mechanism or marketing scheme designed to look green?

It is not easy being sceptical about published work in this area, but increasingly scepticism is what is needed to address some of the issues related to the philosophy and implementation of ecotourism, especially as they relate to ecoresorts.

Will ecotourism's fall from grace be directly attributable to the belief and practice that it fits very nicely as a form of mass tourism, and that mega-ecoresorts are the solution to bring ecotourism to the masses? Is this the rationale for their development—the intrinsic need to not deny the masses their place in the sun (or rather rainforest)?

Or rather is it simply that from an extrinsic motivational perspective, it is big business making money the old-fashioned way? Having seen some of these developments first hand, one merely has to dig a bit more closely at some of the unsustainable features of the development. For example, an ecolodge in Mexico recently developed by a large international company used grass and other materials not indigenous to the area in the design of the facility.

In addition, no interpretive programmes had been developed to enable tourists to learn about or experience the natural and cultural attractions of the area.

Such developments are merely cosmetic, often with few educational and sustainable features, which presumably are important to this segment, and undermine what Hawkins and others have suggested about ecotourism as being minimum density and low impact. Even in cases where ownership is in the hands of one or a handful of individuals, local ownership is rare.

CASE STUDY: GREYLOCK GLEN ECOTOURISM RESORT

This recently approved project is a consortium of state, local, not-for-profit agencies, and private interests which have come together to build a demonstration site for the concept of sustainable development in the region of the Berkshire Mountains region of Massachusetts. The developers hope that this site will be a prototype for similar developments throughout the world.

The resort will operationalise the concepts of sustainable development in offering educational, recreational, and conference-oriented programmes. In particular, visitors will be able to enjoy a golf course (developed from the Audubon Society's guidelines for environmentally sensitive golf courses), a nature centre (a year-round environmental education facility), hiking, Nordic skiing, biking, camping, tennis, swimming, horseback riding, and other recreational activities.

In addition to a 200-room resort, 800 acres will be designated as open, recreational land. The developers (Greylock Management Associates) have specified that the following approaches to sustainability will be followed:

Natural resources: The maintenance of forest integrity and animal preservation will guide all development decisions at Greylock; a natural resource inventory will be compiled.

Cultural resources: All cultural artefacts (e.g. farming fields, old roads, orchards) will be preserved and highlighted.

Energy management: Energy meters will be present and interpret energy usage at the centre.

Water and sewerage: Water-efficient toilets and shower heads will be used. Visitors will be presented with guidelines to help them cut down on water consumption.

Waste management: A recycling programme will be implemented, in addition to composting.

ECOLODGE RESEARCH

As outlined earlier in this chapter, ecotourism and the ecolodge concept have been misused by resort advertisers in the past. For this reason research needs to play a stronger role in providing leadership in this area. The following few examples serve to illustrate some of what exists in the area of ecolodge research.

Russell *et al.* undertook an international ecolodge survey of 28 operators in nine regions around the world (Belize, Costa Rica, Peru, Brazil, Ecuador, the state of Alaska, Australia, New Zealand, and Africa). This study discovered that many of the lodges were found in or adjacent to protected areas, with outstanding natural beauty acting as a key to success of the operation.

Most of the ecolodges sampled were small in size, accommodating about 24 guests, with some successful operations in Amazonia catering up to 100 guests. Prices for accommodation (single night), meals, and local transportation were approximately US$130-170. The authors felt that although most of the ownership had been typically small scale and independent, corporate ownership was becoming more common.

They cited the P&O line in Australia and the Hilton in Kenya as two examples of this recent phenomenon. Finally, they suggested that very few such lodges exist in North America owing to the existing reliance on camping and other, more comfortable recreational lodges.

This finding is supported in a recent market study of ecotourism in Alberta and British Columbia (ARA Consultants 1994). However, according to Wight , this is not necessarily what is happening. She feels that market research does not indicate that such a trend is due to market preference, but rather it is due to the demand for a range of accommodation.

To Wight, a better question would be to ascertain the range of accommodation types supplied by the region or destination area, where, she feels, there is an abundance of the conventional hotel/motel opportunities. She does, however, feel that there is a distinct lack of adventure-type, small-scale, fixed-roof accommodation.

The hard aspects of ecotourism can be identified, at least in part, by non-permanent types of dwellings, including tents and hammocks. The ecotourism experience grows continually softer through fixed-roof units (cabins and lodges) on-site, and through fixed-roof dwellings off-site, usually in the form of hostels, hotels, and resorts.

This hard-soft accommodation continuum relates in part to the work of Laarman and Durst , at least in part, who suggested that one of the hard and soft dimensions of ecotourism was the physical rigour of the trip. Those who were prepared to walk extensively in back-country regions, sleep in camps or crude shelters, or tolerate poorer sanitary conditions were said to have been interested in more of a hard-path ecotourism experience.

If this continuum is to apply to North America, it is logical to ask whether or not such operations are applicable to consumptive or non-consumptive forms of recreation.

This issue has not been adequately addressed in the literature, at least from the Canadian perspective, and is an issue that is of the utmost importance as outfitters and operators wrestle with how to refit their enterprises to accommodate the changing recreational focus in the north, because, as Anderson/Fast (1996a:5-4) suggest, 'depending on the characteristics of the package and the participating tourists, outfitter camps [the only form of accommodation in many remote regions of Canada's north] may or may not be appropriate'.

Finally, literature on ecoresorts seems to indicate that accommodation, although important, is not the overriding motivation for visiting regions. ARA , for example, places accommodation below the natural setting and wildlife viewing (of primary importance), and other secondary activities related to the experience.

To this, Wight adds support by suggesting that accommodation is an enabler of the overall ecotourism experience; basically tourists select the experience, then choose the accommodation.

Often, though, prearranged package tours dictate much of the on-site experience, including choice of accommodation, restricting the opportunity for ecotourists to choose lodging, and reinforcing the point that there is an element of ambiguity as to just what ecotourism entails. According to Grenier *et al.* (1993:9), 'one person's ecotourism dream may be another's touristic nightmare'.

One of the unfortunate realities of ecotourism is that despite its altruistic intentions, to date there is little evidence that it is less intrusive than other types of tourism development. It is indeed frustrating that we continue to talk of appropriate means by which to control development, yet have very few successes to report on.

Those who do report success have perhaps not been operating long enough to let, for instance, the destination life cycle unfold. In many localities around the world, local initiatives are chipping away at the conditions or circumstances that continue to plague ecotourism development. It is within the local arena that such change must occur.

There does seem to be pressure from international development firms to integrate the concept of ecotourism at a grander scale. While there certainly appears to be the opportunity to provide the tourist with a degree of the ecotourism experience at such a scale, caution needs to be used in promoting such areas as true ecotourism sites.

Where this relationship between mass tourism resorts and ecotourism breaks down seems to be in relation to the elements of ownership and control at the destination, with international or multinational domination of the industry still in existence.

Regions intent on the development of ecotourism must be able to secure both consensus within the community and the means, i.e. the decision-making responsibilities, to move away from many of the conventional global tourism development dysfunctions that are so prevalent within the industry.

Chapter 9

The other Side of Leisure

Aristotle said, "We work in order to have leisure. " Who of us can seriously disagree with this statement? Another line from Aristotle, "we are unleisurely in order to achieve leisure" Could anything be clearer? And yet according to the statistics generated by the Department of Labour, as adults there is nothing we do more with our lives than work. From approximately the ages of 21 to 70, we will spend our lives working.

We will not sleep as much, spend as much time with our families, eat as much, or recreate and rest as much as we will work. Whether we love our work or hate it, succeed in it or fail, achieve fame or infamy through it, we are all, like Sisyphus, condemned to push and chase that thing we call our job, our career, our work all of our days.

"Even those of us who desperately don't want to work, " said Ogden Nash, "must work in order to earn enough money so that they won't have to work anymore!" Like it or not, our collective leitmotif is not leisure but labour!

America has always been a land and a society of contrasts and paradoxes. One of the most glaring conflicts in our constellation of cultural values is our duplicitous attitude in regard to the Protestant work ethic. On the one hand, we have always praised work.

We have cultivated an almost mystical reverence in its regard. We have preached that all honest work is character building and the means by which individuals achieve identity, integrity, and admission into the "club of adulthood." To deliberately choose not to work, not to have a job when work is available, is to be a social outcast. Worse yet, it means your mother now has the right to call you a bum!

On the other hand, let's be frank, we also think that work stinks! We just don't say it out loud all that often. Although work preoccupies our adult lives, most of us don't want it to. Few of us eagerly seek it out. Fewer still happily embrace its burdens and demands. And given the option, a lot of us would gladly never work again.

When you think about it, the only people who praise work are historians, politicians, or business owners who have to because it's in their best interest—it's their job! (Oh sure, you'll find the likes of Wendell Berry, farmer, poet, and essayist, praising—at least in public prose—the virtue of drudgery.

But believe me, he's the exception to the rule, and, again, it's his job!) Studs Terkel is right. Don't ask bosses about work. What do you expect them to say? Of course, they're going to be for it. If you really want to know what people think of work, talk to workers. Chances are, says Terkel, they'll tell you stuff that would make Benjamin Franklin, Martin Luther, and John Calvin shake their heads in disbelief and blush with embarrassment.

American popular culture, says Julia Keller, *Chicago Tribune* columnist, is a much more accurate barometer of what people think about work than an academic survey or an uplifting oped piece written for Labour Day. The unruly truth that lies beneath the surface of our national commitment to the sacred icon of the Protestant work ethic, says Keller, is that "work is for saps" and should be avoided whenever possible.

A lot of us may have nightmares about the job, but what most of us fantasize about is—not working! We dream about having unlimited leisure. We imagine lives that are idle, lax, lazy, and, of course, rich too! We yearn for an existence that is exclusively directed at "working at play" and having fun. For most of us, work is a means to an end: status, stuff, cash, and lots of time off.

We put up with it because we have to, but in our heart of hearts, many of us secretly wish we had been born into the J. Paul Getty or Bill Gates families. And even more of us are in complete agreement with yet another icon of American culture, Abraham Lincoln.

My father taught me to work, but not to love it. I never did like to work, and I don't deny it. I'd rather read, tell stories, crack jokes, talk, laugh—anything but work.

The philosopher Josef Pieper said that "we are fettered to the process of work. " Translation: We are captives of our jobs; we are consumed and time bound by what we do. Well, you don't have to be a scholar or a sage to know, or at least feel, that Pieper is right.

Our lives do seem busier, fuller, more fatiguing than ever before. The sociologist Arlie Russell Hochschild suggests that modern workers talk about sleep in the same way that hungry people talk about food.

A lot of us know all too well that we put a lot of time in on the job, and there is a raft of statistical sources that reinforces this feeling. The economist Juliet Schor estimates that annual hours on the job, across all industries and occupations, have been increasing over the last twenty years, so that the average employee is now on the job an additional 163 hours, or the equivalent of an extra month per year.

In her 1991 best-seller, *The Overworked American,* she claimed that one-fourth of all full-time workers spent 49 or more hours on the job each week. Of these, almost half were at work 60 hours or more. The management guru Charles Hardy noted in 1994 that the typical American worked 47 hours per week, for an annual total of 2,330 hours, and that in 2014 the average American worker would put in 3,000 hours per year on the job.

In 1996, Thomas Geoghegan, labour lawyer and syndicated columnist, estimated that middle-management types and senior executives endure a 55-to-65-hour week, and that 11 per cent of all workers report working more than 65 hours per week. In 1997, in her important analysis on work and the family, *The Time Bind,* Arlie Russell Hochschild reported that both men and women workers average slightly more than 47 hours a week.

Finally, in a 1999 study, a Cornell University research

project found that, on average, Americans work 350 hours more per year than Europeans—and 70 hours more a year than even the Japanese, whose language contains the word karoshi, which means "death from overwork. " If some of these figures and projections are accurate, by the year 2010, the average workweek could exceed 58 hours.

What has to be kept in mind, of course, is that these figures reflect only hours on the job and do not represent the other aspects of our workday such as getting to and from the job as well as household and family responsibilities.

A 1993 survey conducted by the Families and Work Institute of New York concluded that both spouses in a double-income household with kids put in a minimum of fifteen hours a day on work, commuting, chores and children. These figures, based on a Monday-through-Friday schedule, mean that both spouses have already "logged in" seventy-five hours before the weekend.

Moreover, although Sundays in many households are still reserved for family outings and social events, Saturdays are usually just another workday "Honey-do lists" are drawn up, chores are assigned, projects are attended to, and kids are schlepped to music lessons and the mall.

Whatever the exact amount of time each of us is putting into the job, it is both palpably and statistically clear to most of us that we are working harder and longer than ever before. And more than just the extra time we are putting in on the job, the tempo, intensity, and stresses associated with our work seem to "Great News" by Horsey. Seattle Post-Intelligencer Tribune Media Services.

Used with permission be accelerating. We cram more and more into each day, and yet we feel that we never have enough time to do all that must be done. In a 2001 phone survey of over a thousand households, the Families and Work Institute discovered that American families feel overworked and that they are doing too much on the job.

Of those surveyed 55 per cent reported feeling overwhelmed by how much work they have to do; 45 per cent felt that they have to do many jobs at once and multitask too often; 59 per cent complained that they were unable to reflect on and perfect the work they were doing; and, finally, 90 per cent agreed strongly that they work "too fast" and "too hard" and they "never have enough time to get a job done properly. "

Some scholars of American culture claim that we are a nation "predisposed to hard work, " that the "elevation of work over leisure" is an ethos that has long permeated our lives, and that we have made a religion out of our commitment to work. My question is: Who have these scholars been talking to? I'm sure that's exactly the kind of puritanical response you'd expect to get from Cotton Mather or from the nineteenth-century industrialist John D. Rockefeller, or perhaps find in the pseudopsychological scribblings of Frederick Winslow Taylor. But it's certainly not the kind of comment most workers would come up with.

Oh sure, there are people who really love their jobs, people for whom the line between work and play has vanished, people who find meaning and purpose in what they do. People who eagerly seek out their jobs, everyday But let's not kid ourselves—these happy few represent a minority of the workforce!

For most of us—white collar or blue, good job or bad, decent pay or not—work is a chore, a task, a responsibility, a duty, something we are required to do to earn a living or maintain a lifestyle. Work for too many of us is perceived as "down-time, " "dead time"—something that must be done, but there's little or no fun to be had in doing it.

Most of us endure our jobs and put up with them because we have to, because we want to get paid. Perhaps the late *Chicago Tribune* columnist Mike Royko comes closest to the spirit of the "common man's" feeling about work when his alter ego in the column, Slats, says:

Why do we think the lottery is so popular? Do you think anybody would play if the super payoff was a job on the night shift in a meat packing plant? People play it so if they win they can be rich and idle...like I told you years ago—if work is so good, how come they have to pay us to do it?

During the Viagra economy of the Clinton administration,

the unemployment rate hit an unprecedented low of 3.9 per cent. Perhaps for the first time ever, employees in every skill set were in demand, and employers from McDonald's to Microsoft were vigorously pursuing them with offers of high wages and big benefits.

Employees, at least for a short time, were in the driver's seat and they knew it. They wanted to be courted. They wanted to be wooed. They wanted benefits and perks, and next to more money and meaningful work, they wanted time off.

According to a Families and Work Institute 1999 study, 63 per cent of Americans say they want to work less, up from only 17 per cent in 1994. In another 1999 study conducted by New York University and the University of Pennsylvania it was found that "45 to 50 per cent of workers (and 80 per cent of those working more than 50 hours a week) said they would prefer to work fewer hours, and more than 25 per cent said they would take a pay cut to make it happen. "

Another survey in 2000 found that even college students and recent graduates place "flexible hours" at the top of the list of the job benefits they most desire—above health insurance, vacations, and stock options. The moral of all this seems clear.

Workers are united in their belief that even a good job, a great job, a job with terrific pay, perks, and prestige can demand too much of us. Jobs can eat up too much of our time, our energy, our passion, and our inner selves.

When Merle Haggard bellowed the lyrics "Take this job and shove it!" and Dolly Parton belted out "Nine to Five, " both were voicing the frustrations of millions of us. Bad jobs suck!

Even good jobs can be overrated! In fact, no job would be ideal! To quote poetry rather than country and western music, in the words of Philip Larkin (former poet laureate of England and definitely not a saloon singer):

Why should I let the toad work
Squat on my life?
Can't I use my wit as a pitch fork
And drive the brute off?

The double irony in all of this is, of course, that although survey after survey reports that we do not like our jobs and that most of us would prefer not to work as much as we do, statistics suggest that given the raw hours we put in on the job, we are fast becoming a nation of workaholics.

Former Secretary of Labour Robert Reich, in his book *The Future of Success,* says that the causes of our workaholism are both immediate and international: our consumer culture, advances in technology, increased competition, and the global marketplace. He is, of course, undoubtedly right. But I also think that the root cause of our workaholism is connected in large part to who we are as a nation and as a people.

As a society, we are obsessed with time. We have always been so; it's part of our national character. In this society, time is money and we always try to spend it well. We fail to understand and often scoff at the tradition of the siesta in Italy, Spain, and Mexico.

We smirk at the French practice of closing down in August and Sweden's mandated five-week minimum vacation policy We have never been comfortable with the abstract notion of free time. It is not in our nature to just let time pass. Unstructured time, dead time, downtime, wasted time—makes us ill at ease.

We see time as our most precious commodity We try to make the most of our time. We fill time, use time, invest and manage time. We strive to be productive with our time. We live by schedules and lists. We micromanage all of our worktime, much of our playtime, and, increasingly, more and more of our family/private time.

We have embraced Thomas Alva Edison's admonition that success is dependent upon "one-per cent inspiration and ninety-nine per cent perspiration. " We pursue success by pouring our sweat and our energy into time. We believe that successful people always have time to do something more, and unsuccessful people never have enough time to do what must be done.

Although perception does not always equal reality, our perception that time must be used wisely and well does, in fact, constitute how we view reality. We have equated time with productivity and success. We desire time, covet time, and our greatest fear is the loss of time. We are in a constant race with and against time.

Historically, Americans have always viewed the active life as morally superior. The tradition of "busyness" is part of our moral fabric; we accord kudos to those individuals who make every moment count and whose every movement is regulated by the clock.

Traditionally, in this society, we measure meaning by productivity. And our obsession with time has always been directly connected to our addiction to work. The University of Iowa historian Benjamin K. Hunnicutt has suggested that whether by choice or circumstances, we have always lived in "a culture of work. " As a people, we have always been compulsive about what we do and how we do it.

How else can we explain this nation's accomplishments in such a relatively short period of time? The nineteenth-century union demand for a limited workday was not about our unwillingness to work. It was about our unwillingness to work long hours for bad pay, in horrible conditions, and without the realistic possibility of improving our lot in terms of cash, possessions, and class.

In a quintessential American way being busy, being overworked conveys status and self-worth. The busier our schedules, the more important we feel and the more we are able to acquire the possessions and things that supposedly constitute the good life.

The lesson we learned as a nation from the Depression is that no matter what abuses can occur, no matter how vulnerable the individual worker can be, no matter what the threats to the human and civil rights of workers, "there is nothing better than work."

After we had endured the stark reality of no work and doing without for too long, all work, any work seemed preferable. We have learned too well that without work, time is unstructured, unproductive, and lacking in both purpose and profit.

As a nation, we came out of the deprivations of the Depression and the rationed priorities of World War II seeking not to escape from or transcend work but rather to find transcendence through our work.

In this society, workaholism is considered to be a clean addiction, and one prized by businesses and corporations. After all, what company wouldn't rather have a workaholic instead of an alcoholic employee? Workaholics produce worth, make money, achieve success.

Workaholism is one of the only addictions that is not merely condoned but actually rewarded. It is socially accepted and promoted because it is socially productive. We all know people who brag about working sixty, seventy, or even eighty hours per week.

Workaholics in effect say: "I know I'm a workaholic, but it's better than a lot of other things I could be! I'm not sailing a yacht. I'm not playing all day long. I'm not taking exotic trips. I'm working my damn ass off!" They assume, as do their families, friends, and colleagues, that they are being dutiful, industrious, and on the fast track to success as it's prescribed in the American Dream.

According to Diane Fassel in her important but underappreciated book, *Working Ourselves to Death*, the American/Protestant work ethic and workaholism are two separate and distinct phenomena. The work ethic is about the role and acceptance of work in our lives. It's about God's calling to work, the dignity and duty of work, the value and purpose of work.

It's about personal and communal fulfillment and survival through work. The work ethic is about life and living. Workaholism, says Fassel, is just the opposite. Workaholism is a substitute for life. It's about self-absorbed, compulsive behaviour and performance fixation. Workaholism is about addiction.

As an addiction, work becomes a narcotic: our surrogate, our palliative, our coping mechanism for life. Workaholism insulates and isolates us from life. It is an opiate that buffers us from ourselves and others.

Workaholism is one way of dealing with reality when other options are unavailable. Work addiction may not be our first or best option, but it is a familiar and well-sanctioned one. "Workaholics, " says Fassel, "are no longer 'showing up' for life.

They are alienated from their own bodies, from their own feelings, from their creativity, and from family and friends. They have been taken over by the compulsion to work and are slaves to it. They no longer own their lives. " Workaholism, she warns, is a progressively fatal disease, "which masquerades as a positive trait (or at least, an acceptable vice) in the cultural lore of our nation. "

Moreover, says Fassel, workaholics are not just job addicts. The addiction does not stop at the front door. It comes with you wherever you go. The workaholic lacks boundaries; the work process provides everything. Workaholics take work to bed, take it home on weekends, take it on vacation.

The workaholic is never without work, because work is the fix. Many children of workaholic parents, Fassel said, describe vacations as whirlwinds of exhausting activity. Their parents did vacations the way they did work—full tilt and nonstop. In its narrowest sense, argues Fassel, workaholism is an addiction to action. The type of action may vary, but the process is the same: you leave yourself by losing yourself in your action/work. Workaholics cannot say no to work and its demands. As addicts, they are driven by the compulsion to work. Work orientates them, affirms them, comforts them, holds out to them the possibility of happiness.

Of course, says Fassel, for the true addict, the work is never done. Thus happiness dangles like the proverbial carrot: it's always the next project away. Then they will have succeeded; then they will be happy; then they will be able to provide for all of their family s wants and needs.

Unfortunately, says Fassel, what compounds the problem for the workaholic is a social and business structure that actively rewards work addiction. We are a nation of addicted workers primarily because we are a nation of addictive work organizations.

In an addictive society, says Fassel, workaholism does not shock us: there is no dissonance in this disease; it feels normal because it is the norm. We are used to it because it is part of what we are used to. Workaholism is the status quo.

We have created a series of positive myths about workaholism: "No one ever died of hard work. " "Workaholism is always profitable for individuals and corporations." "Workaholics always get ahead. " "Hard work keeps you out of trouble."

"No effort goes unrewarded. " "Success comes to those who work for it. " "Work proves worth. " "Fitness addicts have good bodies; workaholics make more money" "Having it all is not an illusion." "The only line is the bottom line." "Business is war; to the victors go the spoils.

"Homilies such as these comfort and numb us. We have adapted to workaholism, says Fassel, in much the same way a frog can adapt to a pot of boiling water. If you suddenly drop a frog into boiling water it will leap out immediately But, says Fassel, if you put a frog in a pot of cool water and gradually heat the water to the boiling point, it will remain in the pot until it dies. Fassel contends that this is the perfect metaphor for the state of workaholism in our society today.

Whether we are all becoming certifiable workaholics or not (and yes, there is a nationally based Workaholics Anonymous Association), the bottom line is that as a nation we are working more and more and recreating less and less. According to a 2001 survey by Oxford Health Plans, an East Coast health care provider, one in six U. S. employees ends up not taking all of their annual vacation time because of the demands of the job.

The survey further pointed out that 34 per cent of workers report that they have no downtime on the job; 32 per cent don't leave the building at all during the day; 19 per cent of respondents said they feel obliged to go to work even when they're ill; 17 per cent said it's hard to take time off, even for an emergency; and, 8 per cent believe they'd be fired or demoted if they became seriously ill. In another survey, conducted by the Wall *Street Journal*, some workers claim that all too often vacations don't even seem like real vacations. At Dallas-based 7-Eleven Inc., for example, most headquarters employees feel pressured, if not directly ordered or obligated, to take their cell phones and laptops with them on vacation. And, Seattle's Real Networks, Inc., requires anyone asking for more than ten days off at a time to make the request through a vice president rather than through a manager.

According to Joe Robinson, former editor of an adventure-travel magazine, "we're the most vacation-starved country in the world. " There is only one other country with fewer vacation days than America (ten to thirteen) and that is Mexico (six). And what is worse is that in America these vacation days are not required by law but rather are the result of negotiated contracts or custom and tradition.

In comparison to the mandated vacation schedules of other industrialized nations, American workers are suffering from a serious leisure lag: Italy, forty-two days; Germany, thirty-five; Sweden, thirty-two; Spain, thirty; Denmark, thirty; Ireland, twenty-eight; and even the work-addicted Japanese, twenty-five mandated vacation days a year.

Financially speaking, all the hours we have put in on the job have not necessarily gone unrewarded. According to the Federal Reserve (January 2000) 12.6 per cent of all households earn less than $10,000 annually; 24.8 per cent earn between $10,000 and $24,999; 28.8 per cent earn between $25,000 and $49,999; 25.2 per cent earn between $50,000 and $99,999; and 8.6 per cent earn $ 100,000 or more a year.

As of this writing, the median American household income is in excess of $41,000. On average, more working households are doing better than ever before. More of us own homes than at any other time in our history. Two-car families are now the norm. Shopping malls are everywhere, and consumer products are abundant and widely distributed.

We make more than ever before. We own more than ever before. And, of course, we owe more than ever before. The problem is, we work more and more in the manic pursuit to maintain our lives and our lifestyles.

The reality is that all too often we have neither the time

nor the energy to enjoy the fruits of our labour. As a society, we are suffering from frenzy, frustration, and fatigue. To turn around the words of Thorstein Veblen, we have become a "harried working class" rather than a "leisure class."

Hallmark cards, those almost unnerving barometers of American mores, at one time marketed a series of cards that perhaps all too accurately captures the pace of our lives and the busyness of our days.

They were greeting cards for absent working parents to slip under cereal boxes in the morning with the message: "Have a super day at school," or to place on a child's pillow at night: "I wish I were there to tuck you in."

To paraphrase the Bard of Stratford—*Hamlet,* Act 1, Scene 1, Line 67—Me thinks there is something rotten in the state of Denmark!

Anna Quindlen of *Newsweek* has offered us two apparently contradictory pieces of wisdom about the importance of work in our lives.

- "There is nothing so grand in all the world as watching a person who loves what he does do it.
- "You cannot be really first-rate at your work if your work is all you are.

" The bridge between these two seemingly disconnected truths and what puts them into proper perspective, at the individual level, is how we portion out and deal with the rest of our lives. That is, how we handle our nonwork lives, our time off the job, our downtime, our leisure. (Better known in the U. K. as le zh' er and in the U. S. A. as lç'zh er.)

What Quindlen is implying is that to do a job well and enjoy the job you are doing, you have to be suited for it, like it, and not do so much of it that you get lost in it, and forget why you're doing it and/or why it should be done. It's what the actor George C. Scott meant when he explained why, although he preferred the stage to films, he would never do a Broadway show for longer than six months: "You can't do a matinee and two supper shows everyday, week in and week out, and still stay fresh enough to bring anything new to the role."

Exaggeration and details aside (matinees are only on Wednesdays and Saturdays and double evening performances occur only on Friday and Saturday nights, if they happen at all), Scott's meaning is right on target.

Even when you love the job you're doing, you can't do it all the time without losing something. To do almost anything well, you must have time off from it. Time away from constantly doing it. Time to recover and relax. Time to do something else. Time to just forget about it.

Although Mel Brooks as writer, producer, and director of The Producers, and the recipient of twelve Tony Awards, can pull it off, it's still not considered "politically correct" to quote a Nazi, even a repentant one.

Nevertheless, I'm going to anyway Albert Speer, Third Reich minister of technology and armaments, argues in his memoir, *Spandau,* that intentions and ideology aside (no small achievement, of course), Hitler's chief failings as a military leader were overextension, overexertion, and fatigue.

Hitler, said Speer, especially when the war began to turn against Germany, never seriously rested or recreated or could find any downtime, away time from the all-consuming particulars of the war. He took on too much, said Speer, and micromanaged too much. He got lost in the details, and his fatigue often blinded him to the obvious logic of the situation.

History, not so surprisingly, tells us there were other factors in play as well. These were, of course, Hitler's raging paranoia, his all-consuming myopia and narcissism, and his total lack of formal military training. Nevertheless, Speer s insights remain cogent.

Fatigue and the frenzy of overstimulation can block objectivity, delimit perspective, and often deaden our ability to calculate and evaluate logically. Vince Lombardi, NFL coach and football legend, is reported to have said that "fatigue makes cowards and fools of us all and more often than not results in mediocrity. " Another American legend, Gary Cooper, in a less-than-legendary 1953 film, *Seminole,* perhaps put it most succinctly: "Never decide or do anything when you're tired."

A less controversial student of leadership, James MacGregor Burns, suggests that one of the essential qualities of leadership is to bring a "fresh perspective" to the problem, "to think outside the box, " to see beyond the "minutia of excessive details. " Effective leadership, suggests Burns in his Pulitzer Prize-winning study *Leadership*, needs to balance "total immersion" in the issues with "time away" from the issues and problems at hand.

Rest, recreation, and regular vacations should be part of the job description of all forms of leadership. Working longer and working harder does not mean that a leader or any worker is necessarily working smarter or better. As the reclusive philosopher Baruch Spinoza suggested, in order to gain perspective, we need to step back; insight and wisdom are very often best achieved in moments away from the task at hand.

Robert Reich argues that more of us are more prosperous and better off than ever before. We make more. We do more. We own more. But, he said, there is a price to be paid for this prosperity. Paid work is demanding more of our time, more of our energy, and more and more of our emotional and psychological reserves.

He suggests that another big part of the price we pay for our progress and prosperity is that we have lost, if we ever truly understood, the meaning and importance of leisure in our lives.

According to the social commentator Witold Rybczynskl, most Americans are so immersed in the pace, meter, and ethos of their workaday lives that they find it hard to distinguish among such key nonwork terms as lazy, recreation, and leisure and often use them more or less interchangeably. This inability, suggests Rybczynski, may not be critical in regard to common usage, but it does delimit and diminish us both as individuals and as a society.

LAZY

Wayne E. Oates, psychologist, pastoral counselor, and the inventor of the term *workaholic,* argues that as a culture we are steadfastly schizophrenic about our understanding of the term lazy. On the one hand, in our workaday world of intense competition, productivity, and status seeking, to be called lazy is to be despised by others and often by ourselves as well.

"Lazy" is often used as a four-letter word to ridicule individuals who lack energy and effort, or who are slow-moving, sluggish, slothful, or just plain goofing off. To be labeled lazy is to be thought of as immature, undependable, irresponsible, indolent, and/or uselessly idle.

On the other hand, says Oates, we long to be lazy, to do nothing, to be purposely inactive. We crave lazy summer afternoons. We brag about lazy winter weekends or, at the very least, the luxury of "long lazy Sunday mornings with the New York Times.

"In one sense, says Oates, we see being lazy as a status symbol, a badge of honour, a privilege and a right. Although we do not see it as "an inalienable right from birth, " we do think of it as a right we have earned by the fruit of our labour. To be rightfully idle, to be righteously lazy, purposeless, with no tasks to do is a direct reflection of our success at work.

To openly rest, relax, recuperate, to redux (to recover, return to health) without worrying about what others might think is testimony to our success and status as workers. After all, besides being judged by what we do, how much we earn, where we live, and what we own, another index of prestige and pedigree is "acquired time off the job. "

Part of the true luxury of "earned laziness" are the bragging rights that come along with being purposefully and publicly lazy. It is a badge of distinction, an emblem of success, without having to say too much about it.

It labels us, affords us kudos, and raises our profile in the "pecking order" of our fellow troglodytes. It says to others, "See, I've done so well that I can afford to do nothing at all whenever I so choose!" Citing the historian Sebastian de Grazia, Oates reinforces the "importance of being lazy" as both a private and a public good.

Perhaps we can judge the inner health of a land by the capacity of its people to do nothing—to lie in a bed, to amble about aimlessly, to sit having a coffee—because whoever can do nothing, letting his thoughts go where they may, must be at peace with himself.

RECREATION

We all seek to be idle, to be lazy, to enjoy rest as a natural antidote to the fatigue and frustrations of the job. As U. S. Supreme Court Justice Thurgood Marshall, when asked about his plans after retirement, so prosaically put it, "Sit on my rear end!" But even well practiced lassitude has its limits. No one can remain idle forever, except possibly my son—at least when he was a teenager.

After a while, even the benefits of laziness can become a burden or at the very least lead to boredom and the kind of anxiety that results from being excessively idle. All of us naturally seek some form of diversion or recreation. Activities that change the pace, change the place, or change the nature of our usual habits. Activities that effect our enjoyment or relieve our stress. In common parlance, this is what most of us mean by the term *play*.

According to the philosopher Hannah Arendt, from the standpoint of "making a living" every activity which is unconnected to labour and is not necessary either for the life of the individual or the life process of society is subsumed under the term *playfulness*.

Play, from the Middle English *plega,* "to leap for joy, to dance, to rejoice, to be glad, " is about activity outside the sphere of the customary, the necessary, or the materially useful.

The poet Diane Ackerman says "play is a refuge from ordinary life, a sanctuary of the mind, where one is exempt from life's customs, methods, and decrees. " Fellow poet Donald Hall suggests that play is about "absorbedness"—"a noun with a lot of verb in it"—which connotes concentration, contentment, loss of self, loss of time, happiness and joy.

For both children and adults, play is about awe, wonder, rapture, and enthusiasm. Play is something we want to do, something we choose to do that is not work, that we enjoy, and that gives us gratification and fun.

In play, we drop inhibitions, give ourselves permission to imagine, to be creative, to be curious. Play, like laughter, is an end in itself, something done without any other incentive except for the pleasure involved in the activity itself.

Unfortunately, for too many of us our various forms of recreation and play are really about rehabilitation, recuperation, and recovery rather than rapture and the possibility of the rediscovery of self.

This is because, for many of us, our play or diversions are really only momentary distractions from the usual pace of life. They are designed to overcome fatigue, numb awareness, or appease a particular appetite—all for the purpose of reinvigorating and restoring us to the work task at hand.

In other words, a lot of what we do, how we spend our time off the job—hobbies, clubs, organizations, going to films, theater, listening to music, working out, friends, vegging out in front of the TV, whatever—is really about taking a break, filling in time, catching up, recharging our batteries, overcoming our fatigue and feelings of stupification so that we go back to the job to endure and earn more.

Revitalization and rejuvenation, not refinement and reformulation, are really at the heart of much of our nonwork activities. For a lot of us, recreation is therapy, a placebo, or an opiate to get us by and keep us going.

Even actions, activities, or hobbies that seem wholesome, worthwhile, or of some benefit to the actor can be engaged in for all the wrong reasons—to kill time, to provide a socially acceptable form of anesthetic diversion—and thereby do not constitute true play.

I've played a game called handball for thirty years. I love the sport because it requires a combination of strength, endurance, agility, and quick decision making. Unfortunately these are traits and talents I am woefully deficient in. Over the years I have spent a small fortune on magazines, books, group clinics, and private lessons in an attempt to improve my game.

But even with all of this, I remain an erratic and mediocre player. Nevertheless, I play every chance I get for the conditioning effects, because it allows me to be playfully competitive, and because it's a lot of fun.

A number of years ago, I would occasionally play handball before going off to work with a group of men at my local YMCA. One of the guys I was regularly paired with was a solid player who was always looking for a fresh victim.

Although I could stay with him for a while, I could never beat him. He was too talented and tough for me, and although my age, he was in much better shape than I was. Besides playing handball every day, he regularly skipped lunch for an aerobics class, and every other evening he ran three to five miles.

One morning over a postgame cup of coffee, I found out that his workout habits were not based on love of the game, middle-age machismo, or the simple pursuit of physical fitness. He said he played a lot of ball and drove himself hard athletically because he was "bored senseless" with his job, he was caught in a "bad marriage, " and he needed an outlet to maintain his sanity.

He said he had tried drinking for a while, but he just didn't like what the booze did to him. He also said he tried the other "usual male forms" of diversion and escape, but his conscience bothered him too much. So, he said, he had played handball in college and he picked it up again.

"Don't get me wrong, " he told me, "playing a lot of handball doesn't make the job or home any better. But it gives me something to do, someplace to be, and something to look forward to. Think about it. There are a lot worse ways to keep yourself busy!"

LEISURE

Because too many of us live in a world of total work, we think that leisure is at least minimally achieved by the mere absence of work. Because we are so eager to escape the burdens of work, we think that any form of nonwork—quiet time, downtime, doing no-thing in regard to a job time—constitutes some form of rest, recreation, and/or leisure.

Well, we're wrong. To be idle, to be without a task, to be

doing no-thing are prerequisites but not sufficient conditions for the achievement of genuine leisure.

G. K. Chesterton, English essayist, editor, critic, novelist, lecturer, broadcaster—and, ironically, a card-carrying workaholic—spent a great deal of time and energy writing about the exact nature and necessity of leisure. Chesterton argues, like the *Oxford English Dictionary*, that leisure is about "free time, " "time which one can spend as one pleases."

The root of the word leisure comes from the Latin licere, which means "to be permitted, " suggesting that leisure is about unstructured, free-choice time. But, says Chesterton, there are wiser and lesser choices one can make in regard to one's free time. Leisure, he said, can be used to describe three different sorts of things.

"The first (and the most common form of leisure) is being allowed to do something (something other than work). The second is being allowed to do anything (anything that engages your interest or desires). And the third is being allowed to do nothing (a noble habit that is both difficult and rare). "

For Chesterton the "noble habit of doing nothing" means to do no practical, utilitarian or quotidian task. He does not mean that leisure is equal to inertia or tc do nothing at all. Rather, leisure is the opportunity to do other than that which is necessary or required. To do as one pleases. To be freed from the mundane. To be free to pursue the unusual, the inexplicable, the irrelevant, the interesting, and the idiosyncratic.

According to the psychiatrist Leonard Fagin, the concept of control is the crucial psychological distinction between work and leisure.

What characterizes leisure is the feeling, if not the reality, of greater control over one's activity; leisure implies doing what one wants to do with one's "free" or "non-work time. " Fagin argues that although work does not imply a total loss of autonomy and control, one's activities at work are never totally arbitrary and without purpose.

Rather, they are structured, goal oriented, and, more often than not, supervised and monitored. At the very least, says

Fagin, in work one temporarily hands over control to the other agencies.

Ostensibly, this sacrifice of control is done in return for financial gain, which offers the possibility of control over one's "non-work time." Conventional wisdom is clear on the matter: leisure is our time; work belongs to another.

Chesterton's own choices and leisure pastimes included an eclectic mix of the unusual and eccentric—sketching, collecting weapons, and playing with the cardboard cutouts of his toy theater. Another famous Englishman, Winston Churchill, had a few eccentric passions of his own. Churchill was both an accomplished painter (on canvas, not walls) and a bricklayer.

At Chartwell, his rural estate, he built two cottages, a playhouse, and several walls. Both men were amateurs in the best sense of the word. Amateur comes from the Latin *amare*, which means "to love" and connotes "doing something that you love," "doing something without obligation," "doing something as a dilettante or in a nonprofessional capacity." Both men were convinced that leisure meant time free of the encumbrance of convention, free from "business-busyness," free of the constraints of social obligation and duty.

Josef Pieper, in his cult classic *Leisure: The Basis of Culture*, argues that leisure is a necessary condition for both individual and communal survival, growth, and progress. Pieper claims that because so many of us are addicted, by choice or circumstances, to the idolatry of work, we are not sure of what leisure is, and even worse, in the words of Bertrand Russell, we have been tricked into accepting a life without leisure as normal.

Strictly speaking, for Pieper, leisure is not simply a form of recreation or diversion, nor is it the natural result of rest, relaxation, or amusement. Although, it is necessary to be free of the toil and moil of the everyday burdens of work for it to occur, according to Pieper leisure is primarily a mental set, a psychological orientation, a condition of one's soul or spirit.

For Pieper, leisure is an attitude of nonactivity, of not being busy, of inner calm, a commitment to silence, meditation, observation, and letting things be. Leisure is a way of life and not just the inevitable by-product of holidays, spare time, weekends, or a vacation.

> Leisure is a form of silence, of that silence which is the prerequisite of the apprehension of reality...For leisure is a receptive attitude of the mind, a contemplative attitude...
>
> Leisure, like contemplation, is of a higher order than the *vita activa* [active life]...It is only in and through leisure that the "gate of freedom" is opened and man can escape from the closed circle of that "latent dread and anxiety"...the mark of the world of work.

To be leisurely, said Josef Pieper, is a choice. To be leisurely is to be disengaged from the tedium of tasks—to be open, observant, and receptive to issues outside of self and one's immediate needs. Leisure is time given to contemplation, wonder, awe, and the development of ideas. Leisure is about creativity, insight, unregulated thoughts.

It is about intellectual activity, but not intellectual work or utilitarian problem solving. It is about desire, wonder, and unbridled curiosity. For Thomas Aquinas, leisure is the vehicle, the necessary condition for the *vita contemplative* (life of the mind), which is the "noblest mode of human life" and the primary means by which we transcend the limits of the human condition.

Like Aristotle before him, Pieper believed that leisure is the catalyst for culture and the development of philosophy, theology, poetry, and the arts. Culture, for Pieper, is all that which is beyond the immediate sphere of wants and needs. Culture is that which is not absolutely necessary, useful, or utilitarian, but that which ultimately defines us as a species or a group.

In both the *Nicomachean Ethics* and the *Politics* Aristotle argued that leisure is the centre point about which everything revolves. It is leisure, says Aristotle, that is the source of distinction between *artes liberales* (fine arts, liberal arts, an end in itself) and the *artes serviles* (physical and domestic work, for a practical purpose).

For Aristotle it is leisure that distinguishes between a high and low calling, between menial and mental tasks, between physical necessity and intellectual curiosity. Of course, Aristotle had a rather skewed and parochial perspective on exactly who should work and who should enjoy leisure.

To the ancient Greeks, whose physical labour was, in large part, done by slaves, work brutalized the mind and made men unfit for the practice of gentlemanly virtues. The Greeks regarded work as a curse, a drudgery and a heavy-hearted activity.

Plutarch in his chapter on Pericles remarks that no well-born man would want to be the craftsman Phidias. While a gentleman enjoys the contemplation of the sculptor's masterpieces, he himself would never consider using a hammer and chisel and being covered with dust, sweat, and grime.

The Greeks felt that work enslaved the worker, chained him to the will of others, and corrupted his soul. Work by its very nature inhibited the use of reason and thereby impeded the search for the ultimate ends of life. Work was accepted not as an end in itself but as a means by which some might be freed to pursue higher goals.

Aristotle declared that just as the goal of war was peace, so the object of work was leisure. Leisure meant activity pursued free of compulsion or desire for gain, free for the contemplation of philosophical issues and truths. Aristotle would have found the Protestant work ethic's commitment to "work as duty" and "work for work sake alone" completely foreign concepts.

Aristotle saw physical work as a burden which he had no duty to bear. He himself never worked, accepting the slavery of others because it freed him for leisure and the "work of the mind."

Although Josef Pieper 's definition of leisure is drawn from classic, medieval, and Victorian sources, his analysis remains, at least in principle, at the core of two contemporary cultural institutions: vacations and the observation of the Sabbath. In Latin the word for vacation is vacare, "to be empty, nonoccupied, " "to suspend activity, " "to do nothing. " Work represents the everyday routine, and vacations are temporary interruptions.

On vacations we turn aside, go in the opposite direction, vacate ourselves from our usual course or purpose. Vacations connote downtime, choice, freedom, personal discretion, and activities an individual engage in for his or her own purposes and pleasures.

Vacations are seen as an antidote to work. They are medicine, a remedy for counteracting the effects of labour. The psychologist Wayne E. Oates believes that vacations offer us an opportunity to "empty ourselves of our multiple roles in life." Vacations allow us to be away from the job, to change the patterns of our day, to alter our routine, to reconfigure our actions and habits, to rediscover ourselves.

Although it is not true for everyone, we commonly associate vacations or vacationing with traveling. In traveling, we take ourselves outside of ourselves, our normal life, our usual patterns. In traveling we seek delight, diversion, and differences. In traveling, there is the opportunity or potential for solitude, speculation, wonder, and awe.

The Chinese philosopher Lin Yutang said that the true purpose of travel is not rest or recovery but rediscovery and renewal. In travel, he said, we "should become lost and unknown. " He chides vacationers who bring along with them handfuls of letters of introduction so that they will become known wherever they are.

Anonymity, he claims, is far better. To have no fixed hours, no inquisitive neighbors, no mail, no e-mails, telephone calls, or faxes offers us a chance to expand our horizons and reevaluate and possibly redefine who we are. For Lin Yutang, vacations are opportunities to rediscover our basic humanness apart from our accustomed personas and roles in life.

Within the Jewish tradition, the Sabbath (in Hebrew, *Shabbat*, "to rest") is Saturday, the seventh day of the week, a day specifically set aside for rest and religious observance. According to the Book of Exodus, the Fourth Commandment enjoined the Jews: "Six days you shall labour, and do all your work; but the seventh day is a Sabbath to the Lord your God, in it you shall not do any manner of work. "In most Christian traditions, the Sabbath is the first day of the week, Sunday (in Latin, *dies solis*, "day of the sun"). It is observed as a holy day and a holiday in commemoration of the resurrection of Christ.

Although the terms *Sunday* and *Sabbath* are not strictly synonymous, they both connote the imperative to set aside work for the purposes of celebration, recreation, and religious festivity. Moreover, the notion of a "day free from labour" is a cross-cultural historical constant that can be found in numerous ethnic and religious groups—Greeks, Romans, Chinese, Hindus, Buddhists, Taoists, Muslims—and even Marxists.

For the observant Jew, there are in excess of thirty-nine specific Talmudic prohibitions against work on the Sabbath. Since God created all in just six days and rested on the seventh, for men to work or to create on the Sabbath would make them guilty of, at least, vanity and hubris and, possibly, sacrilege. (In the ancient texts, tasks such as sowing, plowing, reaping, threshing, and winnowing are among those things expressly prohibited, as are grinding, sifting, weaving, hunting, and slaughtering, building, hammering, and transporting.

And there are, of course, by way of analogy a whole host of modern prohibitions such as not turning on an electric light, watching TV, or using the phone.) But at the heart of Sabbath prohibitions lies a larger and more humanly profound message.

The Sabbath is a day of celebration and joy. On the Sabbath, the good Jew is required by rule to be thankful for all of God's goodness and to celebrate that goodness with one's friends and family with wine, fun, and play. In other words, they are required to show their gratitude for life by giving themselves over to leisure and play

The Christian version of this Commandment reads: "Remember to keep holy the Lord's Day. " Within the Catholic Church it was a mortal sin (punishable by eternal damnation) not to attend church or to do any unnecessary or avoidable work on a Sunday. It was also considered a venial sin (a blot on one's soul, but not one warranting absolute damnation) to go shopping on a Sunday. Within all Christian sects, the Lord's Day was a day committed to prayer, leisure, and family.

The theologian Matthew Fox observes that the purpose behind all these various religious rules and restrictions was to disconnect us from the world of work and the usual rhythms of life in order to remind ourselves of higher values and greater purposes.

Jesus told us, says Fox, "that the Sabbath is for people, not the people for Sabbath. " Sabbath is not about the rules, per se. It is about wonder, joy, and delight. It is about the "sanctity of time," the "architecture of time," and the "architect of time." It is about marveling at the complexity and mystery of reality. It is an interlude from the tyranny of the commonplace.

It is being able to do something without a why It is the celebration of the obvious and the obtuse. It is about relaxation, effortlessness. It is a pause, a moment for a brief spiritual vacation and renewal. Sabbath, suggests Fox, is space and time created to say yes to spirituality, sensuality, sexuality, prayer, rest, song, and delight. Only when we cease our daily labour do we have time for love, friendship, God, and ourselves. In celebrating Sabbath we are saying to the world, "Today I'm going to pamper my soul. "

In the Middle Ages, Thomas Aquinas wrote: "It is necessary for the perfection of human society that there should be men [people] who devote their lives to contemplation. " He believed leisure was essential to civilization because leisure allows us the serenity to recognize the differences between the mysterious and the mundane.

Leisure offers us openness to ourselves and others. Leisure allows us to muse, meditate, and wonder, to find perspective beyond the immediate and the necessary Leisure allows us to be more than workers; to no longer be mere functionaries of the system; to be "unfettered from the process of work. "

The bottom line seems fairly obvious. We are marked, molded, identified, and known to ourselves and others by what we do for a living (work) and how we play (leisure). The question is, have we made the equation too one-sided? Is the world too busy for genuine leisure anymore? Are we all too addicted, too dependent, too needful of work to step away from it, even for a while?

Why is it that for so many of us, leisure has been reduced to recuperation and indulgence? Why is it that so many of us have neither the time, the discipline, nor the tolerance for quiet, solitude, and wonder? Why is it that so many of us think that constant busyness and noise are normal, and that silence is a void waiting to be filled? Why is it that so many of us need to "fill in" and "fill up" all of our time both on and off the job? Why is it that so many of us work at play as hard as or harder than we do at work?

Chapter 10

Vacations and Traveling

According to family folklore, except for a few brief honeymoons, none of us had taken a real vacation until 1954. That summer, my father, mother, aunt, uncle, and myself piled into my dad's brand new, sky-blue Oldsmobile Rocket 88 (eight cylinders, 320 horsepower, hydromatic drive, oversized white-wall tires, AM-radio, and no air conditioner!), and we drove cross-country from Chicago to Boise to Los Angeles to the Grand Canyon, and back to Chicago again—all in two weeks, to see family, friends, and the wild, wild west! It was like undergoing two weeks of root canal surgery. Surprisingly, we all got along amazingly well. The problems were not with the personalities involved, but the amenities of the road.

You've got to remember that these were the days before chain restaurants, chain motels, and an interlinking chain of interstate highways with restrooms and information kiosks regularly dotting the roadway.

The song may have said, "Get your kicks on Route 66, " but kicks were pretty hard to come by when the only thing out there for hundreds of miles at a time was an occasional Stuckeys or a Texaco gas station with dirty bathrooms and a Coca-Cola machine which was invariably empty or broken.

And then there was the problem of lodging. The hotels (or motor courts as I believe they were then called) that were available were either tiny cubicles, freestanding cabins or huts, or something right out of Alfred Hitchcock—Mrs. Bates' Hotel/Motel, "Travelers Welcome!" Believe me, Chevy Chase's odyssey to Wally World with his collective menagerie had nothing on us!

Since the 1950s, generations of American families have been taking cross-country vacations just as we did. According to the American Automobile Association, motoring remains the number one way families travel while on vacation. There are, however, some important differences and nuances between motoring then and now.

To begin with, the sedans of yesterday have been replaced with vans and SUVs. Air conditioning is now considered standard, AM-radio has been augmented by FM-radio, cassette players, CD players, and, in trucks and vans, TV monitors and VCR players. Rest stops with clean restrooms are at regular intervals on President Eisenhower's legacy of 43,000-plus miles of stoplight-free roads linking every major city in America.

Restaurants catering to the needs of families on the go can be found at almost every exit. And, finally, motel chains are everywhere. They all may be cookie-cutter in design, but most of them are safe, clean, reasonably priced, and convenient. (Of course, certain things never change. Both then and now, each room comes with its own copy of the Gideon Bible in either a standard or pocket-size book format.)

The other major differences, I think, came about because of changes in the structure of families, job demands, kids' schedules, and finances.

For example, the standard two-week vacation is a thing of the past. Most road trips now range from two to five days, and of course cover shorter distances. Most trips are to a specific location and not simply an attempt to fulfill Dinah Shore's commercial jingle from the early 1950s: "See the USA in your Chevrolet, America is waiting for you to call. Drive your Chevrolet across the USA, America is the greatest land of all."

And yet, for all these differences, there are some things that remain the same: kids asking, "Are we there yet?"; fights over radio stations, music selection, and volume; mothers yelling, "Can't you two play nicely together?"; and—the dire warning of dads—"Listen, if I have to, I'll turn this car around right now! Believe me, I will do it! And, you will be sorry!" (Yeah, right!)

Cruising cross-country to California in my dad's Oldsmobile was the last family vacation we ever took, and the very last vacation I was ever on until I took my family in the early 1970s to Colorado in the claustrophobic confines of a Volkswagen Beetle. (Isn't it funny how ontogeny reduplicates phylogeny?)

After my childhood California extravaganza, vacations to me meant being out of school, staying at grandma's, playing baseball almost every day, going to a double feature on Wednesdays, taking the bus to the beach, and every once in a while, going on a picnic in a local forest preserve.

My parents always took their vacation time, but they didn't do anything with it. We stayed pretty much close to home. My dad had more days off than my mom. But most of the time he worked a second job, or played golf (his one great passion), or did chores around the house. None of my grandparents went on vacation either.

The only traveling they had ever done was when they migrated to this country from Italy. In fact, my father and both my grandfathers complained that the only time they had traveled—for my dad to fight in World War II and for my grandfathers in third-class steerage from Naples to New York—they hated it.

So why, they asked, would they choose to do it again? The only member of my family to travel was my Uncle Joe. He and my Aunt Theresa took every chance they could to go on vacation. I thought them exotic world travelers. At least three times a year, they went to Wisconsin to fish!

In some sense the history of my family reflects the history and evolution of vacationing in this country. Vacations are both a private event and a social institution. As a private event, they say something about us at the level of class, cash, and culture. The same must be said of vacation as a social institution.

When vacations become part of a society, they say something about the pedigree of that society at the level of education, finance, infrastructure, social enlightenment, and civil rights. Vacations do not occur in a vacuum. They are the result and the expression of other economic, political, and philosophical values.

As Professor Cindy S. Aron has argued in her insightful and informative study *Working at Play: A History of Vacations in America*, vacations tell us much about the society and even more about the vacationer. "More than just yearly rituals…," argues Aron, "vacations are also exercises in self-definition. In affording time away from the demands of everyday life, vacations disclose what people choose to do rather than are required to do."

For the most part, until well into the twentieth century, travel of any kind was a restricted prerogative of the wealthy or an absolute necessity for the desperate and the poor. Whether motivated by desire or need, traveling by any means (ship, rail, or coach) was arduous, complicated, slow, and costly.

One needed a strong stomach, a hearty constitution, steady sea legs, patience, and goodly amounts of cash to endure the ordeal. Even in the later part of the nineteenth century, in the age of advanced sail (clipper ships and combination steam and sail vessels), few individuals gladly embraced or eagerly sought out a two-to-four-week transatlantic crossing unless the motivation was necessity, business, or the prospect of high adventure.

None of this means, of course, that everyone stayed home. The seventeenth, eighteenth, and nineteenth centuries were, according to the historian Daniel J. Boorstin, all part of the "great age of discovery and exploration." Led, first, by explorers and adventurers, followed by soldiers, missionaries, and merchants—as well as economic misfits and political and religious malcontents—hundreds of thousands sought out the "New World" for a chance at a new beginning.

In 1565, Pedro Menendez de Auiles, a Spanish smuggler and soldier of fortune with a ragtag army of 1,500, built the first permanent European settlement on American soil at St. Augustine, Florida. In 1620 the good ship *Mayflower* deposited its 101 seasick and disoriented passengers on the rocky shores of Plymouth, Massachusetts.

And between 1815 and 1914, more than 30 million Europeans left their homelands to settle in the "New World." It was by far the greatest mass movement in human history.

During these years, the trail of traffic was not just one-way and not only limited to the purposes of commerce and migration. There was also a small but steady reverse flow of travelers from the "New World" back to the "Old."

In the main, most traveled for business, but increasingly after the Civil War more and more traveled for culture and play For those afflicted with wanderlust and possessing the wherewithal to act on it, Boston and New York were regular points of departure for Europe and other ports of call. If one were looking for a typical family of nineteenth-century travelers, I believe the Henry James family of New York, Massachusetts, Rhode Island, and points beyond would do nicely.

Henry James Sr. was the son and heir of a successful businessman who left him with an income of $10,000 a year. Freed of the necessity of earning a living, Henry pursued philosophy, religion, and the international education of his five children, the two oldest being William James (the philosopher who wrote like a novelist) and Henry James Jr. (the novelist who wrote like a philosopher).

From the time they were toddlers to teenagers, Henry Sr. shepherded his children along with his wife and a gaggle of nannies, relatives, and friends, plus steamer trunks and boxes of books, back and forth across the Atlantic (at least ten times) in the pursuit of special classes, tutors, exhibitions, and historic points of interest.

Although the family usually traveled first-class and had the financial means to insulate themselves from the usual indignities and inefficiencies of travel, according to family letters and diaries, the children loathed the transatlantic passages and considered them an ordeal rather than an opportunity. Only the stubborn determination and the deep pockets of Henry Sr. kept them at it.

Today, thanks to a long series of economic and technological innovations, you no longer have to be a scion of wealth or a sadist to take your family to Europe or other faraway places on a regular basis. (During the economic good times of the Clinton years, round trip New York to London by air was just over $400 a ticket.

And Chicago to Cape Town could be had for $1,600.) In general, Americans' appetite for traveling has grown exponentially It is estimated that we spend in excess of half a trillion dollars a year on vacations, and the international airlines industry claims to handle an estimated 670 million passengers a year.

For our immediate purposes, let's set aside the small fraction of the population that sailed the high seas in pursuit of business and commerce or leisure and play, and briefly look at how most Americans have historically sought to use their vacation time. To begin with, prior to the 1850s, few Americans would have used the word *vacation* to describe pleasure travel or time devoted to recreation, recuperation, or play.

According to Cindy Aron, most Americans used "vacation" or "vacation time" to refer to students' or teachers' breaks from school or college. It was only in the mid-1850s that "vacation" crept into private use and published works to describe something more than just "time off."

For example, an 1855 editorial in the *New York Times* titled "Vacations for Businessmen" urged men to "grasp at less and enjoy more. " Incessant work, the editorial warned, would result in a life "sans health, sans stomach, sans capacity for all better and higher things. "

But more than just a shift in terminology, the mid—nineteenth century saw a shift in how Americans looked at play. Our Puritan heritage saddled us with a legacy that denigrated amusement, pleasure, and play. Recreation, said our Puritan forefathers, is something that restores a person to better work and service.

Amusement left people wasted and exhausted. Amusement was "pleasure for pleasure's sake alone. " Scripture, they claimed, endured recreation but forbade amusement. As a certified curmudgeon, Thomas MacAulay, pointed out: "The Puritan hated bear-baiting not because it gave pain to the bear, but because it gave pleasure to the spectators. " Eventually, of course, the slow decline of strict Calvinist ideas led to a change in our attitude regarding recreation and amusement and to a new "cultural permission" to play.

An 1848 article in the Unitarian magazine *Christian Examiner* argued that "amusements under the plan of Providence, form an essential part of the great system of influence by which human faculties are trained.... A sufficient reason for participating in them is that they give pleasure. "

Again, in 1848 the prominent Congregationalist minister Horace Bushnell preached that "no creature lives that must not work and may not play" Aron interprets Bushnell's message to read: "people work because they must, because prudence impels" and they play because they must as well. Play, for Bushnell, came from "a fund of life that wants to expend itself. " Bushnell saw work as an "activity for an end, " while play was an "activity as an end. " Bushnell thus challenged the reigning "work ethic" that found play acceptable only when it "prepares [us] for new scenes of labour and usefulness!"

Of course, no matter what one's theology, vacations of any kind, under any rubric, and the pursuit of pleasure and play in any form were dependent upon the financial wherewithal to allow for the suspension of work. In other words, as Cindy Aron clearly argues, for a long time in this society only the wealthy and the prominent could actually take a vacation and pursue play.

To paraphrase Ernest Hemingway, the rich have always been different from us. They've got a lot more money, and a lot more options, too!

Long before an American middle class existed at all, a tiny number of eighteenth-century elites made their way to a handful of springs and seaside resorts for the purpose of rest, recuperation, and relaxation.

In the nineteenth century, a slightly expanded privileged elite sought out vacations at posh and very exclusive watering holes both for the purposes of pleasure and play and as a demonstration of their affluence, social standing, and sophistication. In other words, one went to Saratoga Springs, New York, or Berkeley Springs, Virginia to be amused and entertained and, of course, to be seen. The ability to take a vacation, to take time off, to travel, to be seen, was a statement to oneself and others about one's class and social place.

Although the sacred sanctuaries of the elite remained relatively unsullied by the touch or appearance of commoners or clerks, from the middle of the nineteenth through the middle of the twentieth century there has been a steady democratization of vacations starting with the emergence of the middle class and then passing down this privilege to the lower working classes. As Cindy Aron correctly argues, the history of vacations in America is a reflection of the history of America.

As we became an urban society based on industry rather than agriculture, with a growing and increasingly sophisticated transportation network, what resulted was a general increase in prosperity, more free time, and the creation of a large middle class. These changes allowed both a new vacationing public and new vacationing places to develop and take shape.

Just as the privileged elite saw vacations as a social perk and a badge of honour, so did the middle class. Vacationing became one of the central accoutrements of middle-class refinement and status.

According to Cindy Aron:

Historians have determined various ways in which middle class Victorians distinguished themselves from members of the working class: the nature of their non-manual employment, their urban residential patterns, their adoption of a set of values that privileged domesticity and privacy, their embrace of refined manners and the trappings of respectability, and their behaviour as consumers. I argue that vacationing become another critically important marker of middle class status.

Middle class men and women not only claimed the privilege of vacationing, but also made that privilege into a middle class entitlement. By the turn of the twentieth century the middle class had established vacaioning as a requirement for its physical health and for its spiritual and emotional well-being as well.

The arrival of vacations as a mass phenomenon for the working class did not take hold until the mid-1930s. And although many reformers saw it as a simple matter of justice, many who advocated vacations for the working class were motivated by practical and not by philanthropic reasons.

Social critics and businessmen alike argued that it made good sense to rest both the workers and the equipment in order to guarantee the best possible results. After all: "The human machine, like its mechanical namesake, needs a period of rest and recuperation in order to stay fit. "

Aron points out that the "kindheartedness" of other reformers was also less than purely altruistic in its motivation.

Hoping to stabilize their work force and discourage unionization, a few *progressive companies* began to consider plans to improve the quality of workers' lives. A small minority of forward-looking welfare capitalists argued that showers, clean washrooms, dining rooms, company picnics and vacations would increase workers loyalty, raise productivity, and decrease the appeal of labour unions. Happy workers, they suggested, were more productive workers.

Whether or not the workforce was generally happier and more productive because of their vacation time off the job is hard to determine. But what is clear is that after Americans had endured the Great Depression and survived World War II, vacations and vacationing became an entrenched part of their way of life.

While certainly not every worker took exotic trips to faraway places, knowing that they had "time off" coming to them played an important part in maintaining their mental wellbeing.

Safari is a Swahili word meaning "journey" or "to travel, " but it has come to mean so very much more. Imbued with a sense of the exotic, the word has today become symbolic of something far more romantic. It evokes images of adventure and stylish indulgence as portrayed by actors Meryl Streep and Robert Redford in the 1985 film version of Karen Blixen's *Out of Africa*.

Although a good number of us do take "high-end" trips, the vast majority just go on vacation and not on safari. And although our tastes on vacations range from the pedestrian to the posh, most of us settle for the "golden mean" in hopes of getting the biggest bang for our vacation bucks.

But whether we literally head off on a safari or simply set out to see the sites of Williamsburg, Virginia, what we are all secretly seeking is an adventure. Of course, the adventure we are seeking is not necessarily the overhyped Hollywood version of something "unusual, stirring, expensive, and, of course, romantic. " I think the adventure we more realistically desire conforms to the word's original meaning in Latin: *adventura, advenire,* "that which happens without design; chance, happenstance, luck!"

What most of us would gladly settle for on vacation is far from exotic and is definitely not dependent on the daring deeds of Indiana Jones. We want a break from the normal routine: different, interesting, and pleasant surroundings; a couple of laughs; a few decent meals that we don't have to prepare for ourselves; and, hopefully, walking away from it all without the feeling of being financially ripped off or rudely treated along the way It may not be the sum total of the American Dream that our Founding Fathers envisioned, but it sure goes a long way to fulfill at least a part of it: the pursuit of Happiness!

Since World War II, cars, trains, buses, and planes have changed how and when we travel and where we travel to. Convenient means of transportation meant that the vacationing public "no longer needed months of free time or buckets of money to travel." Of course in the last twenty-five years some things have changed.

For example, except for short-distance commuting, trains are really no longer in the "long haul" passenger business; and, rightly or wrongly, buses are, for most travelers, considered déclassé and the transportation vehicle of last resort.

According to the American Automobile Association, what has not changed in decades is that 80 per cent of all Americans who go on vacation drive. Driving remains the number one way to travel up to a thousand miles away from home.

Anyone who has been near a major airport in the summer knows that aviation is the commercial backbone of not just local but global public transportation and travel. The price of gas, the wear and tear on the car, the wear and tear of small children on your psyche, and the fewer number of days we go on vacation have led more and more vacationers (married or single, with or without children) to consider flying a necessity, not an option.

There are, of course, trade-offs: security checks, long delays, overbooking, cramped seating, bad food (airline food—a true oxymoron that cannot be eclipsed even by Enron's recent contribution to the term *business ethics*), and lost luggage, but nobody ever said progress didn't come at a price.

So where do we all go when we go on our private or familial odysseys? Not so surprisingly, an awful lot of us are pretty pedestrian in the use of our vacation time. It has been my experience that if you randomly survey a hundred people about how they spend their vacations the answers you will get are not scientific, and not always exactly the same, but they conform to a strikingly consistent pattern.

Ten per cent will gleefully report about doing something incredibly exotic: flying to Cape Town, South Africa, to go cage diving with great white sharks; sixteen days trekking through Tanzania; or a rafting trip down the Sepik River in Papua, New Guinea. Another 10 per cent will report that they did nothing on their vacation.

That is, due to lack of interest or lack of funds, instead of taking an exotic trip, they did some chores around the house, took a trip to the zoo, took in a few museums, and spent a long day and night at their closest Six Flags amusement park.

About 40 per cent of those polled will tell you that they had a wonderful time on their vacations even if their destinations of choice were not sites "where no man has ever gone before. " These are the folks—"not that there is anything wrong with their choices, " to cite Jerry Seinfeld—who help maintain camping out as our number one outdoor vacation activity.

These are the folks for whom Disneyland and Disney World are the family vacation destinations of choice. Without children, of course, the adult version of Disneyland is Las Vegas. And for salty silver-haired seniors, it would be Branson, Missouri, where Andy Williams sings "Moon River" at three supper shows nightly And, lest we forget, for those who love country and blue grass music, there's the Dolly Parton theme park, Dollywood in Pigeon Forge, Tennessee.

These are the individuals, couples, and families who go on the grand tour of our national treasures and sacred sites: the Grand Canyon, Niagara Falls, Mammoth Cave in Kentucky, Washington, Boston, Mount Vernon, Monticello, and Gettysburg.

These are the folks who attend sports camps, Shakespeare festivals, and/or Bible study camps. These are the people who try to make it to Europe every third year. These are the hard-core vacationers and tourists who make detailed plans and carefully manage their budgets so that they can take an annual vacation.

These are the people who help maintain the collective corporate coffers of the travel industry. And let s give credit where credit is due: these are the people who, though their tastes and destination preferences vary widely, genuinely enjoy traveling. These are the people who hunger for vacation out of inclination, addiction, or desire.

And then there's the surprising 40 per cent of us who report visiting family and friends on their vacations. On reflection, perhaps we really shouldn't be shocked by this statistic. Going to see loved ones has historically always been a major reason for traveling.

And now, given the fluidity of our lives, our mobility, our multiple job changes, more and more of us live away from our families and our friends because they are scattered about everywhere. So naturally, our vacation time may be the only opportunity we have to get together.

Going to see grandma and grandpa, or spending a week with your brother or best friend from college, does not, of course, mean you do nothing else but spend time with them. Visitors usually end up doing a lot of the stuff that tourists usually do—dinners out, shopping, a little sightseeing.

The main problem that was reported to me by a number of people who regularly take "family-visit vacations" is what one of them called "vacation- interruptus" or "vacation-incompletus!"

That is, going to see family and friends is a vacation of sorts—you're someplace else, you're doing things, you're having fun—but you're constantly trying to balance your wants and desires with those of others. Because of all this and the sheer numbers involved in the project, the first casualty is usually the possibility of anything resembling "spontaneity" or "adventure." Moreover, the concepts of silence, solitude, and rest rarely enter into the equation.

Putting aside my limited survey, I have also found a growing number of people for whom vacations are anything but pedestrian. The past few decades have seen the rise of adventure travel, ecotravel, and archaeological travel, and now there are vacations that "take you to the limit"—extreme sports vacations.

What defines an extreme sport? While there is no exact definition, it doesn't take a genius to figure out that all of them have an above-average propensity to result in death, injury, or maiming. Here are just a few examples: rock climbing, bungee jumping, white-water rafting, base jumping [B-A-S-E, an acronym for parachutists jumping off buildings, antennas, spans (bridges), and earth (cliffs)], bridge swinging, street luge, downhill roller blading, surfing in typhoonlike swells, skiing/snowboarding in avalanche country, and aerobatic parachuting.

Although extreme sports can be a local weekend activity (e.g. parachuting), many of them require time and travel (mountain climbing, skiing) and therefore, most extreme sport athletes dedicate their vacation time to their sport of choice. Extreme sports is about pushing boundaries, taking risks, leaving safety behind to leap into the void. Extreme sports is about a radical rush of adrenaline. It's about forgetting about standards of safety. It's about not being cerebral. It's about *not having control* over the elements. It's not about winning, it's about *not losing, not dying*. It's about elevating risk to the extreme. It's about living through the experience. Simply, it's about the afterglow pleasure of survival.

Clearly, extreme sports vacations are not for the faint of heart. The psychologist Frank Farley of Temple University suggests that the rise of extreme sports is a direct reflection of two human characteristics that also have a predominant role in forming our national character. That is, we are a nation of risk takers and we hate being bored so much that we will take outrageous chances to challenge ourselves and overcome the tedium of monotonous regularity

As we function in the new millennium, I do not think that Americans will embark on a national orgy of thrill seeking and risk taking, but I do understand why so many of us are drawn to it: it's a combination of the thrill of the unknown, novelty, dancing with danger, and the irresistible possibility of the joy of play—no matter what the downside. We are, after all, curious creatures and thrill seekers.

According to Eric Perlman, a mountaineer and filmmaker specializing in extreme sports: "Every human being with two legs, two arms is sometime going to wonder how fast, how strong, how enduring he or she is. We are designed to experiment or die."

Hey, football is for weaklings! Why do they need all those pads? Naked bungee jumping, anyone?

Although the concept of vacations is part and parcel of our general cultural expectations, it is not a reality in the life of every worker. According to a 2001 report by the American Family Institute of New York, one-quarter of the American workforce does not take a regular vacation; two-thirds of people who earn $ 10,000 or less a year take less than one week off per year; and, day workers, who regularly experience "enforced time off" (not hired for the day) take zero planned vacation days off.

And let's not forget George Will's assertion that 40 per cent of working Americans work even when they are ostensibly at play, remaining in "daily contact with their offices, by e-mail, from their cabins, by cell phones from their canoes."

The American Family Institute claims that according to this survey what results from no vacation time or too little vacation has immediate and long-term consequences both for the employee and the employer: stress, burnout, lack of focus, increased mistakes, diminished creativity, troubled relationships on and off the job, disruption of sleeping patterns, and health problems.

Garrison Keillor, National Public Radio superstar and official spokesman for the "town that time forgot," Lake Wobegon, Minnesota, recently wrote an essay complaining about spending too much of his life working. Back when he was a kid, said Keillor, he spent his summers picking potatoes at a neighbor's farm.

It was dusty, body-aching, boring work, but he kept at it because he was ashamed and afraid to complain or quit. He had been told that work was a challenge, a duty, and a demonstration of manliness. He was warned that if he quit work, his life would lose meaning and purpose and he would be unable to bear the shame. So, he said, he spent a lot of years dutifully picking potatoes in one form or another.

Finally, however, after achieving fame, fortune, success, and open-heart surgery, he's begun to change his mind.

It's a lovely life, doing nothing. God never intended for me to work hard. I can see that now. My true calling is to live unencumbered and follow the fleeting impulses of my heart and take a nap around 2 P. M. whether I want to or not. I worked hard for years out of plain fear and ignorance and also to impress women and have the funds to take them to restaurants that serve poached salmon with a light saffron sauce on a bed of roses and then bring them home to Tara and when they say, "Wow! What a big house you have!" to say, "Come in and let me show you my art."

Joe Robinson, former editor of the now (sadly) defunct

adventure-travel magazine Escape, completely agrees with Keillor. We have to work less to be more, says Robinson. In this society we perversely allow "downtime for machinery for maintenance and repair, but we don't allow it for the employees. " Americans' most hazardous work-related illness, says Robinson, is vacation deficit disorder or vacation starvation.

Mind you, Robinson, entrepreneur and business owner himself, is not against the work ethic per se. It's the crazed, psychotic overwork ethic, says Robinson, that needs a pink slip. So, he and his fellow workers at the magazine formed a committee called Work to Live.

The purpose of the committee was to gather as many signatures as possible to present to the U. S. Congress to prove that there is an enthusiastic constituency for working to live, not just living to work. Robinson's battle cry is one we've all, sorta, heard before: *Workers and travelers of America, Unite! We have nothing to lose but our stress!"*

Escape's petition for federally required vacation time was nonpartisan and elegantly simple.

We the undersigned urge you to amend the Fair Labour Standards Law so that every American who has worked at a job for at least a year gets three weeks paid leave, increasing to four weeks after three years—by federal law, as Europeans do. In a recent interview Robinson told me that in May 2002 he had presented 50,000 signatures to the labour staffs of Senator Ted Kennedy (Massachusetts) and Representative Henry A. Waxman's (California).

Now, says Robinson, all of his efforts have shifted to lobbying Congress to make required vacations the law of the land. "The key point to keep in mind, " says Robinson, "is that we're the only industrialized nation without a minimum paid leave law.

Furthermore, " he argues, "the lack of legitimization via a law is largely responsible for the squirminess people feel when they're on vacation, and for all the stalling, canceling, and abbreviating of vacations!"

According to Robinson a work to live law would:

- Stipulate minimum paid leave of three weeks for anyone who has worked at a job for over a year, increasing to four weeks after three years
- Protect employees against any retaliation for taking all the vacation coming to them, and end the fear of replacement, demotion, or promotion fallout from taking a vacation
- Protect against employers stalling or chilling vacations with chronic cancellations
- Prevent vacations from shrinking when an employee changes jobs. You will always get three weeks after you spend a year at a job.
- Provide that after three months with a company and up through the first year an employee would receive a pro rated share of vacation. For example, at six months you would get 1.5 weeks off.

In the summer of 2001, before the horrors of September 11 and its terrible aftermath, the nation was scandalized by the behaviour of its new president, George W. Bush. Thankfully, Mr. Bush did not raise our collective eyebrows for any of the reasons his predecessor regularly shocked us. But what he did, did indeed shock and surprise us! He went on vacation for a month!

Of course, the papers, the pundits, and the pollsters had a field day with it. "For an *employee* who's been on the job just eight months, George W. Bush certainly is not shy about using his vacation benefits," chirped the *Chicago Tribune*. "Most of us," declared one slightly outraged radio commentator, "get a week off after one year, two weeks after two, and if we work for a, so called, benevolent company, maybe we get three weeks after ten years on the job! So what's with him?"

A Gallup poll found that 48 per cent of Americans thought that "the President should not take more than three weeks (of vacation)." And lots of other people, in my own informal poll, told me that the presidency was too important a job to take thirty days off.

Actually he revised his plans and took only 27days. (Question: Doesn't anybody remember Jimmy Carter? He was, and is, a great man, the 2002 winner of the Nobel Prize for Peace, but he was not an effective president. Part of the reason, was that he micromanaged everything. He worked long hours every day and never took a vacation if he could avoid it.)

The joke is, of course, that President Bush was, in some sense, on vacation in name only. Yes, he left Washington and went to his Texas ranch. Yes, he played golf with his father and predecessor, George H. Bush.

And, yes, he had some friends over for a barbecue and to watch a ballgame. But at the same time, as president of the United States, custom and statute required that he be briefed daily on domestic and international affairs. He always has with him at least a skeleton staff of advisers and aides who bring him work that has to be done. And, I believe, as commander in chief of the armed forces, he is obligated to travel with a military attaché who has access to our central military command centre should the president need to act on a military emergency.

Let's be honest, the president's vacation was at best "a working vacation. " He spent a little time cutting brush and doing chores around his ranch. Hc put in a couple of hours pounding nails for Habitat for Humanity He went to New Mexico for the first day of school. He made a nationally televised speech on stem cell research. He pressed the flesh with locals around Waco, Texas.

And he talked to local farmers and corn growers about the new global agricultural market. You may call this a vacation, but I won't The president may have wanted to get away, may have wanted to play a little and rest a littlc, and hc did. But it's not all he did.

Mr. Bush is our first MBA president and he has in fact been consciously conducting himself in office as a CEO of a very large business firm. I think his first vacation is a perfect extension of this CEO model—he spent his vacation multitasking! According to a survey by the American Management Association, CEOs and senior executives may travel far away on vacation, but they're never far from the concerns and problems of the officeplace. "Some 26 per cent will be in daily contact with their offices while on vacation, and two-thirds will check in at least once a week.

Of these 34 per cent remain in touch by e-mail and 52 per cent rely on cell phones. " As one chief executive officer put it: "You just keep doing what you do, just from a different location. With e-mail, faxes, and cell phones, you'd have to go to the South Pacific Islands to truly get away from your job. " Except if you were the president, of course. For sure, he'd still be connected.

Well, maybe the president of the United States and the CEOs of Fortune 1000 firms are bad examples of what we mean by going on vacation. But are there any good examples anymore? Can't people go away and stay disconnected, even for a while? Is the new model for vacationing the Gateway computer ad that features a woman working her laptop while paddling a kayak?

Whatever happened to the notion that a well-rested president or ________ (fill in the blank) is a better president or ________ (fill in the blank) ? Whatever happened to the once-time-honored ideals of doing "no-thing" while on vacation? Whatever happened to the notion of lounging, loafing, and just plain old recuperating from our labors?

There are environmental, economic and socio-cultural benefits of ecotourism, all of which can be especially helpful to less developed countries. Often, development of sites for the purpose of ecotourism can result in more careful preservation of the environment and more effort may be dedicated towards the upkeep of the site's natural state. Through increased recognition of the importance of protecting biological diversity, ecotourism may raise appreciation for biological resources and reduce the release of pollution or contaminants into potential sites.

Economically, ecotourism has the potential to be very constructive. Nature tourists bring with them money to spend – strengthening a country's economy. Along with capital generated from the site itself, the business created by ecotourism enterprises includes tour agencies and guide services, lodges and private reserves, as well as a wide variety of food and transportation services. The country is then free to use this generated income in operating and protecting natural habitats as well as building social infrastructure. Locally, the most immediate and direct economic benefits can be seen in improvements made in employment and income.

Local communities living at ecotourism sites generally possess low incomes; ecotourism may be a viable option for bolstering of the local economy with the provision of new jobs. The introduction and subsequent spread of ecotourism may also encourage deviation from the standard logging, mining, land clearing and agricultural practices that are generally featured in such communities. These activities, which may lead to severe environmental damage and ecological imbalance, may be replaced by ecotourism, which altogether may result in a more economically and environmentally sustainable development strategy.

Because the majority of ecotourists are travelers seeking authentic and distinctive experiences, there exists an added incentive for local communities to preserve traditional culture and customs. Preservation of religion, traditional architecture, art and music may be encouraged. Thus, a country's socio-cultural aspects may flourish under the introduction of ecotourism.

Disadvantages of Ecotourism

While there can be advantages associated with ecotourism, there are also costs. One of the most fundamental issues surrounding ecotourism is whether the practice is truly beneficial for the environment — often, economically successful ecotourism, being a primarily consumer-centered activity, requires the construction of water treatment plants, sanitation services, housing facilities and other visitor-targeted buildings.

This construction may cause strain on the environment and, overall, may cause more damage than good. Another basic issue surrounding the practice of ecotourism is the lack of enforced standards regarding its functions. For example, in Costa Rica, there are few national laws or policies that dictate who exactly can carry out and develop ecotourism and also how it must be managed. Licensing procedures are absent and with no formal regulations restricting ecotourism operators, unsafe forms of "ecotourism" harmful to the environment and non-adherence to basic principles of conservation and sustainability are able to grow. Other challenges can be met when ecotourism management institutions fail to distribute money evenly and appropriately. Often, administration teams may dedicate a large amount of the budget to the initial opening cost, leaving little for adequate park management and programming.

As a result, problems such as trail deterioration, habitat disruption and contamination become more common. Over-visitation is another risk and without the proper direction of ecotourists to less fragile areas, environments are more vulnerable to degradation. In addition to the ecological and biophysical problems associated with ecotourism, there are other economic and socio-cultural drawbacks as well.

While ecotourism can be responsible for some development of the local economy, other local economic activities can be disturbed by the introduction of this form of tourism. In some instances, income from ecotourism may be repatriated to a national tour operator or an international tourism agency, with little benefit going toward the betterment of the local community. As well, the strain that an increase in visitors can have on a nation may a detrimental effect on the local cultural practices. Countries that may have been previously isolated from foreign visitation may experience a sudden influx of tourists and may be forced to adapt and as a result, regional culture and lifestyles may suffer.

Ecotourism and Environment

While the success of any ecotourism venture relies on the condition of a nation's ecosystem, some environmentalists believe that the economic benefits ecotourism are not sufficient motivation for true environmental conservation. For instance, while Eva Garen believes that the ideals behind ecotourism are laudable, she claims in the end ecotourism does more harm than good. Deborah McLauren offers a more radical critique of ecotourism, arguing that ecotravel is an oxymoron since travel, at its base, is detrimental to the environment.

She sites the fossil fuels used and pollution that jet airplanes emit as evidence that international travel and environmental protection are mutually exclusive by their very nature. However, despite its inadequacies, ecotourism offers one of the most environmentally friendly travel opportunities available and perhaps should not be discarded so quickly.

Claims that air travel accelerates global warming will not stop a traveler's desire to explore the world and a trip to a rain forest in Costa Rica is overall much more environmentally sound than a week stay at a 4,000 room beach resort in Cancun. Thus, while it is important to identify the environmentally harmful aspects of ecotourism development, the industry should not be disregarded outright as a valid means of environmental protection.

Environmental Benefits

The environmental benefits of ecotourism development in Costa Rica have been far reaching. Since 1963 when the first environmental protection reserve was created, Costa Rica's conservation initiatives have expanded to includc 70 protected areas or national parks covering 21% of the nation's territory, as well as the creation of Costa Rica's National Park Service in 1970. It can be deduced that this incredible increase in the area marked for conservation would not have been possible without the economic incentives of ecotourism.

As locals were relocated and logging industries shut down, Costa Ricans were able to turn to the tourism industry for employment. This would not have been possible if Costa Rica had adhered to former protectionist measures that tended to wall off protected areas from the public. Besides offering an economic incentive for conservation, ecotourism has benefited Costa Rica's environ-ment in several other ways, detailed below.

Alternative to Environmentally Damaging Industries-Without the market demand and political support for environmental protectionism, currently protected areas may have fallen to the demands of farming, logging, or mining industries long ago. Besides the revenue brought in by tourism, protected nature areas also generate income through environmentally sound pharmaceutical research and the sustainable harvest of food products.

For instance, the previously mentioned EARTH research institution has been researching the production of possible banana byproducts such as banana paper made from the generally discarded banana stalk. Also, in 1991 the U.S. based pharmaceutical firm Merck and Co made a deal with Costa Rica's National Biodiversity Institute (INBio) to carry out pharmaceutical research and development in Costa Rica's rainforests.

Encourages Individual Conservation Efforts-One of the main aspects of ecotourism that differentiates it from a day at the beach is that it educates as well as entertains travelers. By experiencing first hand the beauty of the Monteverde Cloud Forest or the majesty of a Red Macaw, tourists may return home wanting to do more to help protect the environment. Informed tour guides and educational pamphlets can incite tourists to become environmentalists, thereby promoting conservation efforts worldwide.

Encourages Small Scale Infrastructure Construction-One of the main benefits of ecotourism is that it brings in foreign exchange without the polluting factories and exploitative manufacturing companies that are spreading throughout the Third World. Instead, the infrastructure demands of an ecotourism industry primarily include the construction of small scale hotels and transportation systems.

By and large, Costa Rica has been careful to encourage small-scale development over the construction of high-rise luxury hotels, thereby maintaining a healthy balance between expanding its tourism industry and protecting its natural resources. For instance, some architects, such as D.L. Andersen, have begun to specialize in the type of environmentally sensitive construction of small lodges ideal for ecotourism.

One of Andersen's designs is the Lapa Rios Resort located on Costa Rica's Pacific coast. To ensure that the resort has as little negative impact as possible on the surrounding environs andersen took into account waste management and utilities, as well as the actual building design. Construction of the Lapa Rios Resort necessitated the removal of only one tree and the completed resort consists of only a main lodge and 14 private bungalows.

ECOTOURISM AND ITS EFFECTS ON NATIVE POPULATIONS

Tourism, especially international tourism, is one of the world's fastest growing industries. The world has seen an "increase in international tourist arrivals from 25 million in 1950 to 664 million in 1999". People have always had a great desire to travel the world, to experience other environments and to simulate foreign ways of life. In its most basic sense, tourism can be defined as "travel outside one's normal home..., the activities undertaken during the stay and the facilities created to cater for tourist needs".

However, this description is not as basic as one might think; rarely are the facilities created to cater for tourist needs discussed in tourism. Tourism is not only the act of a foreigner visiting a foreign land, but also the participation of and effects on the local populations of touristed areas. These facilities and programs become part of the local culture and it is up to the planning of tourism to make sure that they stay within the original framework of the culture.

With the definition of traditional tourism in mind, ecotourism can be discussed as a different entity based on the involvement of local populations in all aspects of tourism. Indigenous populations are the most knowledgeable about the area and they "possess the practical and ancestral knowledge of the natural features of the area". Maintaining this historical bond between the culture and its environment is important to the survival of an ecotourism programme.

This is especially important now, in a time when ecotourism is part of the development strategy of nearly every developing country. Not only is ecotourism an essential part of the development approach for Costa Rica, Tanzania and

Kenya, but it is also the greatest earner of foreign currency in these countries. And while it is important to ensure that cultures are allowed to maintain their sense of identity, it would also be contradictory to expect them to remain static. It is important "that tourism of a culture not inhibit the culture from growing and changing" with the natural flow of expansion.

This seeks to discover the history, the present and the future of ecotourism. This will be done through the analysis of case studies of ecotourism throughout the world, as well as management practices from all levels of ecotourism governance. Analysis of the benefits and consequences of each specific example of ecotourism programs can lead to the ultimate goal of a defined set of ecotourism guidelines. These would have various changes from region to region, culture to culture, depending on the resources available, but the general framework would remain similar.

A successful ecotourism programme must involve aspects of both environmental planning and social planning for the destination regions. Without one or the other, the programme will focus too heavily on the environment or too heavily on the culture at a detriment to the neglected aspect. Ecotourism cannot be developed out of every type of conventional tourism; it takes a conscious effort to maintain the integrity of local cultures and environments.

The World Conservation Strategy laid out by the International Union for the Conservation of Nature and Natural Resources (IUCN) in 1980 echoes this sentiment: "With the emphasis on 'eco-development,' there has been a strong move [to focus on] the interdependencies between environmental and economic [and social] issues".

Environmental Planning

According to Dowling, there are four main dimensions to the environmental maintenance of a successful ecotourism programme: it must have a strong nature base, support for conservation in the area, sustainable management practices and an element of environmental education for locals and tourists. Support for conservation and sustainable management are especially important to ecotourism destinations because they are "usually concentrated in sensitive and unique environments". These unique environments represent different uses to different people.

Locals use their environment delicately to maintain a balance and future for their culture. Foreigners see a unique environment as an untapped source waiting to be developed or harvested for its resources. Also, visitors are mostly unaware of the impact that their presence imposes on these delicate environments. By simply expecting to live at the same standards they do in their home country, tourists use the resources on the local island much more frivolously. These negative consequences to the environment can be eliminated through proper education of both native and foreign people with respect to tourism.

Social Planning

Social planning in a destination region is equally as important as environmental planning for ecotourism. Both locals and tourists must understand the goals of a programme if everyone is to be working towards the same goal. The most important social factor is to make sure that "local populations have a crucial level of awareness of the prospective benefits and costs of tourism to contribute effectively in the planning process". Wearing acknowledges that "the community is rarely asked by private operators about their vision for the area, nor have they been traditionally part of the planning process."

As the study of ecotourism has increased, there has been a trend to include the community more in development. The simplest and most effective way to ensure community involvement in ecotourism is through the development of community organization programs. Members of the community meet with selected ecotourism development officials to discuss their culture, ways of life and visions for ecotourism. The development officials then teach the community about the positive and negative effects of ecotourism.

This input is used to the highest degree to make sure that both groups work together to reach a common goal. A survey developed in Mexico by Diamantis sought to explore and compare the effectiveness of community organization programs, using the cities of San José and Alta Cimas as examples. Each of these cities had an ecotourism programme in effect at the time of the study and the only noted difference between the two is the presence of a community organization programme in Alta Cimas for two years prior to the study, where San José did not have one.

The objective of the programme in Alta Cimas was to allow the citizens equal input into the development of social, economic and conservation projects related to their ecotourism industry. Through a simple survey of the impacts of ecotourism, it was found that the citizens of Alta Cimas were more conscious of the positive and negative impacts of ecotourism than the citizens of San José.

Benefits for Local Communities

Benefits for local communities are wide reaching. Not only is there emphasis on proper environmental management, emphasis on improving social operations has been effective in these areas. Ecotourism provides new jobs in the local community through the growth of hotels, restaurants and guided tours. This creates business growth and provides additional income for often economically unstable areas. Also, an outlet to new markets for local products is created, in that locals are able to sell their goods directly to the consumer without having to use an intermediary.

While this is great for local businesses, the local citizens themselves are put at a disadvantage. The new market for local goods in effect raises their global price, making it harder for locals to afford goods they have grown accustomed to. Other social benefits of ecotourism include improved funding for facilities and an improved infrastructure, the acquisition of new skills and technologies, increased cultural awareness by the culture itself as well as by the rest of the world and also improved land use patterns for development in the area.

Tourist Spending

Tourist money goes to advancing the quality of tourism services as well as the local way of life. In the ideal situation, "a large part of the revenue gained will stay within the region". When the locals are the hotel owners, the restaurant workers and the tour guides, it is only proper business that they get to keep the money that they make and not have to share it with foreign powers.

Problem Description

Ecotourism faces a set of problems that threaten the entire programme. While growth in the popularity of ecotourism may be beneficial monetarily, the growth of "the global tourism industry often does so at the expense of the social and ecological integrity of destination regions".

The social integrity of a region is compromised when development occurs too quickly and without proper input from the local communities. This becomes a major issue with the involvement and control of foreign powers in the development of ecotourism.

The ecological integrity is also compromised with the lack of proper planning, as well as with an influx in tourists who do not understand the delicate balance in the ecological stability of the region.

Developing countries "possess a powerful economic incentive to develop tourism rapidly and with as few constraints as possible". The benefits of tourism on a developing country are immediate and widespread. This presents a danger to the development of ecotourism in a developing country. Ecotourism takes years of planning across many different levels of governance, "including intranational, national, regional, local and site scale".

Locals at the smaller scales have an important level of involvement in ecotourism planning, but without their complete cooperation, it is easy for foreigners at the intranational level to acquire development rights. When offered enough incentives, developing countries can be quick to cede control of tourism development to foreign interests.

Without having full control of tourism planning, "the culture of the host society is as much at risk from tourism as the physical environment". Many indigenous cultures affected by tourism are not accustomed to the fast-paced, material-oriented lifestyle of developers and the tourists that soon follow.

Without trying to demean these people, it is very easy to let foreigners take control of the tourism industry when they promise that the immediate benefits will far exceed the costs, environmentally and socially, in the future. Relinquishing control of the tourism industry makes it easy to then "turn instead to the representation of environments and cultures as 'products'".

The island of Dominica is a prime example of a developing country that rushed into a growing tourism industry. Dominica did not take the time to include community involvement and develop a grand scheme for the management of tourism; the island and its government are examples "of the consequences of naïve opportunism and political corruption".

Now much of the island has become overshadowed by the industry that was supposed to raise their economy. Local cultures are being exploited and misrepresented and the industry promotes further environmental degradation on the island because of poor planning, much to the detriment of those that still rely on the island's natural resources. The island turned to ecotourism "out of a sense of desperation" as their economy moved away from an emphasis on product output like bananas and now they have nothing to fall back on if this programme completely backfires.

The Future of Ecotourism

The discussion of the effects on local populations brings forth another problem. Should the tourism industry be pushing for further development of existing ecotourism destinations, or should the focus be on opening up new destinations for expansion? Existing destinations already have a tourism framework developed into which the ecotourism industry could utilize. These destinations have also already built a name for themselves and people seem to stick with popular places. However, further developing existing destinations could have a completely opposite effect in that it could begin to marginalize the culture and counteract the principles of ecotourism with overdevelopment. The sustainability "of the community in a peripheral area tends to decline as tourism intensifies".

On the other hand, opening up new ecotourism directions could be great for the region of development. Economic and environmental benefits are documented with correct implementation of ecotourism and expansion into new areas could help these areas maximize their resources. Beginning programs in new areas is only going to be successful depending on "the capacity of local peoples to exert some control over the commonly held resources that attract ecotourists". What might more likely happen is the case of Dominica where ecotourism spreads too quickly without proper input from local cultures. There is also conflict with the conventional tourism industry.

It is known that conventional tourism does not always take into account the consequences of their actions, "such as the inclusive resort in which restaurants, shopping and entertainment are... typically isolated from local communities". Local goods and services are ignored for cheaper goods from other places and there is little regulation over the effects of things like excursions into the country where they may cause disturbance. Tourists also can easily get schemed into what seems like an ecotourism site.

Resort developers "are likely to recognize the benefits of luring would be ecotourists by offering nature tours" and cultural events. Without universal standards, ecologically minded people could easily see an event like this and believe that they are experiencing something that they are not. Practices like this by conventional tourist operations are illegal or immoral, but the public who wants to experience true ecotourism needs to be educated as to what the industry entails.

Ecotourism is implemented differently around the world and the impacts on native cultures vary similarly. It is universal that tourism is a crucial industry to provide economic support to developing countries. An international pact in 1996 designated the tourism industry as the paramount economic growth strategy within Central America. Two prime examples of the effect of ecotourism in Central America are Bay Island in Honduras and Ambergris Caye in Belize. While the areas grew dramatically, most of the effects of ecotourism have not been positive.

A similar example to the survey in Alta Cimas and San José, Mexico is the difference between two communities in Indonesia that have ecotourism programs. In this region, the "lack of consultation and participation by local communities has fueled hostilities and loss of trust" by the locals. However, the two communities have very different cultures and the effects of global communication are obvious on one culture compared to the other.

The final example is not in a developing country, but rather in one of the world's most established countries: Canada. The northern regions of the country are popular ecotourism destinations because of the native aboriginal and Inuit populations. The newest Canadian province, Nunavut, became an autonomous territory in 1999 and their government chose ecotourism as their best way to get money. Their approach to the tourism industry is far different and more representative of its original goals.

Bay Island, Honduras

Bay Island, Honduras is an example of where the rapid spread of ecotourism is not sustainable. This region of Honduras still lacks proper sanitation facilities and safe drinking water, but the luring effects of tourism caused them to develop anyway. The population has grown by nearly 50% with the expansion of ecotourism from 10,000 to 90,000 visitors per year. This has led to what is being called a "rapid dilution" of the local culture. The blame is being placed mostly on foreign-based operations. By 1996, approximately 40% of hotel owners and a greater per cent of diving operations were foreign-owned.

There was no dialogue between developers and the entire local community, nor did they take into account the lack of proper facilities. The few locals that do take part in and benefit from ecotourism in Bay Island are those "with sufficient income to invest" in the first place. This unequal distribution of ecotourism wealth in a community can cause hostility. It is apparent why the locals feel resentment towards the tourism industry as it uses up the resources without providing any type of reimbursement.

Ambergris Caye, Belize

The growth of tourism in Ambergris Caye, Belize is very similar to Bay Island. In the ten years between 1984 and 1994, tourism grew by 50% and in this case, nearly 75% of hotels were foreign-owned.

With the expansion of the tourism industry, Belize needed more people to work the new facilities. By the early 1990s, approximately 50% of all Belizeans had a job in the tourism sector. While this continued to provide jobs and allow for local input, the traditional fishing industry that has always thrived in the area has seen a noticeable decrease in skilled and able workers.

This could pose a problem for feeding the locals as well as tourists who come in wanting to experience everything related to the local ways of life. There is a bright side to ecotourism in Ambergris Caye, however. The local government has implemented a plan for more sustainable growth of the industry to limit the continued expansion. Every hotel that is to be built can have a maximum of 60 beds and the total growth per year is 120 beds.

This limits the input of foreign developers because many do not see a 60-bed operation as being a worthwhile investment of time and money. Also, in order to maintain the important tradition in the region of having an unpaved centre of town, the plan forces the construction of further paved roads along the edge of town. The government is working with native cultures to maintain their local traditions much better than the developers of Bay Island, Honduras are doing.

Sulawesi, Indonesia

Indonesia is representative of most remote Pacific Island nations, where ecotourism is of enhanced significance "where opportunities for other forms of economic development may be limited". Local cultures feel the pressure to provide a tourist industry and often they are prime examples of areas that use foreign developers who do not take careful consideration of the culture. Two communities in Indonesia, the Bajau and the Kaledupan, are similar to the communities previously mentioned in Mexico in that one community (Kaledupan) is more aware of the positive and negative impacts of tourism than the other.

This is directly related to the level of remoteness of the community. The Bajau are an interesting people because they once lived entirely at sea. All of their structures were built on the sea and on structures jutting from the land into the water. They only moved to land recently because of pressure by the government of Indonesia. They still remain a remote society, but allow for tourists to bring in supplemental income. The Kaledupan are a very opposite culture.

They are more typical of mainstream Indonesia with jobs in the manufacturing sector and they have "a more formal education and greater access to global media". What truly sets these two cultures apart with respect to ecotourism is that Kaledupan is part of Operation Wallacea. Operation Wallacea is a British ecotourism group that helps assimilate native cultures with a proper tourism programme.

Through a more extensive survey similar to the Mexico study, it was determined that the Kaledupan community is more "aware of the consequences of their actions with regard to the environment" than the Bajau people. It is not known if this type of operation would work with the Bajau people because of the culture's pride in their remoteness, but allowing them to become more aware of the consequences could prove to be beneficial.

Nunavut, Canada

Ecotourism is a long-standing tradition in Canada, especially in the northern provinces. Their interesting history and unique adaptations to their environment have led tourists to the area for years. Canada's established ecotourism industry shows that ecotourism is not only a profitable enterprise in tropical and/or developing countries. The industry throughout Canada is worth approximately $CDN270 million and employs 14,000-16,000 people in mostly seasonal and part time jobs. This makes ecotourism a substantial economic industry in Canada, but what is more impressive is the way ecotourism is implemented in the country.

In 1996, the Aboriginal Tourism Team Canada issued their goal to "represent Aboriginal people as world leaders in tourism in harmony with our culture". And for the most part, they have been successful. They have a high reverence for the environment and it translates directly to their treatment of tourism. The Aboriginals work through themselves to control the tourism industry, not through a foreign party. This allows them to have a full share of the revenue generated and they can divide the profits equally.

The only environmental issue in Nunavut pertaining to the sustainability of tourism is the conflict in how to incorporate hunting and fishing. The environment in northern Canada is not conducive to growing crops, so the culture has adapted to creating a sustainable harvest of wild animals. With a growing tourism industry, it is difficult to allow tourists to participate in hunting and fishing because they do not know the local practices that continue its sustainability. Even more crucially is the problem of what to feed incoming tourists if their presence places stress on their local food habits.

The Aboriginals are currently working on solutions to continue progress with their mission statement. Ecotourism, also known as ecological tourism, is a form of tourism that appeals to ecologically and socially conscious individuals. Generally speaking, ecotourism focuses on volunteering, personal growth and learning new ways to live on the planet; typically involving travel to destinations where flora, fauna and cultural heritage are the primary attractions. Responsible ecotourism includes programs that minimize the negative aspects of conventional tourism on the environment and enhance the cultural integrity of local people. Therefore, in addition to evaluating environmental and cultural factors, an integral part of ecotourism is in the promotion of recycling, energy efficiency, water conservation and creation of economic opportunities for the local communities.

Ideally, ecotourism should satisfy several criteria, such as:

- Conservation of biological diversity and cultural diversity, through ecosystem protection
- Promotion of sustainable use of biodiversity, by providing jobs to local populations
- Sharing of socio-economic benefits with local communities and indigenous people by having their informed consent and participation in the management of ecotourism enterprises.
- Tourism to unspoiled natural resources, with minimal impact on the environment being a primary concern.
- Minimization of tourism's own environmental impact
- Affordability and lack of waste in the form of luxury
- Local culture, flora and fauna being the main attractions

For many countries, ecotourism is not simply a marginal activity to finance protection of the environment but as a major industry of the national economy. For example, in places such as Costa Rica, Ecuador, Nepal, Kenya, Madagascar and Antarctica, ecotourism represents a significant portion of the gross domestic product and economic activity.

The concept of ecotourism is widely misunderstood and in practice is often used as a marketing tool to promote tourism that is related to nature. Critics claim that ecotourism as practiced and abused often consists of placing a hotel in a splendid landscape, to the detriment of the ecosystem.

According to them, ecotourism must above all sensitize people with the beauty and the fragility of nature. They condemn some operators as "greenwashing" their operations;

using the label of "green-friendly", while behaving in environmentally irresponsible ways. Although academics disagree about who can be classified as an ecotourist and there is precious little statistical data, some estimate that more than five million ecotourists-the majority of the ecotourist population-come from the United States, with others from Western Europe, Canada and Australia.

Currently there are various moves to create national and international ecotourism accrediation programs, although the process is also controversial. Ecotourism certificates have been put in place in Costa Rica, although some critics have dismissed these programs as greenwashing.

Ecotourism, responsible tourism and sustainable development have become prevalent concepts since the late 1980s and ecotourism has experienced arguably the fastest growth of all sub-sectors in the tourism industry. The popularity represents a change in tourist perceptions, increased environmental awareness and a desire to explore natural environments. Such changes have become a statement affirming one's social identity, educational sophistication and disposable income as it has about preserving the Amazon rainforest or the Caribbean reef for posterity. With its great potential for environmental protection, the United Nations celebrated the "International Year of Ecotourism" in 2002.

To approach an understanding of the problem, a clear definition must delineate what is and is not, ecotourism. Ideally, ecotourism satisfies several general criteria, including the conservation of biological diversity and cultural diversity through ecosystem protection, promotion of sustainable use of biodiversity, share of socio-economic benefits with local communities through informed consent and participation, increase in environmental and cultural knowledge, affordability and reduced waste and minimization of its own environmental impact. In such ways, it contributes to the long term benefits to both the environment and local communities.

However, in the continuum of tourism activities that stretch from conventional tourism to ecotourism proper, there has been a lot of contention to the limit at which biodiversity preservation, local socio-economic benefits and environmental impact can be considered "ecotourism". For this reason, environmentalists, special interest groups and governments define ecotourism differently. Environmental organizations have generally insisted that ecotourism is nature-based, sustainably managed, conservation supporting and environ-mentally educated. The tourist industry and governments, however, focus more on the product aspect, treating ecotourism as equivalent to any sort of tourism based in nature.

As a further complication, many terms are used under the rubric of ecotourism. Nature tourism, low impact tourism, green tourism, bio-tourism, ecologically responsible tourism and others have been used in literature and marketing, although they are not necessary synonymous with ecotourism.

The problems associated with defining ecotourism have led to confusion among tourists and academics alike. Definitional problems are also subject of considerable public controversy and concern because of greenwashing, a trend towards the commercialization of tourism schemes disguised as sustainable, nature based and environmentally friendly ecotourism.

According to McLaren, these schemes are environmentally destructive, economically exploitative and culturally insensitive at its worst. They are also morally disconcerting because they mislead tourists and manipulate their concerns for the environment. Despite objections, greenwashing continues to grow unabated. The Nature's Sacred Paradise, a theme park in Quintana Roo, Mexico, is responsible for displacing local Mayan communities and illegally keeping endangered species in captivity to attract visitors. The development and success of such large scale, energy intensive and ecologically unsustainable schemes are a testament to the tremendous profits associated with being labeled as ecotourism.

NEGATIVE PSYCHO-SOCIAL IMPACT OF ECOTOURISM

Ecotourism is the trend towards the commercialization of

tourism throughout the nation. This trend has become one of the fastest growing sectors of the tourism industry growing annual 10-15% worldwide. Ecotourism was first introduced in Africa in the 1950's with the legalization of hunting. This need for recreational hunting zones led to the creation of protected areas, national parks and game reserves. Today these areas have become important revenue-earning venues with the establishment of lodges and tourist campsites.

One definition of ecotourism is "the practice of low-impact, educational, ecologically and culturally sensitive travel that benefits local communities and host countries". Many of the ecotourism projects are not meeting these standards. Even if some of the guidelines are being executed, the local communities are still facing other negative impacts. South Africa is one of the countries that are reaping significant economic benefits from ecotourism, but negative effects including physical displacement of persons, gross violation of fundamental rights and environmental hazards far out weigh the medium-term economic benefits.

A tremendous amount of money is being spent and human resources continue to be used for ecotourism despite the lack of success stories and even more money is put into public relation campaigns to dilute the effects of the criticism. Ecotourism channels resources away from other projects that could contribute more sustainable and realistic solutions to pressing social and environmental problems. "The money tourism can generate often ties parks and managements to eco-tourism". But there is a tension in this relationship because eco-tourism often causes conflict and changes in land-use rights, fails to deliver promises of community-level benefits, damages environments and has plenty of other social impacts. Indeed many argue repeatedly that eco-tourism is neither ecologically nor socially beneficial, yet it persists as a strategy for conservation and development. While several studies are being done on ways to improve the ecotourism structure, these examples provide reason that it should just stop all together.

The ecotourism system exercises tremendous financial and political influence. The evidence above shows that at the very least a strong case exists for restraining such activities. Funding could be used for field studies aimed at finding alternative solutions to tourism and the diverse problems Africa faces in result of urbanization, industrialization and over exploitation of agriculture. At the local level ecotourism has become a source of conflict over control of land, resources and tourism profits.

There are many problems with the idea of ecotourism. Environmental, the effects on the local people and conflicts over profit distribution are only a few of the negative effects of ecotourism. In a perfect world more efforts would be made towards educating tourists of the environmental and social effects of their travels. Very few regulations or laws stand in place as boundaries for the investors in ecotourism. These should be implemented to prohibit the promotion of unsustainable ecotourism projects and materials which project false images of destinations, demeaning local and indigenous cultures.

Direct Environmental Impacts

Ecotourism operations typically fail to live up to conservation ideals. It is often overlooked that ecotourism is a highly consumer-centered activity and that environmental conservation is only a means to further economic growth. Although ecotourism is intended for small groups, even a modest increase in population, however temporary, puts extra pressure on the local environment and necessitates the development of additional infrastructure and amenities.

The construction of water treatment plants, sanitation facilities and lodges come with the exploitation of non-renewable energy sources and the utilization of already limited local resources. The conversion of natural land to such tourist infrastructure is implicated in deforestation and habitat deterioration of butterflies in Mexico and squirrel monkeys in Costa Rica. In other cases, the environment suffers because local communities are unable to meet the infrastructure demands of ecotourism.

The lack of adequate sanitation facilities in many East

African parks results in the disposal of campsite sewage in rivers, contaminating the wildlife, livestock and people who draw drinking water from it. Aside from environmental degradation with tourist infrastructure, population pressures from ecotourism also leaves behind garbage and pollution associated with the Western lifestyle. Although ecotourists claim to be educationally sophisticated and environmentally concerned, they rarely understand the ecological consequences of their visits and how their day-to-day activities append physical impacts on the environment.

As one scientist observes, they "rarely acknowledge how the meals they eat, the toilets they flush, the water they drink and so on, are all part of broader regional economic and ecological systems they are helping to reconfigure with their very activities." Nor do ecotourists recognize the great consumption of non-renewable energy required to arrive at their destination, which is typically more remote than conventional tourism destinations. For instance, an exotic journey to a place 10,000 kilometers away consumes about 700 liters of fuel per person.

Ecotourism activities are, in of itself, issues in environmental impact because they disturb fauna and flora. Ecotourists believe that because they are only taking pictures and leaving footprints, they keep ecotourism sites pristine, but even harmless sounding activities such as a nature hike can be ecologically destructive.

In the Annapurna Circuit in Nepal, ecotourists have worn down the marked trails and created alternate routes, contributing to soil impaction, erosion and plant damage. Where the ecotourism activity involves wildlife viewing, it can scare away animals, disrupt their feeding and nesting sites, or acclimate them to the presence of people. In Kenya, disruption of wildlife observers drive cheetahs off their reserves, increasing the risk of inbreeding and further endangering the species.

Environmental Hazards

We already understand that biodiversity and environmentally intact lands form the basis of ecological stability. Unfortunately, industrialization, urbanization and unsustainable agriculture practices have all had serious effects on the environment. Ecotourism is now also playing a role in this depletion. While the term ecotourism may sound relatively benign, one of its most serious impacts is its consumption of virgin territories.

These invasions often include deforestation, disruption of ecological life systems and various forms of pollution, all of which contribute to environmental degrada-tion. The number of motor vehicles crossing the park increases as tour drivers search for rare species. The number of roads has disrupted the grass cover which has serious effects on plant and animal species.

These areas also have a higher rate of disturbances and invasive species because of all the traffic moving off the beaten path into new undiscovered areas. Ecotourism also has an effect on species through the value placed on them. "Certain species have gone from being little known or valued by local people to being highly valued commodities. The commodification of plants may erase their social value and lead to overproduction within protected areas.

Local people and their images can also be turned into commodities". Kamuaro brings up a relatively obvious contradiction, any commercial venture into unspoiled, pristine land with or without the "eco" prefix as a contradiction in terms. To generate revenue you have to have a high number of traffic, tourists, which inevitably means a higher pressure on the environment.

Local People

Most forms of ecotourism are owned by foreign investors and corporations that provide few benefits to local communities. An overwhelming majority of profits are put into the pockets of investors instead of reinvestment into the local economy or environmental protection.

The limited numbers of local people who are employed in the economy enter at its lowest level and are unable to live in tourist areas because of meager wages and a two market system.

In some cases, the resentment by local people results in environmental degradation. As a highly publicized case, the Maasai nomads in Kenya killed wildlife in national parks to show aversion to unfair compensation terms and displacement from traditional lands. The lack of economic opportunities for local people also constrains them to degrade the environment as a means of sustenance. The presence of affluent ecotourists encourages the development of destructive markets in wildlife souvenirs, such as the sale of coral trinkets on tropical islands and animal products in Asia, contributing to illegal harvesting and poaching from the environment. In Surinam, sea turtle reserves use a large portion of their budget to guard against these activities.

Displacement of People

One of the most powerful examples of communities being moved in order to create a park is the story of the Masai. About 70% of national parks and game reserves in East Africa are on Masai land. The first undesirable impact of tourism was that of the extent of land lost from the Masai culture. Local and national governments took advantage of the Masai's ignorance on the situation and robbed them of huge chunks of grazing land, putting to risk their only socio-economic livelihood.

In Kenya the Masai also have not gained any economic benefits. Despite the loss of their land, employment favours better educated workers. Furthermore the investors in this area are not local and have not put profits back into local economy. In some cases game reserves can be created without informing or consulting local people, who come to find out about the situation when an eviction notice is delivered.

Another source of resentment is the manipulation of the local people by their government. "Eco-tourism works to create simplistic images of local people and their uses and understandings of their surroundings. Through the lens of these simplified images, officials direct policies and projects towards the local people and the local people are blamed if the projects fail". Clearly tourism as a trade is not empowering the local people who make it rich and satisfying. Instead ecotourism exploits and depletes, particularly in African Masai tribes. It has to be reoriented if it is to be useful to local communities and to become sustainable.

Threats to Indigenous Cultures

Ecotourism often claims that it preserves and "enhances" local cultures. However, evidence shows that with the establishment of protected areas local people have illegally lost their homes and most often with no compensation. Pushing people onto marginal lands with harsh climates, poor soils, lack of water and infested with livestock and disease does little to enhance livelihoods even when a proportion of ecotourism profits are directed back into the community.

The establishment of parks can create harsh survival realities and deprive the people of their traditional use of land and natural resources. Ethnic groups are increasingly being seen as a "backdrop" to the scenery and wildlife.

The local people struggle for cultural survival and freedom of cultural expression while being "observed" by tourists. Local indigenous people also have strong resentment towards the change, "Tourism has been allowed to develop with virtually no controls. Too many lodges have been built, too much firewood is being used and no limits are being placed on tourism vehicles. They regularly drive off-track and harass the wildlife. Their vehicle tracks criss-cross the entire Masai Mara. Inevitably the bush is becoming eroded and degraded".

Mismanagement

While governments are typically entrusted with the administration and enforcement of environmental protection, they often lack the commitment or capability to manage ecotourism sites effectively. The regulations for environmental protection may be vaguely defined, costly to implement, hard to enforce and uncertain in effectiveness. Government regulatory agencies, as political bodies, are susceptible to making decisions that spend budget on politically beneficial but environmentally unproductive projects. Because of prestige and conspicuousness, the construction of an attractive visitor's centre at an ecotourism site may take precedence over more pressing environmental concerns like acquiring habitat, protecting endemic species and removing invasive ones.

Finally, influential groups can pressure and sway the interests of the government to their favour. The government and its regulators can become vested in the benefits of the ecotourism industry which they are supposed to regulate, causing restrictive environmental regulations and enforcement to become more lenient. Management of ecotourism sites by private ecotourism companies offers an alternative to the cost of regulation and deficiency of government agencies.

It is believed that these companies have a self interest in limited environmental degradation, because tourists will pay more for pristine environments, which translates to higher profit. However, theory indicates that this practice is not economically feasible and will fail to manage the environment.

The model of monopolistic competition states that distinctiveness will entail profits, but profits will promote imitation. A company that protects its ecotourism sites is able to charge a premium for the novel experience and pristine environment. But when other companies view the success of this approach, they also enter the market with similar practices, increasing competition and reducing demand. Eventually, the demand will be reduced until the economic profit is zero.

A cost-benefit analysis shows that the company bears the cost of environmental protection without receiving the gains. Without economic incentive, the whole premise of self interest through environmental protection is quashed; instead, ecotourism companies will minimize environment related expenses and maximize tourism demand.

The tragedy of the commons offers another model for economic unsustainability from environmental protection, in ecotourism sites utilized by many companies. Although there is a communal incentive to protect the environment, maximizing the benefits in the long run, a company will conclude that it is in their best interest to utilize the ecotourism site beyond its sustainable level. By increasing the number of ecotourists, for instance, a company gains all the economic benefit while paying only a part of the environmental cost.

In the same way, a company recognizes that there is no incentive to actively protect the environment; they bear all the costs, while the benefits are shared by all other companies. The result, again, is mismanagement. Taken together, the mobility of foreign investment and lack of economic incentive for environmental protection means that ecotourism companies are disposed to establishing themselves in new sites once their existing one is sufficiently degraded.

Regulation and Accreditation

Because the regulation of ecotourism is poorly implemented or nonexistent, ecologically destructive greenwashed operations like underwater hotels, helicopter tours and wildlife theme parks are categorized as ecotourism along with canoeing, camping, photography and wildlife observation. The failure to acknowledge responsible, low impact ecotourism puts these companies at a competitive disadvantage.

Many environmentalists have argued for a global standard of accreditation, differentiating ecotourism companies based on their level of environmental commitment. A national or international regulatory board would enforce accreditation procedures, with representation from various groups including governments, hotels, tour operators, travel agents, guides, airlines, local authorities, conservation organizations and non-governmental organizations.

The decisions of the board would be sanctioned by governments, so that non-compliant companies would be legally required to disassociate themselves from the use of the ecotourism brand.

Crinion suggests a Green Stars System based on criteria including a management plan, benefit for the local community, small group interaction, education value and staff training. Ecotourists who consider their choices would be confident of a genuine ecotourism experience when they see the higher star rating.

In addition, environmental impact assessments could be used as a form of accreditation. Feasibility is evaluated from a scientific basis and recommendations could be made to optimally plan infrastructure, set tourist capacity and manage the ecology. This form of accreditation is more sensitive to site specific conditions.

Guidelines and Education

An environmental protection strategy must address the issue of ecotourists removed from the cause-and-effect of their actions on the environment. More initiatives should be carried out to improve their awareness, sensitize them to environmental issues and care about the places they visit.

Tour guides are an obvious and direct medium to communicate awareness. With the confidence of ecotourists and intimate knowledge of the environment, they can actively discuss conservation issues. A tour guide training programme in Costa Rica's Tortuguero National Park has helped mitigate negative environmental impacts by providing information and regulating tourists on the parks' beaches used by nesting endangered sea turtles.

Slow Growth and Local Control

The underdevelopment theory of tourism describes a new form of imperialism by multinational corporations that control ecotourism resources. These corporations finance and profit from the development of large scale ecotourism that causes excessive environmental degradation, loss of traditional culture and way of life and exploitation of local labour. In Zimbabwe and Nepal's Annapurna region, where underdevelopment is taking place, more than 90 per cent of ecotourism revenues are expatriated to the parent countries and less than 5 per cent go into local communities.

The lack of sustainability highlights the need for small scale, slow growth and locally based ecotourism. Local peoples have a vested interest in the well being of their community and are therefore more accountable to environmental protection than multinational corporations. The lack of control, westernization, adverse impacts to the environment, loss of culture and traditions outweigh the benefits of establishing large scale ecotourism.

The increased contributions of communities to locally managed ecotourism create viable economic opportunities, including high level management positions and reduce environmental issues associated with poverty and unemployment. Because the ecotourism experience is marketed to a different lifestyle from large scale ecotourism, the development of facilities and infrastructure does not need to conform to corporate Western tourism standards and can be much simpler and less expensive. There is a greater multiplier effect on the economy, because local products, materials and labour are used.

Profits accrue locally and import leakages are reduced. However, even this form of tourism may require foreign investment for promotion or start up. When such investments are required, it is crucial for communities for find a company or non-governmental organization that reflects the philosophy of ecotourism; sensitive to their concerns and willing to cooperate at the expense of profit. The basic assumption of the multiplier effect is that the economy starts off with unused resources, for example, that many workers are cyclically unemployed and much of industrial capacity is sitting idle or incompletely utilized.

By increasing demand in the economy it is then possible to boost production. If the economy was already at full employment, with only structural, frictional, or other supply-side types of unemployment, any attempt to boost demand would only lead to inflation. For various laissez-faire schools of economics which embrace Say's Law and deny the possibility of Keynesian inefficiency and under-employment of resources, therefore, the multiplier concept is irrelevant or wrong-headed.

As an example, consider the government increasing its expenditure on roads by $1 million, without a corresponding increase in taxation. This sum would go to the road builders, who would hire more workers and distribute the money as wages and profits. The households receiving these incomes will save part of the money and spend the rest on consumer goods. These expenditures in turn will generate more jobs, wages and profits and so on with the income and spending circulating around the economy.

The multiplier effect arises because of the induced increases in consumer spending which occur due to the increased incomes and because of the feedback into increasing business revenues, jobs and income again. This process does not lead to an economic explosion not only because of the supply-side barriers at potential output (full employment) but because at each "round", the increase in consumer spending is less than the increase in consumer incomes.

That is, the marginal propensity to consume (mpc) is less than one, so that each round some extra income goes into saving, leaking out of the cumulative process. Each increase in spending is thus smaller than that of the previous round, preventing an explosion. Ecotourism has to be implemented with care.

INTERNATIONAL ECO TOURISM STANDARDS

The International Ecotourism Standard has been developed by the Ecotourism Australia in conjunction with the Cooperative Research Centre (CRC) for Sustainable Tourism of Australia. The International Ecotourism Standard is based on the highly successful Australian Eco Certification Programme, Agenda 21 and guiding principles for sound ecotourism certification (Mohonk Agreement) developed by a gathering of ecotourism certification experts at Mohonk Mountain, New York State, USA in November 2001.

Green Globe 21 has the exclusive licence for the distribution and management of the International Ecotourism Standard. Green Globe 21 is the global Affiliation, Benchmarking and Certifica-tion programme for sustainable travel and tourism. The Green Globe brand signifies better environmental performance, improved community interactions, savings through using fewer resources and greater yields from increased consumer demand.

The International Ecotourism Standard is based principally on the highly regarded Australian Eco Certification Programme Standard combined with elements of the very latest Green Globe Benchmarking performance system. Criteria have been adapted to ensure their applicability in an international setting and both the Standard and Certification Programme incorporate the fundamental principles for sound ecotourism certification identified in the Mohonk Agreement.

The Green Globe 21 International Ecotourism Standard has adopted Ecotourism Australia's definition of ecotourism: "Ecologically sustainable tourism with a primary focus on experiencing natural areas that fosters environmental and cultural understanding, appreciation and conservation." However, a more definitive "definition" of ecotourism is the expansion of this statement into a core set of principles with specific performance indicators (i.e. the key ecotourism performance areas). The core set of eight principles for ecotourism products are:

- *Nature Area Focus:* Focus on giving visitors the opportunity to personally and directly experience nature.
- *Interpretation:* Provide opportunities to experience nature in ways that lead to greater understanding, appreciation and enjoyment.
- *Environmental Sustainability Practice:* Represent best practice for environmentally sustainable tourism.
- *Contribution to Conservation:* Contribute directly to the conservation of natural areas Benefiting Local Communities Provide ongoing contributions to the local community.
- *Cultural Respect:* Be sensitive to, interpret and involve the culture/s existing in the area.
- *Customer Satisfaction:* Consistently meets consumer expectations.

Responsible Marketing

Be marketed and promoted honestly and accurately so that realistic expectations are formed. These principles have been used to develop the Standard criteria – with specific indicators for each of these eight performance areas. The criteria support the major principles and are based on a hybrid of 'process' (i.e. creating a documented procedure) and 'performance' (e.g. that sewage treatment meets certain effluent standards) standards.

Although some criteria are relatively general and rely on a commitment by the operator to implement a process to meet a desired outcomes (e.g. provision of an interpretation plan in order to stimulate better designed interpretative activities, leading to quality experiences) there is distinct emphasis on specific performance indicators. These are technically prescriptive and deliberately target real environmental outcomes. These criteria include quantification of environmental performance for most of the key environmental indicators. This allows recognition and encouragement of ecotourism product that makes measured environmental improvements which result in a more sustainable world.

Local and Global Perspective

Mass tourism causes cultural and environmental damage. Ecotourism is one of the current buzzwords and like all buzzwords it is misused and abused-with few people really knowing what it means. Many tourist operators have used the term to market to an ever growing segment of the tourist market that wants to be environmentally and culturally sensitive. What these operators market is in fact often worse than ordinary tourism, because it uses local communities and the environment for its own benefit, with neither the communities nor the local environment benefiting.

In fact, most times both suffer considerable negative impacts as a result of the activities of these operators. Many operators take tourists to 'natural' environments and 'untouched' cultures and instead of making the tourists adopt to the non-invasive practices of the local people, provide them with hot showers, imported Western foods, Western body care products and other Western 'necessities' that stress the already fragile local infrastructure, resources and traditional culture.

From the perspective of the tourist, ecotourism is ecologically sustainable tourism that has as a primary focus the experiencing of natural areas while fostering environmental and cultural understanding, appreciation and conservation. According to the Quebec Declaration on Ecotourism, ecotourism *embraces the principles of sustainable tourism and the following principles which distinguish it from the wider concept of sustainable tourism:*

- *Contributes actively to the conservation of natural and cultural heritage,*
- *Includes local and indigenous communities in its planning, development and operation, contributing to their well-being,*
- *Interprets the natural and cultural heritage of the destination to the visitor,*
- *Lends itself better to independent travellers, as well as to organised tours for small size groups.*

Ecotourism fits within the larger tourism market place. Tourism can be subdivided into cultural, rural, nature, sun-and-beach, business and fitness-wellness-health. Ecotourism and adventure tourism are to be found within nature tourism and ecotourism has strong links to rural and cultural tourism. Ecotourism differs from adventure tourism in its guiding ethics and principles. Adventure tourism is motivated by a desire to experience physical exercise and challenging situations in natural environments.

Ecotourism has enormous potential to change how we relate to the natural environment and to the diverse range of people who inhabit the earth, through its embedded conservation ethic and ecological perspective. It provides a platform for Western society and less developed societies to converge on middle common ground. As a part of the service industry, ecotourism promotes a change from material to non-material focus.

Ecotourism can fundamentally change the economic dynamics of business because it recognises the ecological and cultural costs of doing business as well as championing local economy. Through ecotourism the community has the potential to become strong and cohesive through developing and managing their resources and visitors to those resources. Ecotourism should in all cases, aim to achieve sustainable development.

Ecotourism is based on principles, guidelines and standards and as a growing industry needs to have a regulatory system of certification. The basic elements of ecotourism must include:

- Ensures prior informed participation of all stakeholders in meaningful decision making;
- Ensures equal, effective and active participation of all stakeholders;
- Contributes to conservation of biodiversity;
- Provides direct financial benefits for conservation;
- Sustains the well-being of local people by providing financial benefits and empowerment;
- Involves responsible action by tourist operators and tourists themselves;
- Is provided to small groups of tourists;
- Provides a positive experience for tourists and local people;
- Involves the least possible consumption of non-renewable resources;
- Supports international human rights and labour agreements; and raises awareness and understanding of environmental, political, social and cultural contextual realities.

Eco-tourism is more than a catch phrase for nature loving travel and recreation. Eco-tourism is consecrated for preserving and sustaining the diversity of the world's natural and cultural environments.

It accommodates and entertains visitors in a way that is minimally intrusive or destructive to the environment and sustains and supports the native cultures in the locations it is operating in. Responsibility of both travellers and service providers is the genuine meaning for eco-tourism. Eco-tourism also endeavours to encourage and support the diversity of local economies for which the tourism-related income is important.

With support from tourists, local services and producers can compete with larger, foreign companies and local families can support themselves. Besides all these, the revenue produced from tourism helps and encourages governments to fund conservation projects and training programs. Saving the environment around you and preserving the natural luxuries and forest life, that's what eco-tourism is all about. Whether it's about a nature camp or organizing trekking trips towards the unspoilt and inaccessible regions, one should always keep in mind not to create any mishap or disturbance in the life cycle of nature. Eco-tourism focuses on local cultures, wilderness adventures, volunteering, personal growth and learning new ways to live on our vulnerable planet.

It is typically defined as travel to destinations where the flora, fauna and cultural heritage are the primary attractions. Responsible Eco-tourism includes programs that minimize the adverse effects of traditional tourism on the natural environment and enhance the cultural integrity of local people. Therefore, in addition to evaluating environmental and cultural factors, initiatives by hospitality providers to promote recycling, energy efficiency, water reuse and the creation of economic opportunities for local communities are an integral part of Eco-tourism.

Historical, biological and cultural conservation, preservation, sustainable development etc. are some of the fields closely related to Eco-Tourism. Many professionals have been involved in formulating and developing eco-tourism policies. They come from the fields of Geographic Information Systems, Wildlife Management, Wildlife Photography, Marine Biology and Oceanography, National and State Park Management, Environmental Sciences, Women in Develop-ment, Historians and Archaeologists, etc.

Eco-tourism is considered the fastest growing market in the tourism industry, according to the World Tourism Organization with an annual growth rate of 5% worldwide and representing 6% of the world gross domestic product, 11.4% of all consumer spending-not a market to be taken lightly.

Fundamentally, eco-tourism means making as little

environmental impact as possible and helping to sustain the indigenous populace, thereby encouraging the preservation of wildlife and habitats when visiting a place. This is responsible form of tourism and tourism development, which encourages going back to natural products in every aspect of life. It is also the key to sustainable ecological development.

Index